Social Policy in the Third World

Social Policy in the Third World

The social dilemmas of underdevelopment

Stewart MacPherson

Lecturer in Social Administration
University of Nottingham

ALLANHELD, OSMUN
Publishers

ALLANHELD, OSMUN & CO. PUBLISHERS, INC.

Published in the United States of America in 1982
by Allanheld, Osmun & Co. Publishers, Inc.
(A Division of Littlefield, Adams & Company)
81 Adams Drive, Totowa, New Jersey 07512

Library of Congress Cataloging in Publication Data

MacPherson, Stewart.
  Social Policy in the Third World.

  Bibliography: p.
  Includes indexes.
  1. Underdeveloped areas − Social conditions.
  2. Underdeveloped areas − Social service.
  I. Title.
HN980.M266   1982   361.6'1'091724   82-6837

ISBN 0-86598-090-X   AACR2

82 83 84/10 9 8 7 6 5 4 3 2 1

Printed in Great Britain

For my Mother
and Catie, James, Grace and Michael

Contents

Preface

This book was written as the result of attempts to teach about social policy and underdevelopment. Despite the enormous literature, experience over ten years has continually shown the need for an introductory book which deals with a range of social issues in relation to some analysis of the processes of development and underdevelopment. The student of social policy in whatever context is faced with a vast range of material which impinges, directly and indirectly, on the understanding of social policy issues. This book attempts only to introduce the reader to some of this material and to indicate the manner in which inquiry might proceed. It has not been possible to cover more than a few major issues; even those which are covered have frequently been dealt with in a summary fashion. I have been biased by my own experience in both the selection of topics and the concentration on particular countries as the sources of examples.

The omissions are many, and certain topics, such as the position of women, have received far too little attention; my only defence is that the literature, until relatively recently, has been weak. I hope the overall approach of the book will lead the reader to the emerging studies which deal with these topics seriously. Similarly there is little, except for some discussion in the concluding chapter, on issues of social planning. I have chosen not to become involved in lengthy discussions of this, not only because my own incompetence does not allow of the specialised treatment necessary, but also because I am concerned to emphasise the vital necessity for widespread awareness of social policy issues. Social policy is not ultimately a matter for professional expertise, however relevant that might be in programme implementation. The fundamental dilemmas which this book identifies are dilemmas which can only be resolved by general awareness of the consequences of underdevelopment.

There is little that is original in terms of material or theoretical perspectives. The intention is that the book should bring together relevant material in a way that is too rarely done. Understandably perhaps, the explosion of information has intensified the degree to which topics are considered in isolation of each other. I hope that the book will be of use to those in the Third World who are trying to find the connections and inter-relationships between issues which are the theme of this book. For students of social policy in the industrialised countries, I hope that this may assist in widening the horizons of approaches which are too often pursued as if the majority of the world did not exist.

My greatest debt is to the students who have endured my teaching. I was especially fortunate to have at Makerere University, Uganda students from Kenya, Uganda and Tanzania who taught me a great deal about those countries, and inspired me to seek alternatives to the irrelevant material which dominated the study of social policy. My experience of teaching at the University in Tanzania gave me a measure of what university teaching could be, which remains with me. Most recently, two years' teaching at the University of Papua New Guinea was profoundly stimulating. I owe a great debt to the students there and to Maev O'Collins, Bruce Yeates, Kuri Dom and Vincent Warakai.

At Nottingham, I continue to be grateful for the tolerance of my colleagues and their support and encouragement. In particular, I must thank Jonathan Silvey, who wrote the chapter on education. The manuscript was typed with great efficiency and good humour by Chris Isaacs.

Finally, I thank my wife and children for their patience and their constant belief that the book would be finished, a belief that I did not always share.

Nottingham, September 1981

Introduction

'Dilemma: a choice between two (or several) alternatives, which are equally unfavourable.'

Oxford English Dictionary

'Dilemma: A situation involving choice between equally unsatisfactory alternatives.'

Webster's Dictionary

Much of the existing literature on social policy in Third World countries is written as if the conditions in those countries were exactly similar to those in the industrialised countries from which most of the literature comes. Even when the scale of social deprivation is acknowledged, the implication of essential similarity remains: the problems are different in degree but not in kind. It is a major theme of the chapters which follow that there are profound differences between contemporary social policy issues in the Third World and superficially similar issues in the historical experience of the industrialised countries. The nature of underdevelopment went unrecognised in much of the older literature on social policy and development. The emergence of new analyses reflects both the rise of indigenous scholarship which has rejected the inadequate explanations and prescriptions of the past, and also the related growth of theories of development and under-development which had undermined prevailing conceptions of the paths Third World countries should follow. While there have been significant changes in stated approaches to social policy and social development in recent years, studies in the field of social policy have only very recently begun to incorporate the theoretical perspectives of underdevelopment. In the chapters which follow a number of social policy issues will be discussed in the light of an overarching analysis of patterns of underdevelopment. A brief review of recent changes in international approaches to development will indicate the need for such study.

Chapter 1 discusses the emergence of new approaches which seriously question earlier emphasis on economic growth as virtually the only measure of development. It was not until the 1970s that social development was clearly identified as the goal of development strategies and not simply as one of the means by which rapid economic growth could be achieved. There emerged what became known as the unified approach; the UN International Development Strategy of 1970 spelled this out:

The ultimate objective of development must be to bring about sustained improvement in the well-being of the individual and bestow benefits on all. If undue privileges, extremes of wealth and social injustice persist, then development fails in its essential purpose . . . qualititive and structural changes in the society must go hand in hand with rapid economic growth, and existing disparities − regional, sectoral and social − should be substantially reduced. These objectives are both determining factors and end results of development; they should therefore be viewed as integrated parts of the same dynamic process, and would require a unified approach. (United Nations, 1979:2)

The discussion of underdevelopment in Chapter 1 and later chapters on specific areas of social policy similarly stress the close relationship between social conditions and economic growth as part of the same dynamic process. But it is in understanding that process as continuing underdevelopment that the dilemmas are exposed; dominant patterns of economic change are a major part of underdevelopment which is characterised by social injustice. By the end of the 1970s, the United Nations found that 'there is not evidence that the real trends of economic growth and social change have corresponded any better than previously to the ultimate objective.' (United Nations, 1979:3). As later chapters show, social objectives were not achieved; inequalities and social injustices had not only persisted but had become worse.

During the 1970s considerable attention was paid to the 'basic needs' approach. The failure of existing programmes to meet the needs of the majority was recognised and in different policy areas basic needs strategies emerged at the international level. As will be shown, these have been adopted to a considerable extent within national development strategies, but the gap between rhetoric and reality remains huge. The essential element in the basic needs strategy is that the needs of the poor must become the core of development policies. Among all the arguments regarding the feasibility of such a strategy, perhaps the most crucial issue is that it demands redistribution. The nature of the redistribution of social resources demanded by a genuine basic needs approach is explored in later chapters, together with discussion of the forces which militate against such redistribution. Among these the inherited patterns of distribution established under colonialism are of major significance. Chapter 2 explores some themes in colonial social policy with particular reference to health services in Papua New Guinea and social services in Tanzania.

As suggested, a major theme is the gap between stated social policy objectives and real trends. In 1979, the United Nations suggested a number of reasons for this gap (United Nations, 1979). First, economic growth in the Third World has not been sufficient to allow for significant allocations to social programmes and other measures to alleviate mass poverty. But it was clearly shown that this was only a very partial explanation. In many countries, high rates of growth during the 1970s had brought no reduction in inequalities. Second, that a number of countries, faced with economic crises with their roots in the operation of the Western-dominated international economy, had abandoned or curtailed their social programmes. Third, that despite the rhetoric of the basic needs approach, there is continuing attachment to the primary importance of rapid economic growth and reluctance to 'confront politically difficult problems of the composition of economic growth, distribution of its fruits and its environmental consequences'. (United Nations, 1979:10) Fourth, that while social programmes have expanded, they have remained over-dependent on the norms and techniques common in the industrialised countries. This again is a theme which recurs throughout the following discussions of social policy issues. Continuing under-development means continuing reinforcement of alien and inappropriate policies which are determined not by the needs of the majority but by the imperatives of externally-oriented economies and their related social formations.

Following the chapters on specific social policy issues, an important theme of alternative strategies − community-based programmes − is explored in a discussion of contrasting approaches to community development, focused on the 'improvement approach' in the case of India, and the 'transformation approach' in the case of Tanzania. A number of the issues raised by this and preceding chapters are related to the general problems of social policy and social planning in the concluding chapter.

1

Development and Underdevelopment

> For the generation of structural underdevelopment, more important still than the drain of economic surplus from the satellite after its incorporation as such into the world capitalist system, is the impregnation of the satellite's domestic economy with the same capitalist structure and its fundamental contradictions. (Frank, 1967:10)

Debate on the nature of development, explanations of the failure of efforts to achieve it, and of the likelihood of alternative strategies succeeding has taken much energy and produced a mountain of books, reports, articles and conference papers. This may indicate many things, but one thing it most certainly demonstrates is the crucial importance, however hidden this may seem at times, of the major questions in the analysis of development. It is not possible here to examine these in detail, only the outlines of the debate will be sketched. Furthermore, it will become clear that later discussion of more specific social policy issues leans heavily on particular theoretical positions outlined here; although the term 'under-development theory' suggests a unity of approach which denies real and important differences. For the purposes of the present study such a distinction is justifiable in so far as it allows a more or less consistent treatment of issues and the possibility of dealing with the problem of social policy as a dynamic in the contemporary of change in the countries of the Third World.

It is only relatively recently that the Third World has emerged as a real force. Until well into the twentieth century it was either literally subject to the capitalist system dominated by the Western industrial nations, or seen as irrelevant. In population terms, the Third World not only contains the majority of the world's population, but is growing the fastest. In economic terms, it has the greatest share of labour power, and by far the largest future markets. Politically, and despite the empty nature of many victories gained at the United Nations and elsewhere, it is now a real force, particularly so when it can affect the balance between the First and Second Worlds.

Despite continuing efforts to the contrary, it is no longer possible to view the whole of the Third World as an essentially undifferentiated mass of societies distinguished only by their 'backwardness'. By mid-century it became necessary for even the most unwilling Western analyst to approach the rest of the world as a complex and changing group of nations which were gaining political independence. There was of course a continuity here: such new nations were seen as in need of guidance and assistance in the achievement of 'modernisation'. In this process many assumptions were made, perhaps the most fundamental being that of 'a common interest' between the developed and underdeveloped. Abu-Lughod (1977:1) suggests this assumption may have been naïve. Given the nature of relationships both before and after political independence and the dynamics of underdevelopment discussed below, perhaps the assumption was not so much naïve as disingenuous. Common interests were as those which may be seen to exist between farmers and locusts: both have an interest in the crop, and indeed both wish the crop to be as big as possible. The modernisation view was dominant for a considerable period, however, and as will be seen embodied many powerful assumptions which in turn had both direct and indirect influence on strategies for development and specific policies within those strategies. Moreover, it is generally the case that such conceptions remain to a large degree in most countries of the Third World and in the international agencies which influence and constrain the development activities of those countries. There is no sense in which various approaches to development follow one upon the other, the new displacing the old. The contemporary reality is of an uneasy, frequently contradictory, set of attitudes, values and techniques drawn from a legacy of changing approaches and shifting circumstances.

The most recent phase may be crudely characterised as one in which the centres of action and sources of informed thinking, if not the real power, have shifted from the West to the Third World itself. Aid and assistance from the West, previously presented as at best epitomising common interests and at worst well-intentioned but perhaps inefficient, is increasingly seen by those at the receiving end with a great deal of suspicion (Arnold, 1979). Many now see these ties as part of a largely successful process by which the West has re-established and maintains in economic terms the hegemony it lost in formal political terms through decolonisation.

Both scholars and political leaders in the Third World have been critical of Western writing on development which justifies continuing exploitation by locating the causes of underdevelopment in the cultures of the Third World itself. 'Blaming the victim' is a familiar phenomenon to those who have studied poverty and in-equality within Western societies (Ryan, 1971). When it is used in explanations of levels of development it deflects attention from historical and international political and economic factors which create massive external obstacles to development.

Increasingly, explanations have come from within the Third World itself and the factors that account for underdevelopment and its continuation are defined, in both theory and practice, by those who have experienced underdevelopment and judged previous theories and explanations against the reality of their experience and their own perceptions of the world.

Important contributions have come from Latin America and Africa in particular. In what has become one of the most influential works in recent times, Fanon (1963) demonstrated the anger of those subject to oppression and exploitation. He also developed the powerful theoretical weapon of 'the psychology of oppression', in which the colonised victim is not only blamed for his own misery, but effectively taught to accept and internalise this view of his own incompetence and inferiority. The theories of dependency have exposed the nature of structural relationships, and suggest that the inequalities between rich and poor, urban and rural areas, those with power and those without, within Third World countries have been engendered and maintained by the very process of their development in subordination to metropolitan economic power (Oxall *et al*, 1975). The theories of the development of under-development make the crucial distinction between underdevelop-ment as a state, as in modernisation theories, and as a process. Conceived as a process, underdevelopment becomes a powerful theoretical weapon, allowing us to see that underdevelopment is not a position from which societies may move forward but the outcome of a continuing process whereby both their external relationships and internal social and economic formations are perverted to ensure progressively more profound integration as exploited parts of the international economy (Frank, 1967; Bernstein, 1973; Amin, 1974; Hoogvelt, 1978; Roxborough, 1979).

A number of underdeveloped societies have attempted to break the chains of underdevelopment and adopt strategies for genuine development. In this context the socialist countries of the Third World, notably Cuba, China and Vietnam, have served as inspiration; but because of profound differences of historical experience, political organisation and levels of ideological development cannot serve as models. Among the non-socialist Third World countries which have had profound influence on their contemporaries, however, both Tanzania and Mozambique have demonstrated, despite massive problems and only partly-achieved goals, that alternative strategies are possible. Julius Nyerere, President of Tanzania since independence, has consistently engaged the fundamental questions of the nature of development. His emphasis on the real purpose of development and the possibilities of a self-reliant development which serves the mass of people has given his writing a unique place in a popular literature which is still dominated by the pronouncements of international agencies which are fundamentally wedded to international capitalist growth (Nyerere, 1966; 1968; 1973).

The rest of this chapter will look in more detail at these questions with the intention of providing an indication of a theoretical framework in which the nature of social policy may be examined.

THE NATURE OF DEVELOPMENT

'Development' is a complex and elusive concept and is clearly fundamental to any discussion of strategies and policies, but is more often than not left undefined. The lack of attention paid to this most basic concept is of course in itself an acceptance of a particular set of assumptions. It is immediately obvious to anyone familiar with both the rich and poor countries of the world that development is a term used almost always in relation to the poor and not to the rich. To the extent that the term is used at all in rich countries it tends to be as part of 'concern' for 'backward' or 'depressed' areas of such countries, or in relation to particular social groups. In both cases the clear intention is that such areas or groups of people need to develop, or be developed to some state where they are more or less indistinguishable in all important respects from the rest of that society. There is thus no attempt to define the concept in terms of its true meaning, but simply an assumption of the rightness of dominant life-styles and socio-economic forms, and the self-evidence of the necessity to 'catch up'. In this regard, it is significant that in Sweden, a country for long regarded as perhaps one of the most fully evolved welfare states, recent debates on future change have focused on the concept of development, with attention being paid to the fundamental nature of the society and recognition that previous assumptions of continuing economic growth are no longer valid.

It should be obvious that more precise definitions of development must be made; the term is used freely, often indiscriminately, in a wide variety of contexts. It may be argued that we are concerned in a general sense with the development of the country, or that a particular policy or set of actions contributes to development or holds back development. Only if we have a clear understanding of the concept do such phrases hold anything more than symbolic meaning. More specifically, only a clear conception will allow meaningful social targets to be agreed upon and progress towards their achievement be measured. Very often, however, the meaning of this most fundamental concept is assumed and not thought out (Baster, 1972).

As soon as we begin to think through this question it is obvious that we cannot avoid value-judgements. Development is inevitably a normative concept − it is self-evidently almost a synonym for improvement. The question which must immediately be asked is from where we are to take our value-judgements about what constitutes improvement and what does not. One answer to this has frequently been that we should take them from governments, that is to say, from the pronouncements regarding desirable improvements which emerge from the various processes resulting in official policy. The most obvious difficulty with this is, of course, its inherent circularity. How can we assess what governments do if we use the criteria they themselves produce? Do we surely not need some more independent measure with which to judge both stated intentions and actual patterns of state action, or inaction?

Another approach, common in practice, has been to copy other countries − to follow their patterns of economic and social change and take, by implication at least, the present state of these countries as the goal. This, as suggested, is very common, particularly so where countries have been exposed to periods of direct rule by colonial powers, together with a continuing process of cultural, social, political and economic transfers which are designed explicitly and implicitly to establish and maintain the hegemony of particular systems of values and economic formations (Long, 1977; Hoogvelt, 1978). The nature of these relationships will be discussed further below, here it perhaps need only be stated that the desirability, leave alone the viablity, of imported concepts of development cannot be assumed, and indeed must surely be rejected unless some notion of the inherent superiority of established and powerful systems is held, and this must be rejected.

We are then obviously led to a position from which the fundamental values which will inform the concept of development must be debated in the context of the society concerned with reference to the nature of that society, its history, its culture and above all the needs of its people. If we begin with the most basic questions, however, it does become obvious that there will be some continuity in the value positions which emerge. We can approach the problem by asking the question 'What are the necessary conditions for a universally acceptable aim, the realisation of the potential of human personality?' (Seers, 1972). This aim is one which must be accepted as valid; if it is not, the concern with development itself is surely facile.

If we ask what is an absolute necessity, one answer is immediately obvious – enough food. Similarly, it is immediately obvious that individuals must have access to resources, either as individuals or as members of families or other social groups, at a level sufficient to enable them to provide for other basic needs such as shelter, clothing and so on. At this point we are avoiding difficult questions of how to measure what is necessary, but the important point is that there are clearly levels below those which enable basic necessities to be provided and that any normative approach to development must be concerned with this. A crucial cautionary note must be entered here. Although concern with subsistence must be fundamental to any concept of development this in no way suggests that the concept of poverty which will determine the perception of problems and the values and goals of development must be limited to an absolute or subsistence concept, as will be seen.

It has been persuasively argued that another basic necessity in human society is employment (Seers, 1972). Given the domination of debates on development by Western-oriented writers, employment has, more often than not, been taken to mean income-producing employment – either wage-employment or self-employment in production for the market. This assumed necessity of cash relationships is of course fundamental to Western-inspired development thinking and embodies within it far more than a simple carry-over of cultural baggage. It is of major importance, for if the place of a person in society is determined by the market relationship, which of course it is in non–socialist societies, then from this will flow a host of other consequences. To view employment as other than market-related is difficult in societies whose very nature is determined by the cash nexus. In other, but increasingly fewer societies alternative conceptions are still more readily understood. What then is meant by employment if not the relation to production familiar in most discussion of this issue? Put simply, the point is that every person must have a socially accepted role, acceptable to both the person and the society in which that person lives. To be unwillingly dependent on others is incompatible with self-respect. Employment viewed this way may thus include studying, working on the land for consumption and not the market, caring for those unable to provide for themselves, and many other roles which have meaning and purpose in a given society. The importance of this approach is that it directs attention away from an exclusive pre-occupation with paid employment. For such an alternative to have any value, however, attitudes to employment must be other than those characteristic of the non-socialist cash economy. In reality, there are few societies not already dramatically affected by the penetration of the cash economy and its attendant values and role definitions. Where this is so the denial of employment to those who have been socialised to prepare for and seek an economically active life is quite obviously a denial of basic human dignity.

Both subsistence poverty and lack of employment are obviously associated with levels of income, where the latter is defined in terms of the flow of resources of all kinds and not simply money. The level of income may then be seen as important, but as should be clear, but is so often conveniently overlooked, even very rapid increases in *per capita* income may not reduce either poverty or unemployment. Indeed, certain kinds of economic growth can easily be accompanied by, and may be seen to cause, unemployment. This leads us inevitably to a concern with distribution of income and all other resources which directly affect the quality of life for the mass of people. If we consider distribution, we must face some fundamental questions regarding equality and inequality.

Any discussion of equality must ultimately devolve on basic moral positions and fundamental perceptions of the nature of human society (Blowers and Thompson, 1976). Here, it must be emphasised, we are concerned with equality of condition, not the often substituted but essentially quite different notion of equality of opportunity. The latter, which may be interpreted as 'equal opportunity to be unequal', accepts inequality as both necessary and desirable, and is concerned above all to ensure that the inequality which results from the competition for unequally distributed privileges should be fair. To the extent that this is accepted, then patterns of inequality are legitimated.

The pursuit of equality does not assume that talent or ability is evenly distributed, but is rather founded on the recognition that every person is of equal worth. The position adopted on this very basic issue is of course of overwhelming significance in determining the goals sought in any society and thus the concept of development which will inform efforts to reach those goals. There is clearly no agreement on this. Many will deny the proposition that equality should be considered an objective in its own right as the third element in development. An alternative view is dramatically illustrated by the Ndegwa Report, produced in Kenya in 1971. Here, the case for structured inequality was clearly and powerfully put, founded on explicit assumptions about the nature of society and the forces which motivate persons in society (Prewitt, 1972).

There is of course a compromise position which may be adopted, and is frequently found. This recognises that an unequal society embodies social barriers which distort that society and prevent the whole population from realising their potential and thus maximising the achievement of the whole society. However arguments of this kind, which are not rooted in the ethical rejection of inequality, are most often variants of the equality of opportunity position suggested earlier. Concern is with inequalities of power, education and access to all kinds of social resources as well as income and wealth, but not, fundamentally, with equality of condition.

If we accept the three concerns of development outlined here – poverty, unemployment and inequality – we may then ask, as a test of a country's development, What has been happening to each of these? If all three have become less severe we may then say there has been a period of development. If one, two, or even three, have become worse, can we say that this is development, even if *per capita* income has increased dramatically? (Seers, 1972).

These three things then are fundamental to the concept of development, and may perhaps be described as first order criteria. There are, of course, many other criteria which although closely related to these may involve other significant value choices. For example, a value may be placed on education, taking the full meaning of that term; participation may be valued of itself, quite beyond any desire to check the excesses of government by participatory forms. Similarly, the complex and profound values implied in the notion of community may be seen as having an important place in the kind of society sought.

The debate on the nature of development has continued for many years and will go on for many more. A recent major event was the public acknowledgement of its importance to the West contained in the Brandt Report *(The Independent Commission on International Development Issues,* 1980). This, despite its rhetoric, essentially argues a case related to the self-interest of the industrial nations and in its discussion of development demonstrates a lack of conviction in its attempt to separate development from growth:

Development never will be, and never can be, defined to universal satisfaction. It refers, broadly speaking, to desirable social and economic progress, and people will always have different views about what is desirable. Certainly development must mean improvement in living conditions for which economic growth and industrialisation are essential. But if there is no attention to the quality of growth and to social change one cannot speak of development.

It is now widely recognised that development involves a profound transformation of the entire economic and social structure. This embraces changes in production and demand as well as improvements in income distribution and employment. *(The Independent Commission on International Development Issues,* 1980:48)

A view of this kind, although it pays attention to non-economic criteria, still places primary emphasis on economic changes; social questions are concerned with the amelioration of what are seen as inevitable patterns of economic change.

Walter Rodney offered a view much closer to that suggested here:

Development in human society is a many-sided process. At the level of the individual, it implies increased skill and capacity, greater freedom, creativity, self-discipline, responsibility and material well-being. Some of these are virtually moral categories and are difficult to evaluate — depending as they do on the age in which one lives, one's class origins and one's personal code of what is right and what is wrong. However, what is indisputable is that the achievement of any of those aspects of personal development is very much tied in with the state of the society as a whole. (1972:9)

This essential focus on people is to be found throughout the writings of Julius Nyerere, whose influence has extended far beyond his own country of Tanzania:

For the truth is that development means the development of *people*. Roads, buildings, the increase of crop output and other things of this nature are not development; they are only tools of development . . . An increase in the number of school buildings only if the buildings can be, and are being, used to develop the minds and the understanding of the people . . . An expansion of [cash] crops is development only if these things can be sold, and the money used for other things which improve the health, comfort and understanding of the people . . . Every proposal must be judged by the criterion of whether it serves the purposes of development—and the purpose of development is the people. (1968: 59/60)

From this cursory examination of the complex concept of development, it is clear that fundamental differences in approach are possible; in practice perhaps the most profound disagreement has been with those who argue the primacy of economic growth and modernisation. As suggested earlier, from the viewpoint of the Western industrialised nations, development could be seen as a process of modernising backward societies; 'a "total" transformation of a traditional or pre-modern society into the types of technology and associated social organisation that characterise the "advanced" economically prosperous and relatively politically stable nations of the Western World'. (Moore, 1963:89)

During the 1950s and 1960s economists were dominant in development literature which took modernisation and development to be synonomous. The problem was seen as essentially a matter of economic growth; of subsidiary interest were problems of social change, and such change was that necessarily associated with economic growth. Lewis put the position succintly: 'First it should be noted that our subject matter is growth, and not distribution.' (1955:9)

As very many writers have argued, the assumptions of modernisation theories can be shown to be false and the models constructed on the basis of such theories largely irrelevant to the countries of the Third World (Long, 1977; Hoogvelt, 1978; Taylor, 1979). Two important points need to be made about such theories, however. First, that 'structural-functionalist theories of modernisation have in fact very usefully served as an ideological mask camouflaging the imperialist nature of Western capitalism' (Hoogvelt, 1978:62). Second, that despite thoroughgoing rejection of such theories on both theoretical and practical grounds they continue to have profound influence on development policies, not least as these are mediated through the major international agencies. As later chapters will show, both national development strategies and specific policies within such strategies still reflect the modernisation approach. Given the relationship between this approach and the imperatives of the international economy this is hardly surprising, but not always sufficiently acknowledged.

Both the recognition that economic growth as such was not development and that modernisation/Westernisation was a weapon of economic imperialism led, by the 1970s, to a surge of alternative analytical effort. In particular the neo-Marxists declared that what was occurring was 'the development of underdevelopment' (Frank, 1969; Booth, 1975). In marked distinction to prevailing views, underdevelopment theories perceive the relations which exist between poor and rich countries as damaging the interests of the former and working to the further advantage of the latter.

UNDERDEVELOPMENT AND DEPENDENCY

It is the intention here only to outline the main features of under-development theory, space does not permit a detailed discussion of the many complex issues involved (Bernstein, 1973; Wallerstein, 1974; Oxaal *et al,* 1975; Hoogvelt, 1978).

From the outset it must be noted that there are a number of differing versions of the theory (Foster-Carter, 1974). There are, however, important themes which distinguish these from the modernisation theories outlined earlier. The neo-Marxist perspective does not assume that either developed or underdeveloped societies are self-sufficient social systems, but rather places emphasis on the interconnections of a global economic and social system. Secondly, in examining historically the causes of social change in underdeveloped countries, it demonstrates that the diffusion of Western systems creates the reverse of development. Rather than greater independence, the nature of change is such as to bring about greater dependence and further entrench exploitative relationships both within underdeveloped countries and between those countries and their infinitely more powerful 'partners in development', to use Lewis' tragically ironic phrase. In outline, the approach to underdevelopment followed here may be summarised crudely as follows (Amarshi *et al,* 1979:xiv/xv).

The world capitalist system matured in the nineteenth century with the emergence of a relatively small number of industrialised states. This system, despite the emergence of a number of non-capitalist states, remains fundamentally intact. Viewed as a total world system, the dominant element is the group of ruling-class interests within the highly industrialised states. By national, international and supranational means, the latter dominated by the giant transnational corporations, these interests exercise massive economic, political and military power. The single most important feature of the world system is the use of this power to ensure that the economies and societies of the rest best serve the needs of an ever-expanding, Western-dominated world economy. This subjection may be seen to operate principally through mechanisms of unequal exchange. There is a group of semi-peripheral states, which, although suffering the effects of this subjection, have nonetheless some semi-independent development and some ability to use the mechanisms of unequal exchange for their own limited advantage. The majority of poor countries, however – those in fact which are generally referred to as the Third World – remain on the periphery of the world capitalist system and are continuously underdeveloped by their relations with the more dominant nations. At this point, it is important to emphasise the difference in meaning given to the term underdevelopment as distinct from earlier, but persisting interpretations. The fundamental feature of under-development as it will be used in later discussion is that it is a process; and it is thus quite unlike the conventional economic and sociological usage which refers to a static condition. Although we may refer to a society as underdeveloped at a point in time, we are by doing so only taking a snapshot view of a process which has gone on, and continues to go on, over a period of time. The distinction is profound; as the term is used here it connotes a pattern of relation-ships and complex process by which a nation-state may *be under-developed*. Griffin's often quoted conclusion is worth repeating here: 'Underdeveloped countries as we observe them today are a product of historical forces especially those released by European expansion and world ascendancy . . . Europe did not "discover" the underdeveloped countries; on the contrary, she created them.' (1968:38)

A number of characteristic features of underdevelopment may be identified, at the obvious risk of over-simplification and generalisa-tion. In the economic sphere there is above all progressive dis-location and distortion of the economy involving restriction of autonomy. Capitalist structures are imposed on already existing economic and social formations. These imposed structures, not being indigenous, widen the divergence between the domestic and export-oriented economies. Thus, as production processes in certain sectors are progressively oriented to the economic needs of the metropolitan countries, there is greater divergence between domestic resources and domestic needs and demand. Production for the satisfaction of domestic needs suffers as a result of a dominant export orientation and characteristically domestic manu-facturing is severely limited with heavy reliance on imported manufactures. The nature of economic relations between the metropolitan countries and the underdeveloped countries is such that the surpluses are transferred to the former, leaving the latter relatively impoverished and chronically dependent. Put simply then, the essential point is the distortion of underdeveloped economies, they may grow, but that growth is primarily geared to the economic interests of the metropolitan powers. The lack of fit between economic activity and the achievement of real development is, to a large extent, the result of this external orientation and the lack of internal dynamics and coherence.

The importance of the process of underdevelopment cannot be over-emphasised; the penetration of the cash economy which now dominates the societies of the Third World not only influences profoundly the contemporary patterns of social formation, but dramatically restricts the range of future options. The majority of Third World populations are in the rural areas. Of these, very few are now untouched by the money economy although large proportions remain primarily within the subsistence economies. In a number of countries the interactions between the 'modern' and the pre-existing subsistence economy and its related social systems is of major significance. A number of those who have argued for alternative development paths stress the values of pre-existing systems and the possibilities of expressing those values in national development strategies which reject the domination of the international capitalist economy and its attendant social forms (Nyerere, 1968).

John Waiko, a young Papua New Guinean in a society undergoing rapid and profound change, has eloquently expressed this position:

Subsistence culture is a total way of life and itself provides an ideology for the subsistence population. What is lacking is leadership; the kind of leadership that can decide now whether the society, or the majority of its members, must live within a cash economy based on intensive capital from outside, or whether it can retain and revitalise the subsistence economy based in primary resources. The latter seems the best alternative for Papua New Guinea, though not for its élite, nor for the international corporations. (Waiko, 1977:427)

In social terms, underdevelopment is characterised above all by the emergence of 'a perverse class structure shaped more by external than by internal pressures'. (Amarshi, 1979:xv) The analysis of class formation in underdeveloped societies has received considerable attention in the literature and is clearly of profound importance to understanding of present dynamics and the direction of future change (Cohen, 1972; Wallerstein, 1974; Good, 1976; Shivji, 1976).

In simple terms it must first of all be noted that pre-existing social formations were not undifferentiated – traditional modes of production carried with them attendant social formations.

However, social classes came with the money economy and, in very many cases, with colonialism. In post-colonial societies two features may be seen to predominate (Gutkind and Wallerstein, 1976; Gutkind and Waterman, 1977): the emergence of a largely urban, largely public service-based wage and salary élite and the beginnings of rural class formation. There is considerable variation in the latter, but typically there is both the growth of a group of rural entrepreneurs and the creation of landless wage labourers in rural areas.

The existence of two modes of production, the traditional and the capitalist, has attracted a good deal of attention. The inter-relations between these has been seen to produce a reality of extreme complexity (Clammer, 1975; Mamdani, 1976; Wallerstein, 1976;). In rural areas the overlaying of traditional social systems by class relations may be complex in detail but clear in its effects – the growth of inequality. In most areas, however, the fundamental source of inequality is the rise of the urban-based classes. As is suggested below, the nature of urban class formations is problematic, and at this point only some general features most closely related to social policy questions are outlined. Typically, the power of the urban areas is very great – the towns and cities dominate the political economy (Lipton, 1977). No discussion of contemporary Third World issues can ignore the significance of relations between urban and rural areas. It is not simply that resources of all kinds are unequally distributed in favour of the urban areas, but that the power which determines the pattern of distribution lies in the urban areas (Lipton, 1977). This is not, of course, to suggest that Third World urban populations are homogeneous. Social relations within urban systems are complex, and relations between specific urban populations and the rural areas are equally so (Castells, 1979; Santos, 1979). Nonetheless, in crude terms, the most important feature of a very large number of social systems in Third World countries is the urban-based élite. In many instances this group is primarily formed from within the public service, and it is essentially a group of state employees in terms of employment location (Markovitz, 1977). In situations where such groups are the heirs to colonial administration, this group has enormous power and, with few exceptions, concomitant privilege. The nature and role of this group are major factors in the formation and implementation of social policy.

Closely related to the nature of this administrative élite is the dominance of the state (Golbourne, 1979). It is clearly impossible to generalise across the whole range of contemporary underdeveloped societies particularly with regard to the crucial relationships between class power and state power; for a not insignificant number, however, we may identify certain common characteristics:

> The state is the principal employer of labour, the chief dispenser of jobs, benefits, patronage, contracts, foreign exchange and licence to trade. Manipulation of the offices and resources of the state by the power elite proved the shortest cut to wealth. It was political power that made possible the creation of economic power, not the other way about. (First, 1970:101)

At this level of analysis, then, it may be clear that the institutions of the state have a profoundly important place in the concrete reality of underdeveloped societies. To move further and attempt to examine the nature of state power is vitally necessary but extremely difficult; it can only be done by analysis of specific formations. While acknowledging that in general the state may be seen as 'exceptional in the sense that is strong and authoritarian'. Roxborough argues that 'the ways in which the interests of the dominant classes are connected with the actual functioning of the state apparatus are highly variable' (1979:119; 121). Of particular concern here, in relation to later discussion of social policy, are three specific aspects of the state. First, the degree to which the apparatus of the state is used to further the class interests of those who are able to use a variety of mechanisms to affect policy formation and implementation. Second, the degree to which this manipulation of state power allows the effective intrusion of foreign interests, directly or indirectly. Third, whether and to what extent those who have gained privileged positions in the state bureaucracy are able to use their power to form themselves as a new class, or as a distinct part of the dominant class. State power and class power are not the same, and the extent to which they are independent is a major question: 'It should be clear that any analysis of the state in the Third World must examine the mechanisms and institutions through which social classes have access to, and influence on, the making of state policy.' (Roxborough, 1979:123)

Social class is thus an essential element in the framework of analysis adopted for the examination of social policy. There is, as suggested earlier, no simple theoretical structure which will encompass the concrete reality of underdevelopment. However, the main lines of colonial class formation may be seen as being centred on an uneven transformation of pre-capitalist societies into bourgeoisie, proletariat and peasantry. The bourgeoisie within underdeveloped societies must be seen in its relations with the 'great absent member' (Amin, 1974:393) — the metropolitan bourgeoisie. Typically, it has a relatively weak position and severely restricted autonomy — the term *comprador* may frequently be encountered in discussion of this group. Historically, this term referred to those who acted as middlemen between foreign economic interests and the internal resources those interests either could not or did not wish to control directly. Given contemporary patterns of international economic activity and the overwhelming dominance of metroplitan-based interests, the bourgeoisie in underdeveloped countries typically has a very restricted economic base, except as dependent or *comprador* in character. Closely related to this must be the activity of the bureaucratic bourgeoisie, by which is meant the more senior state functionaries. This group is sometimes directly involved in the control of the means of production through government regulation of the market economy, the operation of state enterprises, and close involvement with metropolitan interests in the planning and operation of joint ventures (Evans, 1977). As will be stressed in later chapters, the bureaucratic bourgeoisie may have considerable power in relation to the distribution of state resources, these allocations frequently comprising a very large part of national income and are significant in a variety of ways to the interests of the whole bourgeoisie. Furthermore, rewards from employment at senior levels are typically very great and take a huge share of state revenue (Markovitz, 1977). The difficulty of isolating the class elements is illustrated further by the common practice of members of the bureaucratic bourgeoisie using both their relative wealth and privileged positions to involve themselves in outside enterprise (Amin, 1974; Mamdani, 1976). This may be done in co-operation with other members of kinship groups, and if this is so it may be seen as further complicating the complex relations between traditional and capitalist modes of production. The reality of Third World situations can be yet more complex, particularly so when particular strands in a pattern of relationships may reverse the expected flows of obligation or exploitation:

To draw sharp distinctions among the administrative bourgeoisie, the politicians, and the businessmen can be misleading because power and class are not necessarily matters of individuals but of families. The same men can play many roles and take part in politics, administration, and commerce. Their brothers, cousins, fathers and sons can do the same. The result is a web of relations that brings the holders of power into overlapping and sustained contact. (Markovitz, 1977:210)

Thus classes are not clearly demarcated, especially so in a rapidly changing, dependent political economy, and there are 'all sorts of what appear to be intermediate groups and strata and even "overlaps" . . . ' (Shivji, 1975:16). Nonetheless, and especially if class *formation* is the primary concern (Cohen, 1972), the bureaucratic bourgeoisie may be seen to be the dominant exploiting class element within the majority of social formations of the Third World. To the extent that this is so, and later chapters will return in a variety of ways to this theme, this is a crucial element in the understanding of social policy and any consideration of the possibilities for effective, alternative social policy strategies.

SUMMARY

It has been argued that the concept of development is fundamental to any discussion of social policy in the Third World. Although widely used, the term has very frequently not been defined with any rigour. It has often been taken, implicitly and explicitly, as a progressive pattern of change towards an idealised model of Western society. More recently, however, such conceptions have been challenged and modernisation approaches, which placed overwhelming emphasis on economic growth, were supplanted by approaches which recognise the fundamentally normative nature of development and emphasise the real needs of the majority of people. In order to comprehend the reality of contemporary Third world societies, some aspects of underdevelopment have been considered. Above all, it has been stressed that underdevelopment is a powerful and continuing set of processes producing particular kinds of economic and social formations both within developing countries and between those countries and the more powerful nations in the international economy. Although specific forms vary, in general terms the perversion of Third World political economies may be seen as directing change in the interests of external forces. The crucial importance of this perspective is that it enables the economic and social dimensions of what may appear to be vigorous growth and change to be more fully understood. In the chapters which follow the focus of concern is with those economic and social formations within Third World countries which affect the nature of social policy issues and responses. In this chapter, the most significant of these have been identified as patterns of internal dependency, inequality, the role of the state, and class formation. With regard to the latter, the dominance of élite groups and the problematic class position of the administrative bourgeoisie may be seen as being of major importance. A number of these theories will be explored further in later consideration of social policy.

2

The Legacy of Colonialism

We have been oppressed a great deal, we have been exploited a great deal and we have been disregarded a great deal. (Tanu, 1967:5)

This book discusses the social services that have been built up in England and other countries to meet the changing needs of the people, and it suggests ways in which similar services might be developed in countries such as Nigeria and the Gold Coast where the pattern of life is rapidly altering. (Gardiner and Judd, 1954: frontispiece)

Dictionary definitions of the word colony stress the importance of the settlement by emigrants of new territories, remote from but retaining connections with the parent state. Goldthorpe (1975:40) points to 'a curious inversion' in usage during the twentieth century: countries which were colonies in the dictionary sense were called, in British terms, 'Dominions', while countries where most people were not of European descent were called 'Colonies'. The significance of this is not as a contribution to a debate on semantics, but as an important clue to the nature of the relationships between the metropolitan countries and the countries of the Third World. A number of writers have made the distinction between trade and control (Rhodes, 1970). In such analyses, whether a country was incorporated into a colonial structure or not, penetration by expanding Western capitalism in general was a profoundly important factor in determining the nature of change in that country. Formal systems of colonial administration were often necessary in order to stabilise situations of dependency, and where this did occur it may be seen as a formal recognition of the relationship between the metropolitan centre and its dependency. Such a relationship implied the existence of administrative, legislative, military and social control. Thus, although particular attention will be paid here to countries where colonial administrations were relatively well-developed, colonialism is taken as a useful, if somewhat loose, term for the analysis of historical processes which linked the growth of European, and later North American, capitalism with the creation elsewhere in varying forms and to varying extents of underdevelopment. The structural transformation was most often begun in quite modest ways with the establishment of trading posts, missions and agency houses, though in the case of the Spanish involvement in South and Central America force was employed from the outset (Furtado, 1973).

Most contemporary Third World countries experienced direct colonial rule in the past; a few remain colonies even now. A large number gained political independence only relatively recently, in the Indian sub-continent and South Asia there was a 'rush to independence' in the 1940s, while in Africa there was a similar rush in the 1960s. Others have had a form of political independence for very much longer – a number of South American countries gained independence during the first half of the nineteenth century. In a number of these, however, it was the immigrant white communities which achieved political independence and who used it to dominate the majority indigenous populations. Where this is the case, as in South Africa more recently, colonialism may be seen as 'internalised' (Wolpe, 1975).

The age of European expansion falls into two major periods. During the first, from about 1500 to the early nineteenth century, Europeans conquered the Americas and wholly occupied many islands around the world; they remained confined, however, to small enclaves on the coasts of the Asian and African continents. From about the middle of the nineteenth century, they occupied the whole of Africa and parcelled out between them most of the continent of Asia. (Goldthorpe, 1975:40/41)

During the first period identified by Goldthorpe, European colonialism was essentially mercantile, and the fundamental concern was with the extraction of wealth from those areas which could be penetrated. Not least in importance was the trade in human beings; the slave trade was of crucial importance to European economic growth and the biggest movement of population was that of African slaves. During the second period, from the mid-nineteenth century onwards, there was a fundamental change in the nature of colonial domination. The earlier mercantile basis began to change, and new forms of imperialism began to emerge. In terms of territory, the colonialists had been active only at the edges, particularly the coasts. Increasingly they moved inland, seeking and gaining control over large areas of land. In this lies the profound change: these areas were directly controlled and administered. Two closely related sets of factors may be seen as important here. First, although trade remained important, there was a growing desire to exploit directly the natural resources of these new areas; the actual and potential productivity of the colonies was fuel for the engine of economic advance in Europe. The imperatives of European capitalism demanded the exploitation of these areas. Second, however, as Goldthorpe points out, there were a number of technological innovations which enabled this expansion to take place (1975:44), in particular the railway, which permitted rapid and reliable movement of goods from inland areas to the ports. At sea, the steamship allowed faster transportation of primary products, and particularly agricultural products, to the markets of Europe and North America. In addition, of course, the new warships could both protect goods in transit and ensure the continuing subjection of those producing them. Other significant advances of the period include those in medicine, especially the use of quinine in the treatment of malaria, which gave Europeans a higher rate of survival.

The phase of direct European colonial rule was not significantly advanced until the second half of the nineteenth century, the greatest extent of colonial annexation and establishment of administration not taking place until the last quarter of the century. When it occurred, however, it was with a ferocity and rapacity the legacy of which remains today.

The new commercial enterprises which sought to exploit more directly than their trading predecessors began to establish plantations, mines, and other permanent production activities. As they did so, they demanded both protection and services from colonial administrations. Thus the network of administrative outposts was extended, and its functions increased to serve the needs of these new interests. Particularly where commercial interests employed European staff in remoter areas, it was for their benefit that colonial administrations took greater control. As will be seen later, however, plantations and mines needed labour and certain minimal services were required to ensure a regular and reliable supply of such labour. Taxes were imposed on the new colonies to support the growing burden of imposed administration.

COLONIAL SOCIETY

The most important feature of colonial society, and crucial to the patterns of social policy in contemporary Third World countries, was that virtually all the activity of colonial administrations was directed by, and in the interests of, foreigners. For the most part the foreigners were European. Three areas are of significance here: economic formations, missions and patterns of government.

In many instances immediate economic advantage may not have been the major factor governing the acquisition of colonies. Both the requirements of a free-ranging military/diplomatic strategy and the demands of non-economic interests, particularly missions, led the colonial powers to take control of territories from which, initially at least, there was little or no direct economic gain. Both Uganda and Papua, but not New Guinea, may be seen as examples of this (Oliver, 1952; Nelson, 1972). However, although precipitating factors may have varied, it is difficult to discern any areas in which economic advantage was not taken very soon after the establishment of colonial administration even if this had not previously been significant. Furthermore, although it is clearly the case that the annexation of territory with little immediate economic potential was often part of political rivalry between European nations as Midgley suggests (1981:43), this rivalry itself must surely be seen as essentially part of the development of the international capitalist economy in the late nineteenth and early twentieth centuries.

However, for whatever reasons acquired, the new colonies were not seen as liabilities. It was assumed from an early stage in the period of colonial expansion that colonies should meet the costs of their own administration from internally-generated revenues. Any subsidies from the metropolitan power were seen as temporary, and as noted above taxes were imposed on local populations as soon as possible. This leads us to a fundamentally important point – the need for taxes demanded the development of a cash economy in all colonies. In most, the number of Europeans was too small to bear the whole cost of colonial administration and without exception they were resolute in their unwillingness to do so. Thus, in almost all cases, economic activity was encouraged explicitly with the intention of bringing a greater proportion of the local population into the money economy. Where this was insufficient, payments-in-kind, both of goods and labour, were frequently extracted in the place of money taxes, or in addition to them. In specific terms the patterns of economic activity varied considerably. In some areas smallholder, cash crop production was encouraged under the control of the Europeans who bought and transported the products (Seidman, 1980). In others, the nature of the production demanded large-scale activity − for example mining − or European enterprises wished to control more directly the volume and quality of supply. In the latter case large farms and plantations were established. The extent to which these forms were adopted had considerable effects, notably in terms of the existence of substantial settler populations as in Kenya (Leys, 1975), the scale of land alienation, and the use, for example, on plantations of migrant labour both from within the colonies but also from outside (Baran, 1957; Myrdal, 1968).

Colonial economies were externally oriented. Production was of primary products for unprocessed export to the metropolitan countries. In this, the plantations and extractive industries were most completely dominated by reference to external forces. Managed by foreigners, they produced virtually nothing which could be used within the colony. The large farms were different; they could, and did, produce food for local consumption and were frequently run by foreigners who would in time claim rights to large areas of the best agricultural land. But all these activities had in common a demand for cheap labour, and colonial administrations ensured the supply of such labour. Although the most extreme forms of direct compulsion were less used during the twentieth century, alternative 'inducements' were equally effective. The simplest, and widely used, was the requirement to pay money taxes, and in most circumstances the only source of money for taxes was wage labour. The extent of economic activity varied considerably in the colonies, as did the nature of that activity. In a comparison of neighbouring Kenya and Tanzania, Cliffe (1973) provides a useful study of the different patterns of colonial economic activity. Kenya had a substantial settler population and thus a number of large-scale farms, whereas Tanzania did not. Kenya was penetrated by a much more intensive economic infrastructure linked with international capitalism; in Kenya smallholder production for the external market advanced much further during colonialism. However, as Nyerere has pointed out, this relative backwardness may be variously interpreted, 'Tanzania's strength lay in its weakness and in the unity of its people.' (1973:268)

Despite variation in the extent of penetration by the external economy and the particular forms of economic activity, the central features are constant. Both production and its myriad associated activities were dominated by external forces. Under colonial administrations these economies were made into extensions of the metropolitan economies. To the extent that an infrastructure of railways, ports, telephone communications, airstrips, banks, administrative centres and, as will be seen later in more detail, health and welfare services was established, this was related in virtually every case to the needs of European-dominated economic activity. Both in nature and location the infrastructure which supported the economic activity, encouraged by colonial administrations, was informed by needs other than those of the mass of people.

MISSIONS

Missionary activity was an important part of European colonial expansion in several ways. First, the task of 'civilising' local populations which missionaries took upon themselves was very frequently used as a justification for more extensive penetration of territories and greater degrees of control. Both of these were often accomplished by completely uncivilised methods (Fanon, 1967; Rodney, 1972). Second, once established, the missions were important interest groups in the colonies, on occasion in conflict with both administrators and business interests. However, despite such conflicts, it is clear that common interests ultimately outweighed particular differences and the very existence of a significant missionary presence gave legitimacy to continuing colonial domination. Third, missions encouraged the penetration of cash economy both from general assumptions they brought with them regarding the virtues of hard work, thrift and so on, and specific needs for cash to support church activities. They were influential in attempts to shift local people from subsistence production to cash crop production and wage labour. Particularly in remoter areas, the mission stations themselves were significant employers. To the extent that they engaged in the provision of services, for example health and education, and in many areas this role was considerable, their impact was greater still. As will be seen later the impact of mission activity in this regard was, and in some areas remains, considerable; their involvement in education is of major general importance. Proselytisation could succeed only where local populations could be cajoled or persuaded to accept both new ideas and a host of attendant skills and forms of behaviour necessary to the proper expression of these ideas. Thus the incorporation of local populations into the introduced religious institutions demanded both particular kinds of training such as basic literacy, and also the abandonment of traditional forms of all kinds. The total impact of the missions, backed by the power of colonial administrations, must of course be seen in total, but it is in their attack on existing cultures that they may be seen as most explicitly pernicious. Local beliefs and customs were not simply criticised and alternatives offered by example, what already existed was most often reviled and stamped as immoral. Missionaries took with them, and continue to do so, not just their religious beliefs but their own cultural preconceptions. Their success in transferring both are profoundly important. In producing converts in their own image they undermined traditional systems and, as part of doing so, respect for these systems. The relationship between the stated or implied superiority of introduced systems and the acceptance of modernisation is clearly complex, but is nonetheless important. Furthermore, this profound and long-lasting impact may be seen to be deepened by the fact that the churches, as they became localised, provided important channels for upward advancement and mobility in colonial and post-colonial society. Thus it was common to find many leaders of the newly independent nations of the last forty years who had achieved education and position through religious affiliation and activity.

Although the negative effects of missionary activity have so far been stressed, it must also be noted that throughout the colonial period the missions as a whole tended to act on behalf of local populations in conflicts over gross exploitation by economic interests or unjust administrations (Perham, 1962). However, although such examples are numerous and neither the tempering role of missions nor the extent of their direct provision of services can be denied, they were nonetheless deeply embedded in the total system of colonial society. Above all, there was a consistent refusal to challenge the legitimacy of colonial administration itself. 'Rendering unto Caesar' was invoked when conflict threatened to become extreme. The contemporary activities of missionaries in some parts of South America continue the theme; they have faced hostility from their own churches when struggling for the rights of the poor and oppressed (Gallet, 1972).

GOVERNMENT AND ADMINISTRATION

Colonial rule not only imposed systems of administration on areas which had previously governed themselves through distinctly different political and social forms; it created, through the drawing of artificial boundaries, new geo-political entities. Thus from the beginning, competition between the colonisers created borders where none had previously existed, planting the seeds which would later grow into enormous problems. The results of this are well known: current problems of border dispute, non-viability of tiny or land-locked nations, conflict between cultural groups, and difficulties of more recent attempts at reunification all attest to the arbitrary carving-up of the late nineteenth-century empires. There was, of course, enormous variation in existing social and political institutions. It was only when these were recognisable as 'government' by the colonisers that attempts were made to adapt them to their needs. In Uganda, for example, pre-colonial social formations were complex and the related political system equally so. For the British as colonisers this presented considerable problems; they were overcome with characteristic expedition:

It thus became necessary for the metropolitan power to seek allies in its colonial venture. Colonialism – the implantation of the metropolitan state apparatus in a conquered territory – was not possible without *mediating* this rule through classes physically situated in the colony. In the language of British colonialism, 'indirect rule' became a necessity. A class of collaborators – those who would recieve partial treatment in return for helping to maintain law and order – had either to be found among the natives or brought in from other dependencies. In Uganda, Britain resorted to both measures. But Britain's problem . . . was not just to create a collaborating class; there was also a need to come to terms with a ruling class and a monarchy that were both politically organised and militarily powerful . . . Nothing short of undermining the organisation and unity of the Baganda fuedal lords would do. To achieve this the British successfully exploited and furthered existing divisions within this class. Lord Lugard, leading the troops of the Imperial British East Africa Company, had joined forces with the Baganda Protestants to defeat the Baganda Catholics at the Battle of Mengo in 1892. (Mamdani, 1976:41-3).

In this analysis can be seen several important themes. There is the explicit alliance of political, economic and religious interests; the reference to 'indirect rule', and indeed to Lugard himself, closely associated with the concept; above all, to the 'implantation of the metropolitan state apparatus'. It is this which is the key to under-standing of colonial rule. Although specific forms varied, and be-tween, say, the British and French approaches quite substantially, it was always ultimately this which lay at the heart of the functions of the colonial state. The colonial state was a geographical extension of the metropolitan state, and was directly subordinate to it. In the case of British colonial administration this appeared in practice as the subordination of the governor of a colony to the colonial secretary, and of the bureaucracy in the colony to the Colonial Office in London. As Mamdani puts it, 'the colonial state re-presented an absentee ruling class, the metropolitan bourgeoisie, and it performed the functions of both state and ruling class in an "independent" nation'. (1976:142)

Perhaps the most important features of colonial administration which need to be emphasised here are first, the establishment and maintenance of the state apparatus and second, co-option of local groups who would not only allow that apparatus to function but would provide crucial assistance to that apparatus.

The government of colonies was typically regarded as a matter of administration rather than of politics. All the important positions in the colonial administrations were held by officials of the metro-politan country and they were ultimately responsible to the govern-ment of that country rather than to any local body. In the British case, colonial policy was for the greater part of the period fundamentally concerned with the maintenance of order. This involved both the provision of protection to European interests from threats, both real and imaginary, which the local environment and population were seen to pose. But colonial administrations were concerned with order in a more general sense; a major pre-occupation was with ensuring conditions of stability, predictability and rational government — all these of course from the perspective of colonial interests. It was only in the latter part of the colonial period that there was any real concern with the welfare of local populations and the expansion of social, economic and political opportunities. Given the dominant concern with order colonial administrations were, for local populations, essentially authoritarian. Despite later changes in stated policies, the nature of administrative systems continued to be authoritarian, this continuity, in fact, extending beyond independence in the majority of cases. The practices, procedures and precedents associated with the colonial period remained in evidence despite changes in government and personnel (Adu, 1969; Leys, 1969; Hyden, *et al.*, 1970).

Several particular features of colonial administrative systems are worth noting. First, that those systems were essentially bureaucratic; they had clearly defined hierarchical authority structures, a preoccupation with the definition and delimitation of areas of jurisdiction, both geographically and functionally, and they emphasised consistency and replicability within a framework of rules and precedents. They were, as suggested earlier, systems of administration designed for control, the policies they administered were externally derived. Despite the undoubted existence of colonial administrators who were flexible, innovative and sensitive to local needs — and there were some — the patterns of recruitment and promotion in colonial bureaucracies were those to be found in other parts of the metropolitan state bureaucracies (Symonds, 1966). Administering a colony was seen as comparable to administering a government department at home: 'A matter of making sensible rules, and seeing that they were obeyed, collecting revenues and using them efficiently for approved purposes to the satisfaction of a government auditor, and generally attending to the business of government in an orderly manner.' (Goldthorpe, 1975:56)

Second, such bureaucracies produced highly centralised systems of administration. Recent attempts in a number of countries to introduce greater decentralisation of administration and decision making have underlined the significance of this aspect of the colonial legacy (Stohr and Taylor, 1981). Third, the nature of colonial administrations was such that virtually all real power was vested in the bureaucracy, and genuine local political institutions were either impotent or non-existent until very late in the period of colonial rule. Public servants thus had both high status and real power. Although ultimately subject to control by superiors and legislatures in the metropolitan states, the colonial bureaucrats commonly did not have political institutions within the colonies which might control their activities. There was of course considerable variation in this, particularly where a substantial settler population was politically organised (Riggs, 1964).

Colonial administrations were thus powerful, bureaucratic, hierarchical and centralised. Their primary concern was with a routinised administration of policies which were concerned above all with order and stability. Given these functions, one of the most significant and long-lasting impositions was the law and its attendant institutions. Above all, administration existed precisely to ensure that economic interests were served; European lives and property had to be given essentially the same kinds of protection as existed in Britain, France or Germany. But the reality of colonial legal systems went much further than this. As Fitzpatrick argues, the law was used very directly to coerce local populations to respond to the needs of imposed cash economies.

These pre-colonial social formations contained little or no 'free' labour, so the producer had to be separated from the traditional means of production and legally coerced to work in various systems of forced and indentured labour. Taxes were introduced as an incentive to labour to get cash for the tax. Alternative means of getting cash for taxes which would reduce this incentive, such as cash-cropping were often legally prohibited or restricted, especially in settler colonies. Alternatively, with colonial economies based on the creation of a peasantry, peasants often had to be legally coerced into controlled and compulsory schemes of cash-cropping. (Fitzpatrick, 1980:37)

Thus, in addition to the achievement of maximum order and stability in what were essentially unstable conditions, law was used extensively and harshly to engineer change in the directions required for the penetration and entrenchment of external economic interests. As will be seen in the many areas of social policy to be discussed later, the same authoritarian and partial use of law was characteristic of colonial administrations. The legacy of this, and of general patterns of colonial control, will be seen to have had enormous influence on contemporary social issues and social policies.

COLONIAL SOCIAL POLICY

Although it is clear that the imperative of colonial policy and administration was the creation and maintenance of conditions suitable for the economic interests of the metropolitan countries, we are concerned here to examine social policy in the colonial period. As will be seen, this was closely related to the central purpose of colonial policy but there were a number of subsidiary factors which may be seen as important, not least the perception of the 'civilising mission' which is a consistent theme in statements of colonial policy intentions; for example:

There can be no room for doubt that it is the mission of Great Britain to work continuously for the training and education of the Africans towards a higher intellectual, moral and economic level than that which they had reached when the crown assumed responsibility for the administration of this territory. (Great Britain, 1927:2)

Two case studies will be considered here in order to illustrate and elucidate the characteristics of colonial social policy – health services in Papua New Guinea and social services in Tanzania.

COLONIALISM AND HEALTH IN PAPUA NEW GUINEA

It was in 1884 that Britain claimed a protectorate over South East New Guinea (Papua), when the Australian state governments agreed to pay the administrative costs of approximately $30,000 per annum. Germany claimed the north-eastern part (New Guinea) one month later, and so the history of the two areas must initially be considered separately. The first doctor arrived to live in British New Guinea in 1889, he was the administrator, Sir William McGregor. As Blackburn says of him: 'In New Guinea he explored widely and did his best to develop the people – he established the native police force and village constables, but did little medicine.' (1970:252) A second doctor, J.A. Blayney, was appointed in 1897 to the position of Resident Magistrate and Government Medical Officer, 'a not unusual dual appointment' (Blackburn, 1970:253). Blayney was appointed Chief Medical Officer when McGregor left in 1899, but had no medical or para-medical assistance until 1901. According to Blackburn, Blayney's requests for two more medical officers were refused by the Colonial Office.

In 1899, Cecil Vaughan was appointed as Acting Government Medical Officer for the Eastern Districts, stationed at Samarai. Vaughan had come to British New Guinea as manager of a company which intended exploiting rubber, but the project failed. Although unqualified, he was appointed as Medical Officer on the basis of experience in the Indian Medical Service. The fact that his appointment was to Samarai is of some significance. This was the most heavily populated European settlement in British New Guinea at the turn of the century, and the administration was concerned only with the health of Europeans until 1902.

It was in fact in Samarai that the first provision of medical services for the 'natives' was made in 1902. A native hospital was built in that year for $200, by A.J. Craigen, Blayney's replacement as Chief Medical Officer. A similar sum was spent on a native hospital in Port Moresby, the present capital. A European hospital had been built at Samarai by public subscription but closed due to lack of funds, while the planned European hospital at Port Moresby 'could not be built because of shortage of tradesmen' (Blackburn, 1970:253).

There were then, in the early years of colonial administration, virtually no medical services in British New Guinea, and what little did exist was concentrated in the areas of European settlement:

There is little point in discussing medical services before 1906, the year in which the Papua Act 1905 came into force. In 1900-01, for example, the medical department of British New Guinea [as Papau was then called] spent only $1014, or 1.6 per cent of the total administration expenditure. In 1906 — 07 Papuan medical services accounted for $4316, or 4.76 per cent [although] certain principles of health care have been recognised and (Gunther, 1972:749)

The early period in German New Guinea was essentially similar; there was one doctor in Finschhafen, employed by the German New Guinea Company between 1885 and 1889. By 1907, there were still only two doctors, and no hospital. By 1913 there were six doctors 'but they had not evoked the confidence of the native population; however the government and mission doctors were interested in native health and established a type of medical orderly who did village health work after three months' training' (Blackburn, 1970:253). This reference to medical services for the rural population is unusual in the accounts of the early years of colonialism, medical services were either for Europeans or for those native workers engaged in the cash economy. Gunther offers a somewhat generous interpretation of the pattern of medical services which emerged as the country was developed in the twentieth century:

When the medical service of a colony has very limited funds the establishment of priorities is difficult. The expatriate community, accustomed to ready access to medical attention and to hospitals, will press the administering authority to reproduce as far as possible the conditions of the metropolitan country. It is therefore not surprising that in both Papua and New Guinea there was the tendency to establish services in centres of European settlement, and then to extend them to sources of revenue such as the plantations and the mining fields. (Gunther, 1972:748)

In the first quarter of the century large numbers of local workers were engaged in the plantations and goldfields. The extent of sickness and death among these workers was appalling, but the response of the administrations was very often one which emphasised a curative approach to epidemics which got out of hand. On some occasions the reponse was even less than that. In 1907, the request for a medical officer to be stationed at the Yodda goldfield was refused on the grounds that he would have very little work to do; in that year the mortality among Papuan miners and carriers was 177 per 1000. At Lakekamu goldfield in 1910, a death rate of 35 per cent was reported for the native hospital. The Chief Medical Officer reported five European deaths, and that 255 of the 600 natives had died in five months (Blackburn, 1970). The major cause of death was bacillary dysentery. By 1910-12 dysentery was prevalent on the rapidly expanding coconut plantations too. As Lambert put it, 'the isolated white man having lower sanitary standards than the primitive natives'. (Lambert, 1928:362)

Not all medical services were concentrated on the European centres, but the major examples of those which were not were the

three venereal disease hospitals established in the Trobriand
Islands and near Samarai and Rabaul. Venereal diseases were
introduced by Europeans, and despite attempts at control,
gonorrhea in particular had spread throughout both territories by
1925 (Strong, 1926; Maddocks, 1973). Gunther, in assessing the
early provision of medical services, argued that:

In retrospect, two great weaknesses can now be recognised. There was the
failure, especially in Papua, to appreciate fully the patterns and trends of
disease. In both territories there was a failure to train the local people in
medical work, either in sufficient numbers or to an adequate level, so that
they could undertake greater responsibilities. (Gunther, 1972:749)

A crucial example of the failure to appreciate disease patterns,
and of the impact of the plantation system, may be seen in the case
of tuberculosis. No serious effort was made to find and isolate
sufferers until 1939, and the number of officially recorded cases was
small. But in 1923 it had been shown by autopsies that 21 per cent of
deaths in Rabaul were caused by tuberculosis. Furthermore, tests
on plantations showed that while only 5.2 per cent of labourers
newly arriving for work had positive tuberculosis test results, the
proportion rose to 42.8 per cent after one year's service, to 51.6 per
cent after five years, and to 73.3 per cent after ten years (Gunther,
1972). Plantation workers were travelling to and from their home
areas between contracts. Wigley and Russell stated in 1972 that:

The present incidence of infection with tuberculosis is directly proportional
to the degree and duration of contact with European communities, and to
the degree of urbanisation or culture change which has occurred in the
native communities . . . the association between contact and urbanisation
and the incidence of tuberculosis infection is so close that if the geography of
an area and its trading and movement patterns are known, it is possible to
predict the incidence of infection very accurately. (Wigley and Russell,
1972:642)

On the failure of the administrations to train local people in
medical work, Gunther suggests that, 'The attitude to Papuans and
New Guineans playing a more important role in health services may
be summed up in the words of a New Guinean Director of Public
Health in 1929 who said that natives could be trained as dressers,
but not more'. (1972:749) The employment of Papuans for medical
work began in 1912 with native helpers accompanying travelling

medical officers to deal with epidemics. From this developed the position of native medical assistant, and in 1922 a definite policy of training was implemented (Calov, 1929). They were used particularly for the treatment of yaws, but Blackburn states that 'By 1930 they were making independent patrols and reporting in English'. (1970:254) In New Guinea, the German administration introduced a system of medical 'tul-tuls' who were medical orderlies in the rural areas. The low level of education offered to local people was a great barrier, but in 1933 twelve educated Papuans were sent for six months' training at the School of Public Health and Tropical Medicine at the University of Sydney. There is a telling parallel with the contemporary situation in that 'most of them preferred on their return to work as clerks'. (Gunther, 1972:749) By 1936 there were fifty native medical assistants and about fifteen native hospitals, including those operated by missions. In 1935-6, there were thirteen administration medical officers, two doctors were in private practice, two were employed by goldmining companies, and there were five mission doctors.

Until the Second World War then, there was some development of medical services but these were extremely uneven in their distribution, being concentrated in areas of European settlement and cash economy production; mission services were primarily located in coastal areas. Although some training had been given to local people, the medical services available to the overwhelming majority of local people were minimal. Both government and mission services were almost entirely curative and hospital-based; the major emphasis in programmes of treatment for local people was the control of epidemic diseases. As noted earlier, a large part of the disease treated was the result of European exploration, settlement and exploitation, with venereal disease and dysentery as major examples. There were some examples of campaigns against major health problems and here the efforts to eradicate hookworm and yaws may be cited (Cilento, 1927: 1928). These campaigns were marginal, however, to the sum of health provision in the inter-war years. The paucity of services in this period was noted in the 1974-8 Health Plan: 'Before the last war, services were limited in both distribution and effectiveness, although attempts were made to provide medical care to village people through patrolling.' (Papua New Guinea, Department of Public Health, 1974:29).

Mair, writing in 1948 on the policies of the Australian administration prior to the war, was rather more critical:

Until a few years before the Japanese occupation, hospitals for natives were concentrated in areas of European activity rather than those of dense native population, while the medical treatment of native labourers is obviously to their advantage as well as to that of their employers, this does suggest a certain disproportion in a territory purporting to be administered on the principle of trusteeship. The total number of natives treated at hospitals in 1938-9 was 30,000, or one twenty-first of the enumerated native population. The total number of Europeans treated in government hospitals was 1933, or nearly one-third of the white population. (Mair, 1948:180)

There can be no doubt that the dominant purpose of medical services was to enable the development of colonial production both in mining and plantation production (Chinnery, 1923). Services were provided for native labour and to make conditions more tolerable for Europeans. The attempt to control malaria is perhaps the major example of the latter (Black, 1959; Gunther, 1974). There can be no doubt that many medical officers worked extremely hard in very arduous conditions, they were frequently in conflict with both business interests and the adminstration over the effects of colonial exploitation on the health of Papua New Guineans. More often than not, however, they shared the dominant view that economic development was 'natural' and that the 'uncivilised' native population would only achieve 'decent standards' by adopting European customs and habits. Any interest in the specific health problems of the local people tended to reflect a fascination with the exotic (Lambert, 1942). As in many other areas of social policy, the impact of war was of major significance. According to Ryan:

For Papua New Guinea itself the Second World War was the most cataclysmic event in the country's whole history . . . changes occurred or were set in motion which far exceeded in their effects the coming of the white man (which had been local and gradual) or the results of any natural catastrophe of disease or volcanic activity. Hunger, hardship, captivity and violent death were the lot of many of the indigenous people, for whom the war was an almost unrelieved disaster. Yet nearly all the changes, which count today as 'progress' stem in some way from World War II and its aftermath. (Ryan, 1972:1211)

The dual effect of the war on Papua New Guinea was important in relation to health services; on the one hand there was appalling suffering, but on the other the basis for post-war development was laid by the wartime adminstration. During the war, medical services were taken over by the army through the Australian New Guinea Administrative Unit (ANGAU), and for some time 'attention to the health needs of the ordinary people almost ceased, the peacetime anti-yaws and anti-hookworm campaigns were suspended'. (Gunther, 1972:750) Staff of the small, pre-war medical departments who were of military age were assigned to purely military duties, particularly Intelligence. ANGAU included some medical personnel in its field service and in 1942 a separate medical service was created consisting of two medical officers and twelve medical assistants (Ryan, 1968). Gunther acknowledges that in the later years of the war 'increasingly effective health measures were provided for those natives employed as carriers and labourers by the armed servies' (1972:750). Mair, however, attaches much greater importance to the establishment of medical services by ANGAU in the latter part of the war, 'In the sphere of health, a period during which the cost of the war to the people of New Guinea was high was later partially offset by the expenditure of money on a scale which only the resources of the army could have made possible'. (Mair, 1948:197)

In 1943, training courses for both European and local medical personnel were organised and by September 1944, there were ten medical officers, 113 European medical assistants, and 453 native medical orderlies. There were base hospitals for local people at Port Moresby and Lae with full army equipment, and fifty-three other hospitals operated by ANGAU. The significance of the wartime administration of medical services must be seen not so much in what was done during the war years, but in the pattern of services left when the war was over. Although primarily directed at the armed services and those Papua New Guineans assisting them, ANGAU medical services were comprehensively organised and directed over the whole area controlled by the allied forces. Facilities were established in locations which had not previously had services at all, and the programme of training local people as medical orderlies was on a much greater scale than anything which had gone before. It was of course avowedly curative in nature, which is of crucial importance in understanding the pattern of services which succeeded it. After the war, six native medical assistant schools were established with the aim of 'placing a thousand native medical assistants in a thousand villages'. (Gunther, 1972:751) In 1946, Papua New Guinean students were sent to the Central Medical School in Fiji for a five-year course which qualified them as native medical practitioners, later described as assistant medical practitioners, or assistant medical officers (Pathik and Goon, 1978). Although much inferior in status and remuneration to medical doctors recruited from overseas, these graduates did virtually the same work as the doctors, particularly in rural health centres (Calov, 1955). A programme of hospital construction began in 1947, and throughout the 1950s a number of sub-district hospitals were established. When the major hospital was established in Port Moresby in 1957 it had two wings (the differentiation was technically between those who paid fees and those who did not, in fact the division was racial). In 1960 there were ninety-four hospitals, the majority of which had separate paying and non-paying wings. Hospital construction continued through the 1960s with the emphasis on major district and base hospitals which had, in addition to provision of basic curative services, training functions and the provision of 'increasingly advanced and complex treatment at the specialist level'. (Papua New Guinea, Department of Public Health, 1974:29) Although there was provision for aid posts in the 1950s and 1960s, staff at this level were part-time and resources for these facilities were extremely limited; they were almost every-where the responsibility of local authorities and missions. Central government emphasised hospital-based medicine and in particular the recruitment, and later the training, of doctors. A great deal was made of the opportunities for doctors, particularly those with little or no experience (Calov, 1955).

Noting the views of the 1960 visiting mission that targets in the field of public health for the next five years generally are realistic, that progress made in the field of public health has been admirable, and that the high standards of hospital construction and administration which are being set are well justified, and are very much to the credit of the Administration, commends the Administering Authority for the progress being made in the field of public health. (Gunther, 1972:756)

There can be no doubt as to the achievements of the adminis-tration in hospital provision; by 1964 there was a ratio of one hospital bed for every 186 of the population, which compared favourably with many European countries (International Bank for Reconstruction and Development, 1965). But there were great costs. The financial cost was emphasised by the House of Assembly Committee on Public Accounts:

After the Second World War, the Department of Public Health was formed, and within a few years, had managed to bring into being a quite extensive curative health service. By 1947, the Department was operating 55 hospitals, which, in 1966, has been increased to 103 . . . This was not achieved without great expense. During the 1950s the Department received an average 15-20 per cent of the total budget. (Territory of Papua and New Guinea, 1967:7)

Although the proportion of the total territory budget spent on health services had declined to 12 per cent in 1963-4, the 1964 International Bank for Reconstruction and Development Mission devoted considerable attention to what it considered to be 'unrealistically' high levels of expenditure on health services. On the hospital programme the mission certainly did not share the views of the 1962 Trusteeship Council report:

The Mission believes that there has been over-building of hospitals and an extension of hospital facilities at a rate faster than could be properly staffed and effectively used. The Mission also believes that the adoption of Australian standards for the larger new hospitals was not appropriate in the conditions: these buildings are luxurious, unrelated to the standards of most of the people, and the costs are very high, much higher than the Territory without substantial aid has any prospect of being able to afford in the future. (IBRD, 1965:338)

The IBRD development strategy for Papua New Guinea was not eventually accepted in total, although the principle of rapid economic growth based on export production remained central to later development strategies. On health, the Mission's report was concerned above all that Papua New Guinea must live within its actual and projected means. Virtually the whole discussion of health services was in terms of costs, rather than effectiveness. The Mission recommended that there should be no increase in hospital capacity for five years; that charges in cash or kind should be introduced at all levels of health service provision; and that rural health centres should be the basis for the development of both curative and preventative services (IBRD, 1965:340-1). With the emphasis so strongly on the health centres, the Mission saw little potential for development of the aid post system and indeed argued that 'as more rural health centers are established, the present system of aid posts will gradually become subordinate to the health center program' (IBRD, 1965:342) Essentially, the Mission felt that health took too large a share of the Territory budget and that this share should decline:

The health services have now, by the standards of most undeveloped countries, been brought to an advanced level and, in the light of the Mission's view that *future government spending should emphasise economic development rather than social services,* the Mission recommends that spending on health should grow much more slowly than in the past. (IBRD, 1965:354; emphasis added)

On the pattern of health expenditure, the Mission stressed the importance of preventive programmes, although with significant qualifications related to the scale of expenditure. They did however note, with an unusual degree of prescience that 'the hospital and medical program is expensive and absorbs a substantial part of the total budget. The cost will continue to climb and will take a greater proportion of the budget unless action is taken to hold the line on the medical program'. (IBRD, 1965:339) In 1968, the administration acknowledged that although the general principles suggested by the IBRD Mission had been applied, total public expenditure on health had increased more rapidly than foreseen by the Mission, 'owing partly to increases in costs which the Bank Mission did not take into account. Nevertheless, the proportion spent on health has been reduced from 12.3 per cent in 1963-4 to about 10.9 per cent in 1967-8'. (Territory of Papua and New Guinea, 1968:93) It was argued that the proposed five-year health programme gave special emphasis to preventive medicine, medical training and community health education as recommended by the 1964 Bank Mission. But this commitment was significantly qualified by reference to the need to maintain standards of general medical services which, 'although concerned primarily with curative medicine, also provide many of the hospital and other facilities required for preventive medicine and contribute to health education through normal contact with the people'. (Territory of Papua and New Guinea, 1968:93-4). There was only one, general reference to 'other facilities' in the 1968 plan and the specific discussion of medical service facilities was concerned with the expansion of hospital services; there was no discussion of health centres or aid posts (MacPherson, 1980). Throughout the 1960s, the health services continued to be dominated by the hospitals. Despite the many statements made regarding the importance of rural services and preventive health the bias was very clearly to urban, curative services. Although there was some extension of rural services, the relative position of the rural areas grew worse as the administration attempted to reduce the growth of total health expenditure while maintaining, and even expanding, its sophisticated curative facilities. In the mid-1960s the trends were recognised, but reaction to them by the health department was mixed; against the desire to implement sophisticated, Western, curative services there were doubts as to the viability of such a policy. The doubts were still, however, related to finance and not to the appropriateness of hospital-based medical services:

The community has shown continued interest in health activities and hospital services. Demands and requests are coming in from all parts of the country, sometimes from the most remote places which a few years before, did not even have an aid post. This should be considered as a good sign and a recognition of the value of health services, by the people. The question is: 'Will we have the financial ability to meet all expectations in the future?' (Territory of Papua and New Guinea, Department of Public Health, 1966:14)

In March 1971, the Select Committee on Constitutional Development, which had been established by the House of Assembly in June 1969, recommended to the House that the development of Papua New Guinea should be geared to preparing the country for internal self-government with a view to full independence at some future time. By the middle of 1971 that recommendation had been agreed by the House of Assembly, accepted by the Australian Government, and welcomed by the United Nations' Trusteeship Council. Wolfers argues that the Australian administration of the1960s had been marked by a 'benevolent paternalism of government at all levels' (1976:3), and that beneath the apparently open general policy 'there was the undertow of practice, in which the Australian government and its territorial administration seemed to be primarily concerned with maintaining official control over the process of decolonialisation in Papua New Guinea'. (1976:1-2) When self-government came there was a desperate lack of Papua New Guineans in senior positions, and inevitably, expatriate staff continued to dominate government departments. If new health policies were to be formulated and implemented, the stranglehold of colonialism would have to be broken; the administration inherited by a self-governing Papua New Guinea had little chance of even beginning to do this:

The current Public Service structure was one designed to implement policies that had been made elsewhere, rather than for internal ministerial govern-ment. The Ministerial and Assistant Ministerial Members perched precariously atop their various specialist departments, advised by a pre-dominantly expatriate public service . . . In Papua New Guinea, the various departmental heads seemed to be better equipped for day-to-day and specialist administration than for the policy-oriented, generalist approach of a ministry. However, the possibility of reconstructing the current system so as to make the upper echelons more policy-oriented, and to reserve these areas as far as possible to men who were exclusively committed to Papua New Guinea's government semed not to have been considered by officialdom. (Wolfers, 1976:24)

For health services, the limitations of the administrative system were not the only, or indeed the major, problems of the transition from colonial administration to self-government and eventual political independence. The health sector was subject to the same limitations and distortions under colonial rule as other sectors of the political economy; widespread ill-health and especially chronic malnutrition were not primarily internal problems, just as increas-ing inequality was not. They were products of colonial history, continuing dependence, and changing social relations of produc-tion. The structure of dependency created by colonialism was ultimately the determinant of both ill-health and health services. Papua New Guinea, in common with other colonies, was established as an exporter of primary products before domestic needs for food and consumer goods could be met; capitalist relations of production imposed by the colonial government turned land, labour and wealth into commodities, which disturbed the balance between population and resources; and political domination reinforced a social class structure in which Europeans at the top controlled decision making, while Papua New Guineans at the bottom were disenfranchised. In this situation there was little reason to expect either that modern health care could offset the process of emiseration or that health services would conform to egalitarian patterns of distribution or be governed by other than capitalist relations of production. In 1973, when Papua New Guinea effectively gained self-government, the system of health services was that created by colonialism. In the early 1970s there had been some awareness of the inappropriateness of that system and the need to produce policies and programmes relevant to Papua New Guinea.

In general terms, the hospital-centred programmes of the colonial administration were attacked on the grounds that they denied services to a large proportion of the rural population. It was argued that the patterns of morbidity and mortality in Papua New Guinea were such as to demand an emphasis on low-cost basic health services (MacPherson, 1980).

Many of the critiques and proposals for new policies drew heavily on the experiences of the countries of East and Central Africa, and in particular on the work of Professor Maurice King (1966). There was a realisation that although the general patterns of ill-health were known, one of the profound effects of the system of health services which had developed was that available data very often reflected the extent and nature of health services rather than the health needs of the mass of people. A good deal of emphasis was put on the importance of establishing both a more useful picture of health problems in the country, and systems of data collection which could be used to monitor future programmes (Vines, 1970; Bell, 1972; Maddocks and MacKay, 1974).

There were some doubts cast on the benefits to Papua New Guinea of doctors imported from overseas and, in sharp contrast to the dominant views fifteen years before (Calov, 1955), questions were asked regarding the need for doctors at all in basic health services (Vaughan, 1971; Bussim, 1972).

As noted earlier, self-government would mean that policies would be formulated in Papua New Guinea; the health department would no longer simply implement programmes under ultimate direction from Canberra. There was some awareness of the difficulties of comprehensive health planning in Papua New Guinea, but little analysis of these difficulties in relation to the emerging patterns of political, social and economic power (Allbrook, 1972; Ring, 1972; Bell, 1973; Hellberg, 1973a). The position of the missions in the system of health services was seen as a possible source of difficulty, but only in terms of co-ordination and integration of services. There was not, in the published work at this time, any doubt as to the continuation of extensive mission health services and of government subsidies to those services (Hellberg, 1973b; Strang, 1973).

Perhaps the most important contribution to the debate in the early 1970s was that made by Radford in 1971 (Radford, 1972). Radford was then Associate Professor in the University of Papua and New Guinea Faculty of Medicine, and later became Professor of Community Medicine. The focus of his 1971 paper was rural health services and the health needs of the mass of the population. He began with the crucial observation that high national aggregate figures for health spending may have little or no meaning for the majority of people: 'Although almost $10 per head per annum is allocated for all health services in Papua New Guinea on a national basis, at the sub-district level this fell to about $2 per head.' (1972:250) Drawing heavily on King's 'axioms on health care for developing countries' (King, 1966:1.7; 1970:344), Radford argued that the legacy of colonialism in Papua New Guinea would follow the pattern set 'all over the decolonised world' (1972:251), with inappropriate emphasis on expensive Western-style hospitals. Health services, Radford argued, are best received closest to the people they serve; the hospital utilisation data he used demonstrated what had been shown elsewhere, that these facilities were used by a very small proportion of the population from within a relatively small area. The disease pattern in rural areas was such that, in Radford's view, 'a properly trained aid post orderly, or village health orderly, is potentially capable of curing approximately three-quarters of all fatal illnesses at a fraction of the cost of hospital care'. (1972:256)

To avoid the worst features of health systems in other decolonised countries, Radford argued for a 'best chance pathway' which would redesign the Papua New Guinean health services from the bottom up. He put considerable emphasis on the aid post orderly and on the involvement of local communities. He proposed that the construction of expensive hospital buildings should be stopped immediately, as they resulted in 'the extension of health care to a privileged few at the expense of some care for many'. (1972:263) In relation to mission health services, Radford noted their significant contribution in rural areas, but pointed out an important feature of their contribution to the legacy of colonialism from which an independent Papua New Guinea would have to build its health services:

One unfortunate feature of mission medical services is that they have established in many remote areas hospital buildings of sophisticated design and equipment. While they are built and maintained from overseas sources one can only regret that the money is not being used to its best advantage, but after independence it will be unfortunate if a high proportion of national health funds are channelled into the maintenance of such structures. (1972:270-1)

Radford was essentially applying the experience of other developing countries, and in particular the countries of Eastern and Central Africa, to the situation in Papua New Guinea. He suggested that there were many signs that the African trends would be repeated. Despite the mass of evidence in support of a system of basic health services related to the dominant patterns of morbidity and mortality, he was ultimately pessimistic, suggesting that 'there is a very grave danger of administrations implementing policies based on the pressures of politicians and professionals expressing the people's "wants" in terms of their own immediate political and professional security rather than the actual needs of the population'. (1972:258)

The National Health Plan was produced against the background of the criticisms of the early 1970s, and indeed many of the critics, including Radford, were involved in its preparation. It was presented as an attempt to overcome the problems of the existing health system, but the rhetoric of its boldly-stated aims was quite clearly at variance with the realities of the emerging political economy within which the plan was to be administered (Mac-Pherson, 1979). The plan was produced in 1974 and reflected the recently adopted development strategy. It stated clearly an awareness of many of the issues outlined:

In recent years, it has become widely recognised that equitable, meaningful and effective distribution of health resources in a developing country depends upon the application of certain principles. These principles differ in many respects from those currently practised in Western medicine and are designed to ensure that scarce resources are applied to maximise the social and economic benefits of health services for all the people . . . [although] certain principles of health care have been recognised and practised for a long time in the country . . . there has not as yet, been a systematic attempt either to define or implement all relevant principles appropriate to the provision of health services in this country. This has led to an unplanned approach which is vulnerable to professional, political and self interest demands. (Papua New Guinea, Department of Health, 1974:48)

The plan laid down principles 'appropriate to the provision of health services' and stated that these were the bases of the strategy outlined in the remainder of the plan. The stated principles drew heavily on King's 'axioms of health care', the influence of which has already been noted. Indeed the health plan used several of them directly, and paraphrased others. The plan argued for an emphasis on low-cost basic health services, the importance of prevention and health education, and community participation. In doing so, it accepted what the critics of the late 1960s and early 1970s had begun to argue — the hospitals drained a huge proportion of resources, but contributed little to the health of the majority of the population. This was reinforced in the plan by reference to the maldistribution of health facilities. It was estimated that 10 per cent of the population had no reasonable access to health facilities of any kind; only 23 per cent had reasonable access to a health centre; 16 per cent had access to a district hospital, and only 9 per cent to a base hospital. A very small proportion of the population had access to those facilities which were consuming the greater part of health expenditure; most relied on aid posts alone. Considerable emphasis was given to the achievement of an 'equitable distribution of health services' and the provision of 'a comprehensive health service for all people'.

Papua New Guinea gained political independence in 1975, its achievement of the health objectives stated in the period of self-government preceding independence is problematic (MacPherson, 1980). The attempts made to shift the direction of health policy and bring about an essentially different pattern of health service are indicative of the failure of colonial health policies to meet the health needs of the Papua New Guinean population. The immense difficulties faced in implementing new policies illustrate the enormous and continuing influence of health policies and institutions developed under colonialism.

Although the available data have serious limitations, it is clear that the pattern of ill-health in Papua New Guinea is similar to that found in most developing countries; infectious diseases, faecally-transmitted intestinal conditions, and malnutrition are of major importance. The greater part of morbidity and mortality is susceptible to changes in socio-economic and environmental conditions; treatment for most cases is relatively simple and can be given by low-level health manpower. The pattern of health services which developed under colonial administration was hospital-oriented and biased towards curative medicine. The distribution of facilities reflected the patterns of European settlement and economic penetration. Missions played an important role in the provision of services both before and after independence. Health policies in the years prior to independence reflected dominant views on appropriate development strategy. They continued to do so when, with political independence, Papua New Guinea adopted a national development strategy which attempted to redress inherited inequalities in access to resources within the framework of an economic strategy which emphasised the rapid growth of primary production for export. The National Health Plan of 1974-8 placed great stress on the progressive correction of imbalances in health expenditure, in particular those between urban and rural areas and between curative and preventive services. The stated intention of using budgetary strategy as a planning mechanism to ensure the growth of basic health services, did not succeed during the period of the plan in reversing expenditure trends. Overall expenditure remains biased towards urban curative services and there have been no significant shifts in inter-provincial inequalities in access to health services.

Although the imposition of colonial rule in Papua New Guinea did not end until some time after that in many other Third World countries, the main features of its colonial experience in relation to health may be seen as typical. Doyal and Pennell, for example, in a discussion of colonial health policies in East Africa identify very similar patterns to those in Papua New Guinea, both in terms of the disastrous effects of colonial expansion on the health of local populations and the nature of health services established in the colonial period:

Initially, both British and German colonies were served by a handful of doctors who were directly employed by their respective trading companies and were required simply to attend to the immediate health problems of the small white community. By the turn of the century, commercial interests had in each case transferred responsibility for health to the imperial state, but for many years the scale of official medical provision was derisory. This was in keeping with the limited objectives of colonial health policy, which was set out in a directive to British medical administrators in 1903. The East African medical department was instructed firstly, to 'preserve the health' of the European community, secondly to keep the African and Asian labour force in reasonable working condition, and lastly, to prevent the spread of epidemics. (Doyal and Pennell, 1979:241)

As will be seen in later discussion of contemporary health policy dilemmas, the colonial legacy of curative bias, extreme maldistribution of services, extreme inequalities in access, and the dominance of Western medicine are of profound importance. To a certain extent present problems will be seen to result from the inheritance itself, in terms of infrastructure, staff and policies. However, it is the continuing dependence of Third World societies which is crucial in perpetuating and extending earlier inequalities. Economically, dependence means that a considerable part of the economic surplus continues to be taken off, reducing severely the level of resources available to underdeveloped countries for developing social programmes. But, as earlier discussion of the nature of underdevelopment suggested, it is not simply a lack of resources which affects the nature of social provision. Incorporation into the international system is marked by the emergence within the periphery of social structures which are responsive to the dynamics of metropolitan capitalism. In particular, the role characteristically taken by the state and by the dominant classes in Third World countries which determines the nature of social policies for health.

SOCIAL SERVICES IN TANZANIA

Organised social welfare was minimal in Tanganyika during the period of German control and there is no evidence of a relationship between German colonisation and the institution of social welfare as developed by the British, and later by the independent government of Tanzania. Thus in terms of the history of social welfare policy, it is to the British colonial administration that we must turn. The first act of the British parliament to allocate money to the African colonies ostensibly for the welfare of the colonies was in fact disguised. The 1929 Colonial Development Act, the manifest motive of which was the agricultural and industrial development of the colonies was, in fact, an Act designed to help Britain cope with its severe unemployment problem:

Those who are familiar with the Debates of 1929 will remember that even then the primary purpose of our legislation was not to help colonial development for its own sake but in order to stimulate that development mainly to bring additional work to idle hands in this country. It was devised as part of our scheme to solve our own unemployment problems. (House of Commons Debates, 1940:Col.45)

Although passed by a Labour government, the Act quite clearly represented the laissez-faire economic ideology. The predominant belief was that the colonies were to be self-sufficient, despite the fact that virtually the whole of the wealth extracted from the colonies went to Britain; social welfare was to be financed by local taxes and voluntary charities (Mair, 1944). It was not until 1940 that the British parliament passed the Colonial Development and Welfare Act, which may be seen as the beginning of formal, organised social welfare in the colonies, including Tanganyika. Prior to colonialism, political, economic and social systems had been developed to cope with environmental and social needs. Social problems were essentially local, dealt with by the internal systems of the family, clan and tribal structures. Colonisation not only resulted in the collapse of many of these systems, but brought with it foreign problems with which these pre-existing structures could not cope. Colonialism robbed the society of its people and its land; it split up families and disbanded whole tribes. A complete change of the political and economic structure was initiated, particularly associated with the penetration of market values; the communal foundation of the social structure was infused with the concept of individualism (Nyerere, 1966; Rodney, 1972).

The institution of social welfare programmes outside the social tribal structure began with colonialism. These programmes were very limited in scope and almost exclusively the responsibility of missions and large-scale employers of labour (Heisler, 1970). To the extent that services were available to the African population, the focus was on public health, minimal education and tied housing. In its direct dealing with the social problems of the people the concern was with containment rather than contentment.

The major part of the responsibility for dealing with the needs of the victims of rapid social change was assumed by the people themselves. In Tanganyika the Maji Maji rising of 1907 may be seen as an attempt to throw off the imposed colonial control which prevented Africans from benefiting from the resources of the land, and controlling the direction of change. The Maji Maji leaders felt that colonial control stifled creative ability to absorb the stresses that were continuously imposed on the society; their solution was to overthrow the colonial structure. With the failure of the uprising the society may be seen to have turned inwards and to attempt to solve its problems through self-improvement, with more education and better economic conditions. There were various movements organised to protest the lack of educational facilities and to demand more opportunities at the higher levels of education. Organisations were founded to demand a greater voice in the government of the area and a greater share in the profits from agricultural production (Kimambo and Temu, 1969; Ranger, 1969).

Although the grass roots of the struggles to overcome these problems were in the rural areas, the planning and co-ordinating centres were the towns. As migration to the towns increased rapidly in the 1930s the social conditions worsened, and problems of housing, unemployment and a lack of family, clan and tribal support intensified. New organisations were formed in the towns, very often to combat these problems; unions, clubs and other voluntary associations were established to which members contributed. Strikes were conspicuously unsuccessful, however, and it was apparent to those involved that the movement for self-improvement very quickly led to conflict with the colonial administration; nothing less than independence would leave the people free to control the nature and progress of their society.

Thus, prior to the establishment of formal social welfare systems, the social and economic needs of the African population were met through the family system, land tenure, some wage-employment, religious bodies and their social welfare systems, semi-tribal societies and a few voluntary associations; thus social and economic security needs were met by a system of mixed status and contract. By the 1940s the traditional systems were beginning to disintegrate, immigration to the towns was increasing, a money economy had been introduced, those who had some education or skill might find wage-employment but many would not. For increasing numbers, the family system no longer provided social or economic security, and the traditional systems for meeting social welfare needs were becoming obsolete in the context of colonial development and were indeed unavailable and inadequate in many circumstances (Tanganyika Development Commission, 1946).

There were, as discussed later, particular factors influencing the establishment of social welfare institutions in Tanganyika after the Second World War. A United Nations report in 1964 suggested more general reasons for the establishment of social welfare programmes in the British colonies (UN, 1964). First, the report suggests, there was the influence of moral principles, although these have consistently demonstrated a poor record of translation into action and also considerable flexibility in practice. Second, there were practical considerations of industrial efficiency; such arguments abound in the history of social welfare legislation in Britain, and in Tanganyika were used in the early part of the century to justify the provision of services to employees. Third, the report argues that pressure in Britain for welfare state provision served to focus attention on the well-being of the people in the colonies. Fourth, and clearly related to the last point, provision of welfare services had come to be regarded as a necessary function of government in Britain, and therefore the colonial administrations were obliged to assume social welfare responsibilities previously held by missionaries, tribal structures, voluntary associations, and the 'lady bountiful' activities of European colonists. Fifth, social welfare services were perceived by the British government as a means of preparing the Africans for eventual self-rule. There is quite obviously a good deal in this point with the crucial caveat that we need to be aware what the British envisaged self-rule to mean (Great Britain, 1940). Finally, the report argues that the doctrines of freedom, equality and democracy, symbolised in the fighting of the Second World War in which Africans fought for Britain, together with the numerous African risings, increased the pressure on Britain to assume more responsbility for the well-being of Africans. Whatever may be made of this argument in general terms, it can be seen to apply to the development of formal social welfare institutions in Tanganyika with almost startling directness.

A social welfare department was established in 1945 for the purpose of assisting some 68,000 discharged African soldiers to become 're-absorbed' in the territory. A social welfare organiser was put in charge of the small social development division of the Ministry of Local Government and Housing. Welfare centres were built in forty-two district headquarters and the services provided at these were meeting-rooms, reading-rooms, lectures, discussions, film shows and dances. The department had a general respon-sibility, though no specific powers or resources, for public health, education for social development and housing in the territory. In 1950 the objectives of the department were re-examined and defined – it became the Department of Social Development and included the probation division (Moffett, 1955).

An examination of the development of the Social Development Department provides a clear illustration of colonial administration. It is important to bear in mind here that there was considerable confusion during the 1940s and early 1950s as to what exactly was intended by the use of the term social welfare (Colonial Office, 1948). The term was variously used to embrace all those activities related to social development through to a narrow usage concerned simply with 'personal social services'. The British colonial govern-ment, after the Second World War, was most concerned with maintaining law and order, and indeed this was the latent motive for the establishment of social welfare in most of its colonies at various times. The British Colonial Office believed, probably quite correctly, that unless some social welfare services were provided for these newly arriving African servicemen they would create unrest. These men had helped Britain fight for democracy and freedom and had a change in outlook – they knew a better life was possible and wished to share it.

Britain, however, was concerned to develop and exploit the natural resources of Tanganyika. Despite the vast flow of wealth to Britain from her colonies, including Tanganyika, the argument that was consistently used was that social development must await economic development. Put quite simply, the African population was told that they could have a bigger slice of cake, but only by producing a bigger cake. In the ten-year-plan produced in 1946 it was stated that:

Full consideration has been given to the Secretary of State's views [of] April 27 1945. . . . that a disproportionate share of the total cost of the programme had been allocated to social services, public works and buildings, township developments, etc., and an insufficient sum to economic development. In this connection the Secretary of State pointed out that the extent to which the territory could afford the proposed expansion of the social and other services described . . . would depend very largely on the extent of economic development. (Tanganyika Development Commission, 1946:2)

The philosophy of social welfare underlying the programmes in Tanganyika was essentially that which dominated the social policies of Britain herself; there was an export of principles, but without any export or reduction in import of resources. Britain's use of the principles of indirect rule or native administration affected social welfare development in Tanganyika because, as it was applied, it required the native administrators to finance, plan and administer their own programmes (Wicker, 1958).

The stated objective of the Department of Social Development in 1950 was to raise the standard of living of the people in rural and urban areas (Moffett, 1955:69). There are two major reasons why there was hardly any progress towards this objective. First, the overriding policy imperative referred to above of giving emphasis to economic development; throughout the 1950s this became well-entrenched in legislative council planning. By 1960, the development plan explicitly stated that it was based on this assumption of priority for economic development. The estimated budget, therefore, included a small allocation to social welfare and public health of £303,000 for 1961-2, while allocating £11,019,000 for economic development.

Second, the values imported from Britain determined the nature of the social welfare system, in fact stultifying the growth of relevant social welfare activity. The public social welfare agencies which emerged in the 1940s were superimposed on the voluntary organisation of welfare undertaken by missions and industry and were clearly intended to ameliorate the worst effects of urbanisation, 'rehabilitate' the returning soldiers, and meet the social welfare demands of the European population (Colonial Office, 1945).

Ideas current in Britain which were exported with little thought to their relevance were 'the value of voluntary effort', 'government from below' and 'decentralisation'. These were expressed in the encouragement and subsidisation of effort not direclty managed by the colonial administration itself. The voluntary organisations, and particularly the missions, dominated social welfare provision and these were supported and encouraged – there was however no statutory relationship between voluntary organisations and government programmes. It was not until 1964 that serious attempts were made to co-ordinate their activities, leave alone to direct them. Despite the lack of a statutory relationship between government and voluntary organisations, the government did provide some resources to voluntary organisations, both in finance and staff. As will be seen later, this relationship still exists and produces a situation in which development is piecemeal and un-directed. The nature of social welfare programmes in the ten years before independence was essentially determined by the voluntary organisations, most of which were European in origin, attitude and in many cases controlling staff (Tanzania, Ministry of Health and Social Welfare, 1970).

This was consonant with the general thrust of colonial policies noted earlier. Despite recognition of social needs in both official statements and outside criticisms of practice (Hinden, 1946), virtually total emphasis was given to economic expansion. Expenditure on social welfare was seen as a wasteful form of consumption which would detract from efforts to achieve rapid economic growth. In the late 1940s and 1950s there was some relaxation of the old doctrine of colonial self-sufficiency in favour of a policy of assisted development. As Doyal and Pennell suggest, 'bilateral aid such as that provided through successive Colonial Development and Welfare Acts during the 1940s and 1950s can be seen as a counterpart to the growth of state intervention in the metropolitan economies'. (1979:254) But such aid was given primarily for infrastructural projects closely related to the needs of economic expansion, thus perpetuating both the link between welfare services and the pattern of economic activity and the low level of such services.

Thus, expenditure on social services was minimal and it was assumed that social needs in general could only be met by the transformation of traditional economies. Despite this, certain minimum levels of provision were found to be inevitable, especially those dealing with social problems such as crime and delinquency, and prostitution and vagrancy, which were regarded as a nuisance and actually or potentially threatening to the European population. Services were thus minimal and remedial, and were fundamentally an extension of the continuing concern with law and order. More specifically the kind of provision introduced may be seen to embody the importation of British models of social service facilities. There was emphasis on probation, substitute care of children, social work services, recreational work with young people and approved schools. The colonial adminstration was concerned with the growing problems of crime and vagrancy in urban areas and, following contemporary practice in Britain, made special provision for young offenders. Remand homes and reformatories were built and a probation service established (Clifford, 1966). At the time when the Poor Law in Britain was finally repealed, legislation was enacted which enabled the colonial administration to deal with beggars and the destitute − the original purpose of the Poor Law in England 400 years before. Marking still further the Poor Law legacy, institutions were established in which the destitute had to stay in order to receive relief, and the police were given powers to commit vagrants to such institutions or to repatriate them to rural areas (Farrant, 1974).

The use of probation as a method of dealing with offenders began in the late 1940s with the release of young offenders into the care of 'guardians'. Later, the courts began to employ 'enquiry officers' for supervision; it is interesting to note that these were originally missionaries. The institution of a formal probation system came with the Probation Ordinance of 1948; a British officer was appointed in 1949. The service grew steadily from then on, being extended to the local courts in the mid-1950s and gradually taking on a wider range of responsibilities such as matrimonial conciliation, school truancy, problems of delinquent children, administration of approved schools, family and child welfare, services to the blind and to unmarried mothers. The probation service was almost entirely urban-based and, as can be seen from the growing list of responsibilities, grew into a more general social welfare service. It is important to stress that as far as state activity in social welfare was concerned, this was carried out through the growth of a service with its roots very firmly in concerns for law and order in the towns.

As a final example of social services in colonial Tanzania, child welfare services may be seen in contrast to the law and order concerns outlined above. Although the most visible problems of child neglect or abandonment began to arise in the urban areas, the penetration of the cash economy, and in particular the impact of the migrant labour system, led to considerable child welfare problems in rural areas (Mwambene, 1970). The colonial administration encouraged voluntary organisations to respond to these problems, and the first child welfare services in Tanzania were orphanages established by the missions. The first of these was established in 1940 and others soon followed, each contradicting traditional patterns of kinship responsibility for children in need of care. By 1964 there were thirty children's homes all run by non-government agencies, mainly mission-based. Very often the children were quite young, and would return to their families after a time; as the provision increased, however, so too did the proportion of children who were older and with whom their families had lost contact. It was not until several years after independence that government sought a measure of control over the provision of child welfare services; for the whole period of post-war colonial administration policy and provision in this area was left almost entirely to non-government agencies which essentially replicated patterns of provision to be found in Britain and introduced these into both urban and rural Tanzania.

In conclusion, the motives of the Colonial Office in creating and encouraging institutions of social welfare can be seen as a mixture of humanitarianism, pragmatism, enlightened self-interest and imperialism. These motives affected profoundly the nature of social welfare which was developed.

Imperialism can be considered in part to account for the fact that the British form of social welfare was introduced without consideration to the nature of the cultural systems of Tanganyika. While the British utilised some of the tribal structures, they did not take into account the basic functions which these structures performed, but simply converted them to the form they wished them to have for administrative purposes.

Enlightened self-interest can, in part, account for the fact that initial social welfare services were primarily directed to returning soldiers and juvenile delinquents. These services were essentially concerned with repatriation. Social welfare, as imported from Britain, was seen as ameliorative and remedial. Programmes were designed in response to risings – actual or potential, juvenile crime, and the 'threat from the urban areas'.

Later, social welfare was directed to remedial functions in relation to the vulnerable population groups: orphans, the destitute and the handicapped. Provision in these areas was dominated by the missions and in most cases depended on locally generated resources.

The fundamental feature of social welfare as developed by the colonial administration was that it was rooted in the premise that welfare would drain rather than contribute to the economic resources of the country. The colonial administration had a tendency to operate pragmatically, and therefore established primarily remedial types of programmes in response to specific pressing problems:

Social welfare services, which were established in the colonies before independence, were based on practices in the metropolitan countries . . . Social welfare legislation in the British territories was often based on the English statutes . . . in many, the English Children and Young Persons' Act of 1933 was copied verbatim by officials responsible for drafting colonial laws. To administer these services, social workers from the metropolitan countries were recruited into the colonial service and although they were allowed limited resources and were responsible often to indifferent superiors, gradually they were given greater autonomy and scope . . . [But] in keeping with the economic development priorities at the time, residual social welfare policies, which dealt with the most conspicuous manifestations of need at minimum cost, were adopted. (Midgley, 1981:52-3)

It was not until some time after independence that the leaders of independent Tanzania recognised that social welfare was not necessarily a liability, but that economic and social development are each basic elements in the equation of national development. The inheritance from colonial rule was a system of social welfare institutions which prevented development. The impact of this inheritance will be examined in more deatil in later discussion of contemporary social service policy issues.

SUMMARY

The legacy of colonialism in Third World countries is of massive significance. Of overwhelming importance is the establishment and maintenance of the social, political and economic formations characteristic of the 'development of underdevelopment'. The imperatives of economic expansion and exploitation during the colonial period determined both the nature and extent of social provision. The main features illustrated by the two case studies examined here may be seen as typical of most colonial situations; the primacy of economic development, the protection and extension of European interests, urban bias, centralised bureaucratic administration heavily dependent on an authoritarian legal system, the significance of the missions and the pervasive importation of ideas and approaches from the metropolitan countries. Dependency and underdevelopment, with roots in colonialism, are as important to an understanding of contemporary social policy as they are to the economic plight of the Third World.

3

Education

Jonathan Silvey

If education is the answer, what is the question? (Weeks, 1977)

In 1974, when its whole aid and development strategy was in the process of major change to a 'basic needs approach', the World Bank answered with five brief questions which together sum up the issues of education policy: 'Who shall be educated? How? For what? At whose expense? At what expense?' (World Bank, 1974a:11). To see how such fundamental questions could still be at issue, we must look at how Third World education came to be as it is.

In order to reproduce its cultural heritage from generation to generation, every society must have an education system (Bourdieu and Passeron, 1977). It is a mistake, therefore, to assume that education is an alien, Western-imposed weapon of cultural imperialism. A developing society, in order to enable its members to obtain the information they need to adapt to change, must promote literacy and numeracy.

The skills needed for life in traditional subsistence societies were generally conveyed in informal settings or in what we would now call on-the-job situations. Society's religious and social beliefs and rules were also usually inculcated informally. Children learnt about clearing land, planting, tending and harvesting crops, working alongside others. They absorbed the values of their society, its magico-religious beliefs, their social rights and obligations, through its oral literature, rituals and by direct instruction. In many societies, a system of age-grades or quasi-apprenticeships facilitated the learning necessary to become a responsible adult.

Formal education is characterised by paid teachers performing roles within institutional settings (schools) usually with age-specific groups of students. Apart from a few instances such as Muslim schools, formal education was first introduced by missionaries from the colonial or other metropolitan powers. In Papua New Guinea, for example, where certain areas of the country were not declared 'open' to all-comers until two or three decades ago, the first non-governmental outsiders to move in were missionaries from Australia (Catholics and Apostolics) and the United States (Lutherans and Seventh Day Adventists) (Runawery and Weeks, 1980; Hecht, 1981).

Some societies were under the influence of one of the world religions before the advent of colonialism or the development process. There were Koranic schools in Islamic areas (Wagner and Lotfi, 1980) and Christian schools in Ethiopia (Kalewold, 1970), for example. The religions of conversion are 'religions of the book' (Goody,1968:2) and hence the earliest formal Western-style schools in future developing countries were religious schools. This fact, as we shall see, has had important consequences for many countries over issues of school control, open entry, curriculum content and the styles of learning which are reinforced.

The missionaries first needed local people to act as their interpreters in making contact with the indigeneous population, and later they needed evangelists, clerks, skilled and semi-skilled workers in addition to unskilled porters and general labourers. It was natural for them to satisfy these needs by establishing schools to train their own personnel. The first schools, therefore, taught basic literacy and numeracy, as well as religious beliefs.

With the growth of churches, congregations, trade, cash-cropping and husbandry, and administration, school became the essential avenue to a desirable, new life-style in the modern sector. Children were sent to school in order to get a wage-earning job, preferably one which did not mean getting their hands dirty. Parents and relatives were prepared to pay school fees and expenses not only for their child's sake, but also because they had a prescriptive right to help from the children for the rest of their lives.

This identification of schools with white-collar jobs is very significant because of the effect it has had on the difficulties of changing the 'How?' and 'For what?' issues raised by the World Bank.

EDUCATION FOR WHAT?

The ability to read, write and calculate at levels appropriate to a person's future life would generally be agreed to form a minimum core of secular education. Beyond this common core, every education system aims to provide other ingredients. These may be extra skills, values or areas of knowledge; every system has its unique set of components, even though it may be virtually impossible to get agreement on what these ingredients are or how they should be mixed.

But even before a common core of skills can be identified, judgements have to be made on the kind of life education should be preparing children for. Is it to be life in a society which is not very dissimilar from today's? If the answer is yes, the implication is that little change can be expected in the life circumstances of the majority who receive only the core education. This may be by design, as in the educational system provided in South Africa for the black majority whom the government wishes to prevent competing with the whites.

It may also be a reluctant admission by a government that the pace and scale of change needed to alter the majority's circumstances radically cannot be achieved, as in Tanzania. In *Education for Self-Reliance,* President Nyerere called for education to adapt to the realities of Tanzania's situation.

[We] will continue to have a predominantly rural economy for a long time to come . . . It would be grossly unrealistic to imagine that in the near future more than a small proportion of our people will live in towns and work in modern industrial enterprises . . . Our educational system . . . must also prepare young people for the work they will be called upon to do in the society which exists in Tanzania today − a rural society where improvement will depend largely upon the efforts of the people in agriculture and in village development. (Nyerere, 1968:51-2)

On the other hand, if education is intended to prepare youngsters for a life with substantially more opportunities and expanded horizons than, say, their parents' generation, it may be that the consequences of rising expectations will be a generation of school leavers with frustrated ambitions, reluctant to accept a social and political structure which denies them the opportunities they had expected. These youngsters are overwhelmingly from the rural areas, and their search for wage-earning jobs takes large numbers of them to the cities and urban areas. As Todaro (1980:179) puts it:

Numerous studies of migration in the developing countries have documented the positive relationship between the educational attainment of an individual and his or her propensity to migrate from rural . . . areas. Essentially, this is because individuals with more education face wider urban—rural income differentials and higher probabilities of obtaining modern sector jobs than those with less education. In particular, it is the greater probability of finding a good urban job which explains the continual influx of educated rural migrants, in the face of rising urban unemployment.

Sri Lanka and Kenya (Kinyanjui, 1973; Dore, 1976: 60-9)' and Papua New Guinea (Conroy, 1976) provide three examples among many of this situation.

Thus the question of what education should be about is a major political issue for any country, for it involves questions of the allocation of scarce resources to a limited number of beneficiaries. Since the adoption of the 'basic human needs' approach by the world's multilateral agencies in the late 1970s, the significance of education to the development process has been seen as threefold:

As a basic human need . . . education becomes a necessary condition for the ability of the individual to identify with the prevailing culture. '*As a means of meeting other human needs'*, [it] influences and is in turn influenced by access to other basic needs — adequate nutrition, safe drinking water, health services, and shelter . . . '*As an activity that sustains and accelerates overall development'*, education plays several roles. (World Bank, 1980c:13)

First, it produces the trained personnel needed to manage all sectors of the economy. Secondly, it facilitates the advancement of knowledge in pure and applied fields, and thirdly the better use of energy, the environment and human resources. Fourthly, 'the ability of individuals to identify with their changing culture and find constructive roles in society depends, to a large extent, on what education can provide by way of self-understanding, better knowledge of the choices available to society, and a criticial view of the culture'. (World Bank, 1980c:13)

Among the most obvious examples of this approach in practice are China, Cuba, and Tanzania (Williamson, 1979:153-206).

Widespread basic education is not, therefore, solely a capitalist approach. The three examples illustrate that the strategy is more likely to be successful where this transformation has been part of a greater mobilisation of national resources and effort. Education cannot be divorced from its larger social and political context.

Just how successful they have been is problematic, because publication of such systematic evaluations as there have been is rare (Foster and Sheffield, 1975:206). Nyerere has indicated that he is relatively satisfied with the progress made in the decade since the Arusha Declaration ushered in the 'education for self-reliance' policy, Universal primary education has been introduced, nearly two million adults have passed the functional literacy test, the curriculum has given extra emphasis to technical, agricultural and scientific training where it was most appropriate. Admission to university is from jobs, not straight from school, and partly dependent on character references from workmates. There has been positive discrimination to women in entry to university as a temporary compensation for past disadvantages (Nyerere, 1977: 11-14).

These three socialist countries, and South Africa at the opposite extreme, are all using the educational system as a means of social engineering to produce their own kind of society. Within more pluralist societies, where changes in the education system are not part of a more massive general transformation or control policy, the possibility of inducing significant social change through schools is much more limited.

With ever increasing numbers entering school, the mismatch between the number of jobs available and the numbers moving from school to the job market becomes worse. The school leaver problem is the result of both more enrolments and a declining number of new jobs in countries hit by a recession in world trade and commodity prices, and population growth exceeding economic growth rates. It is made more serious by 'qualification inflation', the process by which the excess demand over supply for jobs leads to increasingly high educational qualifications however irrelevant to the job in question being required by employers.

Whether it occurs because employers believe that by taking the applicant with more schooling they are getting a better bargain, or whether it is simply a relatively easy way to eliminate large numbers of applicants, is unclear. It has the paradoxical effect, however, that the worse unemployment becomes, and the more a given school certificate is devalued, the stronger becomes the pressure for more education (Dore, 1976:4). It is increasingly important for a student to progress to the next stage of education because there are very few alternative routes to paid employment.

The kind of education provided by the schools, both the early mission schools and later government schools, tended to be academic and book-oriented. It was geared to produce enough individuals for the needs of a modern society, individuals who could be selected from amongst all those leaving school for further training, on-the-job or in higher educational institutions. So secondary schools determined what and how primary schools should teach,³ and their emphasis was in turn determined by universities and colleges.

Competition for entry to the next stage of school has always been fierce (Silvey, 1981), because the proportion who can be admitted is small, and because the differential rewards for the next certificate were so great. In the early 1970s, it was estimated that the average earnings of a higher education graduate were 6.4 times those of a primary school leaver in the less developed countries, compared with 2.4 times in typical developed countries (Psacharopoulos, 1973:132).

The naïve assumption that social pressures can be counteracted by education ('Education is the answer'), or the failure to recognise these pressures, has led to many disappointing attempts to introduce more vocational curricula into Third World schools.

Agriculture has been introduced into primary and secondary school curricula, but unless it is treated as an examinable subject equal in status to the traditional academic subjects, it has usually been devalued by both staff and students. All too often, it is actually treated as a punishment – 'two hours on the school gardens'. Vocational schools have been established as alternatives to secondary schools, but again they are regarded as second-best alternatives. Their graduates frequently use them as stepping stones to re-enter the academic stream or to migrate to the cities in search of urban jobs.

Foster argues that such experiments illustrate what has come to be called 'the vocational school fallacy'.

The present employment crisis [is attributed to] the provision of a particular form of academic education that has generated unrealistic employment expectations for clerical work, caused a flight from the rural areas, and induced in students a disdain for manual occupations. If this diagnosis of the situation is correct then the solution is simple: change the curricula of the schools to provide instruction based upon agriculture and technical subjects and the aspirations of young people will, in consequence, be directed towards agricultural activities: the flight from the land will be checked and unemployment will correspondingly be diminished. (Foster, 1966:172-4)

In Foster's view, Third World children enter school and compete so hard to remain in the system because school is the only gateway into the modern sector of the economy: African parents sent their children to school to maximise their opportunities for access to the occupations with the highest prestige and, more importantly, the highest pay in the economy. (Foster, 1965b:145)

Their vocational aspirations are almost exclusively determined by factors which lie outside the schools. No amount of technical, vocational or agricultural instruction taken alone within the formal educational system is going to check the movement from rural areas or reduce the volume of unemployment . . . The crucial variables lie in the structure of incentives within the economic system and the degree to which [it] . . . supports entrepreneurial activity. (Foster, 1966:174)

He has always argued that student aspirations are realistic, and that when they opt for an academic education they are choosing the most suitable *vocational* course. In recent years, he acknowledges that student expectations are shifting with the changing opportunities open to them, and that many who drift to the town in search of work will return to the rural areas after a short stay. In these circumstances schools should still concentrate upon what they do best: literacy, elementary numerical skills and the rudiments of a general education, for these are the foundations for more specifically vocational training, best provided after ten to twelve years' general schooling (Foster, 1968:95-7).

Foster's diagnosis has been widely accepted by policy promoting institutions like the World Bank and the International Labour Office, as well as by academics and educational planners. His evidence comes from his fieldwork in West Africa in the 1960s, and later impressions gained around the world. Because of its influence on educational policy makers, the challenges to it are important. The *Comparative Education Review* devoted a whole issue to it in 1975, and other critics include Marvin (1975) and Pettman and Weeks (1978). Critics have suggested that his explanation is simplistic, and that it has gained acceptance because it suits many of those interested, especially economists, to be able to demonstrate that the African parent is acting as a rational, 'economic man' (Marvin, 1975). If an economic man model can be accepted, then it follows that the behaviour of parents and their children can be manipulated by changing the conditions of the market without altering what goes on inside the schools.

But can such a complex behaviour be reduced to a single motivation? Can one imagine a single acceptable explanation of why, say, people go to church? Granted that the economic rationale for education may be very powerful, it does not necessarily preclude all others. One can think of many competitors: to learn religious and/or social values, for the companionship of peers, to foster a child's potential, to avoid not conforming to community norms or social pressures, to help children cope better with *rural* life. Foster's thesis implies that if parents believed there to be almost no chance of economic betterment, enrolments would collapse. One has only to instance the Harambee secondary schools in Kenya, which offer very little possibility of a reasonable school certificate at the end, to find disconfirmation of this prediction.

Although there are signs of falling enrolments in some parts of the world, there is no evidence that this is due to Foster's causes rather than any competing explanation. One can equally speculate that it is due to difficulties in finding the fees, disillusionment with the moral behaviour of teachers and school leavers, or the need for children's help in daily activities as more of the able-bodied migrate to the cities.

Sensitive investigators, alert to the possibility of multiple causes, have given a richer picture of parental attitudes. Kemelfield, for example, in an interview study of 400 rural families throughout Papua New Guinea concludes that:

Parents put strong emphasis on the importance of their children's education being directly useful to them in their home communities. Many stress that if their children cannot gain entrance to further education and urban employ- ment (and thus pay back their people by contributing money, food and skills to the village) they should alternatively learn practical skills, particularly those relating to commercial farming and fishing so that they can help develop businesses in their own community. Many parents also wish that those with further education and experience of urban employment should eventually return home with capital and skills to benefit the village. These findings suggest that a number of parents might welcome the imparting of practical skills alongside more academic learning. (Quoted in Weeks, 1978:30)

The significance of the Foster fallacy controversy is that it highlights the limits of curriculum engineering as a lever of social change, and re-emphasises the extent to which what schools can achieve must depend on the social context in which they operate.

One of the reasons why vocationalising primary and secondary schools appears to be so unsuccessful is that leavers are simply too young to be economically independent, and the traditional setting rarely allows it even if, as is rarely the case now, land were available. They need to learn responsibility and maturity under the guidance of kin or those already practising a trade or craft. They need time and experience to build up their resources and to acquire the necessary equipment, however rudimentary, for their occupation. If they are working with others who are more experienced, they cannot be expected to implement what they have learnt in vocational training without the risk of causing resentment by appearing arrogant.

This practical objection to vocational primary education has led Nyerere (1968:61) to propose raising the age of entry to primary school. Modest as this proposal is, it recognises the reality that seven or eight years will be the only education that most in Tanzania will receive for the foreseeable future. Others elsewhere have been led to support eight or nine years as necessary for the primary schooling.

Another approach has been to incorporate a 'transition into work' phase after primary school. In Botswana, the Serowe Brigades act as both productive enterprises and centres for skill-training and general education. Most of the training takes place on a farm, building site or in the workshop. Brigade trainees' production helps pay for their training, and their work supervisors are also their skill teachers. Trainees are released for periods of theoretical training and general education in English, development and cultural studies, and basic science.

As the difficulties of obtaining jobs on leaving grew due to the adoption of an enclave economy in Botswana, production units were established to provide work for ex-trainees. By 1977, it was reported that 400 people were being trained in twenty-five different skills, and that the system provided employment for 300, including the production workers. 70 per cent of the costs of training, education, production costs and overheads were covered by the income generated. (*Guardian*, 18 March 1981)

In Papua New Guinea, rather different prescriptions have been drawn from a basic acceptance of the Foster diagnosis. School leavers there, as elsewhere, migrate to the towns in search of work and further education, but there is reason to think that village life has a relatively strong appeal if they could make money there. Many return home if they are unsuccessful in the town, and probably more would do so if they could find the fare. A large-scale survey of urban migrants showed that most migrants maintain links with their villages and intend to return, the educated more so than the uneducated (Garnaut, Wright and Curtain, 1977:Ch.5). But while in school the most popular goal is to gain entry to higher education or high-level job training.

Faced with increases in unemployed secondary school leavers, the Education Department is experimenting with a partially vocationalised curriculum which incorporates the students' main goal of further education. In a few secondary schools, the curriculum has been broadened so that a third of the pupils' time is spent on community extension projects. In these projects, the emphasis is on reinforcing theoretical classroom learning by practical application − 'learning by doing' (Vulliamy, 1981:95). But students at these schools (who are not specially recruited) compete in the same examinations as other schools for tertiary education and salaried employment training. This is a two-stage examination, in which schools first compete on a national scale for the fixed quotas of distinction and credit level passes. When each school as a whole knows how many it has earned, it then decides by internal assessment procedures which of its candidates shall be awarded them. This means that while the experimental schools cannot afford to lower their academic standards, they can reward individuals with high level certificates on the basis of more than academic achievement. They also take account of 'application, innovation, leadership success and a wide range of personal attributes and attitudes designed to reward those who excel in the practical implementation of the curriculum.' (Vulliamy, 1981:96). Thus the carrot of opportunity of access to further education is used to stimulate students to apply the knowledge they have learnt in the classroom to the problems of village development. It is hoped, but too early to tell yet, that the majority for whom secondary school will terminate their education, will have developed more applicable skills and the motivation to apply them in their rural community without having to sacrifice a general education.

These attempts to answer the question, 'Education for what?' have been carried out in countries not attempting a total transformation of their society. But what of those countries where education policy has been determined by its part in a general transformation approach?

The best known example is China, but it is very difficult to make any assessment of the lasting accomplishments of the last thirty years when currently so much is apparently being reversed. During that period, education was used emphatically as a tool of development, both in terms of changing attitudes and of increasing production. Unlike other developing countries, China had a long tradition of its own formal system of education, the baleful influence of which was deeply ingrained. The system was authoritarian, encouraged respect for hierarchy, was élitist and was dominated by examinations.

Every poor boy aspired to become a scholar so that he could ultimately become an official. So ingrained was the idea of 'official' in Chinese minds that even the name for the supreme deity was 'heavenly official'. (Schurman and Schell, quoted in Williamson, 1979:197)

China's unique innovations in educational reform date from the Great Leap Forward with the abandonment of the slogan 'Learn from the Soviet Union'. The break with Russia meant a sudden loss of expertise, which the Chinese responded to with an emphasis on production and self-reliance. There were moves to reduce the number of years of compulsory attendance so that young people entered the labour pool after nine years' schooling, and to make schools into half-work, half-study institutions. Curriculum control was decentralised to emphasise local initiative and relevance. Admission criteria for higher education were altered to increase the proportion of workers' and peasants' children entering. (Munro, 1973:133-134; Dore, 1976:168-9)

Although China may be modifying some of these reforms, in the post-Gang of Four era, Dore believes that:

The legitimacy, the social fairness, of the new pattern seem widely accepted. While it may not use the nation's best intellectual talent to fullest
advantage, it will improve traditional agriculture and the small-scale agricultural based industrial sector in the rural communes. (Dore, 1976:175-6)

Cuba too has put great emphasis on integrating school and work
as a means of mass participation in production and mobilisation.
Cuba's changes have been made largely as a result of deliberate
trial-and-error processes, searching for new forms to meet emerging social and economic needs. The ideology of revolutionary Cuba
stresses the need for a 'New Man': 'the aims of our education
[are] . . . the interests of the workers, peasants, intellectuals, and
the middle strata of the population', it was stated in an official
report by the Cuban government to a UNESCO conference in 1962:

The two basic aims . . . are the linking of education with productive labour
as a means of developing men in every respect. Educating in productive
labour, making the students familiar with the details of production through
practical experience, enabling them to learn its laws and organisation as
processes; that is, educating them in the very root of all cultural, technical,
and scientific progress, and giving them ideological and moral training
leading to an all-round education. (Carnoy and Wertheim, 1979:55-6)

At the primary level, the major innovation has been the introduction of universal primary schooling, with Castro already talking
of secondary education as a universal right (Dore, 1976:107).
Secondary education has seen the most radical changes. Enrolments tripled in the decade up to 1968. After 1964, the decision to
make agriculture the lead sector of the development programme
had profound effects on education, resulting in a new kind of school
combining study and agricultural production together. By 1974-5,
more than 25 per cent of students in the first cycle of secondary
school were enrolled in 'schools in the countryside', which had
grown out of the earlier 'schools to the countryside' programme
(Dore, 1976:101). In this, whole secondary schools moved to the
countryside for about eight weeks a year, spending half their time
studying and half working in the fields. The increased mechanisa-
tion of labour in the 1970s made 'schools in the countryside' less of
an agricultural necessity, but it has continued because of its success

in socialising students into the collective work ethic of the 'New Man' (Dore, 1976:95). Moral incentives, 'socialist emulation' and mass participation continue to be stressed in the schools, even as an increased use of material incentives were being restored in factories (Dore, 1976:4). 'Schools in the countryside', which were intended to cover all junior high schools by 1980, work half a day in agriculture and half on school work. They are boarding schools, but most students are able to return home at weekends, and in the vacation the agricultural work is continued by students' relatives who are offered the use of the school with all its facilities as a vacation centre in exchange for two hours' work a day. It is estimated that the schools' output covers their recurrent costs and produce a 4 per cent return on capital invested (Dore, 1976:103).

The second major innovation is the 'circles of interest', a way of involving students in scientific subjects and their practical application, such as biochemistry, photography, meteorology, soil science and geology. As Bowles points out, by capturing the interest of students through substantive knowledge of an area, these clubs provide an alternative means of encouraging entrants to selected occupations when wage differentials are usually minimal (Bowles, 1971:489).

Cuba's policy of integrating school and work raises the question of a possible decline in the quality of academic achievement. It is, of course, a matter for each country to set its own standards; the question is whether the Cubans themselves are worried about falling standards. Castro claimed in 1972 that achievement tests (*sic*, even in socialist Cuba) were leading to higher promotion rates in the 'schools in the countryside' than in traditional schools. One can see reasons for this encouraging trend. As boarding schools, more time and trained help are possible, and absenteeism is virtually eliminated. In new schools, equipment and facilities tend to be new and of high quality. It is said that the work/study programme has produced improved relationships between staff and students, and that the introduction of peer teaching has also contibuted to higher test results (Carnoy and Wertheim, 1979:119).

On the other hand, the rapid expansion of the educational system has resulted in shortages of properly qualified staff at all levels, although teacher/student ratios have improved substantially (Carnoy and Wertheim, 1979: Table 12). There are apparently serious dropout and repeater rates in both primary and secondary schools. Carnoy and Wetheim, generally sympathetic observers, argue that:

Implicit in much of the dropout problems . . . is that the Cuban economy at this stage of development has greatly reduced the economic pressure to get into higher levels of schooling by the income guarantees it provides, while at the same time the level of consciousness about work and doing better have not taken hold. When Castro refers to the 'persisting lack of awareness about the importance of schooling', he is dealing with the lack of values which make people want to know more and have their children know more in order to help the collectivity do better, since the personal incentive to do materially better has been greatly reduced. The solution to the motivation problem, therefore, lies in the long-term re-education of Cubans into the new value system, and this either requires getting them into schools or reaching them by mass moblisation programmes. (Carnoy and Wertheim, 1979:116)

WHO SHALL BE EDUCATED?

Although the World Bank posed as its first question in 1974, 'Who shall be educated?' rather than 'Education for what?' which logically take precedence, this perhaps reflected the shift in its policies then occurring. From giving priority to financing the training of middle and high-level manpower needs of developing countries, the strategy now was 'a fuller use of all available human resources, particularly in traditional and transitional sectors of the economy' (World Bank, 1975a:269-70).

In the discussion so far, we have focused on the formal sector of education, in schools, of young people. But what of the estimated 32 per cent of adults who were illiterate in 1975 (World Bank, 1980c:23)? The provision of a minimum education is an essential condition for effective participation in the development process, the Bank had declared in 1974, but an efficient means of eradicating adult illiteracy had not been found in most countries. During the 1950s and 1960s, more than one hundred countries supported general adult literacy campaigns, but they seldom proved effective. In consequence, UNESCO promoted experimental functional literacy campaigns in several countries, projects aimed at teaching basic reading and arithmetic as part of the training for particular occupations (not necessarily employments). Again, they were generally unsuccessful. Largely due to high wastage rates, it has been estimated that the cost of producing a successful graduate from this programme was actually greater than providing six years' primary schooling (Simmons, 1980:51).

Although professing the need for improvements in adult literacy, the World Bank's latest education policy document has more to say about the constraints on promoting it, than how they propose encouraging it.

The target population is dispersed and heterogeneous in its needs and aspirations. The kinds of education and training needed are many, diverse and often small in scale; the dividends, especially in skills for living, are not readily apparent . . . Poor people are simply not buying the service. (World Bank, 1980c:25)

Yet there have been highly successful mass literacy campaigns, most notably in Cuba and China. The difference in these two countries was that literacy was part and parcel of a total transformation, mass involvement in the revolutionary struggles to overcome years of neglect. In Cuba, Castro designated 1961 as the 'Year of Education', closed down all schools for eight months, and used all staff and students as a teaching force to eradicate illiteracy in a year. The campaign had three stages; the first was a national campaign to locate and reigster all illiterates, resulting in an official estimate of 21 per cent of the adult population. In the second, student brigades were trained under the leadership of a local leader; and in the third the brigades went to their areas, and lived with and successfully taught about 72 per cent of those located. The campaign to locate and register all illiterates, resulting in an official offering the inducement of involvement in managing the new co-operatives.

Apart from its quantitative success in reducing the official literacy rate at the end of the year to 3 per cent, its immeasurable achievements included bringing Cubans who knew little of each other into direct contact within the framework of the Revolution, a clear benefit in unifying the nation (Jolly, 1964: *passim*; Carnoy and Wertheim, 1979:68-76). After 1961, the campaign was followed up with post-literacy adult education in continuation classes and 'family circles'. In the late 1960s, part-time secondary schooling and pre-university courses in worker-peasant faculties were begun in many workplaces (Williamson, 1979:186).

Functional literacy campaigns, by contrast, are intended to do just that, to enable one to function within, rather than transform, one's situation. In the non-socialist world, Paulo Freire is the best known advocate of mass literacy. He insists that literacy must be treated as more than a mechanical problem. He argues that the poorest are reluctant to learn to read if their new skill is used as a further means to ensure their domestication into an unjust, exploited role (Freire, 1972). When he was appointed Director of Brazil's National Literacy Programme, Freire drew up plans based on the Cuban example to reach two million people. Prospective students were encouraged to join 'culture circles', in which they discussed their shared position and tried to discover ways in which reading, writing and speaking skills could be used to improve their status. Even without Freire's explicit linking of literacy with revolutionary social change, mass literacy posed a political threat to the *status quo,* where illiterates were disenfranchised. Two million new voters threatened political stability. Not surprisingly, the programme was closed down after the military *coup* of 1964, and Freire was arrested and exiled (Mackie, 1980:4-5).

The adult education budgets of most countries are typically a tiny fraction of the total spent on education. In part this reflects the actuality of expenditure, but it also partly reflects uncertainty on which government department, if any single one, should be responsible. Literacy as such is clearly an educational function, but it is increasingly recognised that it cannot be taught in isolation from other prospective improvements in the learner's life. Other adult education may be carried out under the rubric of the Departments of Health (nutrition, mother and child clinics, for example) and Agriculture (extension training) and community development. We discuss in the final section why, wherever adult education expenditure is hidden away, it remains so low despite its importance.

Besides adults who have missed out on schooling, there are of course those children who either never start school, or who drop out before completing primary school. Most countries cannot afford to provide universal primary education, though it is a high priority for most. In countries with *per capita* incomes of less than $520 in 1975, between 40 and 50 per cent of school-age children are not enrolled (World Bank, 1980:18). Less than half the children who did enter the first year were still attending in the fifth, the stage at which UNESCO assumes that permanent literacy had been achieved (World Bank, 1980c:30) (though empirical evidence suggests that twice that period might be a better assumption (Simmons, 1980:44)). In addition, 15 — 20 per cent of primary education places are occupied by 'repeaters' — children who are repeating a year in order to improve their chances of promotion to secondary school.

Dropping out and 'repeating', represent significant inefficiencies in the use of the school places which poor countries do manage to provide. In terms of equity, non-enrolments, drop-outs and 'repeating' are all found more in the poorer and more isolated sections of the community, and amongst girls more than boys.

These groups — the rural, especially the remote rural, and girls — also lose out in admissions to secondary and higher education, even discounting the smaller proportions who survive to become candidates for selection (Silvey, 1981). This has led some countries to stipulate entry quotas for underprivileged groups, to ensure that they do not miss out completely in the competition for the élite positions in society which higher education offers. Quotas, in so far as they interfere with selection on the basis of public examination results, are politically controversial. Ostensibly objective exams and tests confer legitimacy on the claims of those who do best in them. It is hard to justify to the parents of an excluded child why another pupil who has done less well is preferred. In so far as the 'best' results are determined by environmental advantages rather than innate abilities, public examination results favour those from the more literate, educated, healthy families who use the language of instruction at home, and those able to get into better staffed, better equipped schools.

In countries where governments have imposed few, if any, restrictions on the free play of examination forces, dual or even triple systems of education have emerged. In Kenya, for example, the schools which catered for European children under the colonial administration offer the best teaching and obtain the best results at relatively high fees. The educated élites who took over power at independence did not abolish this privileged sector, they merely opened it up to their own children by abolishing the racial restrictions on entry. Consequently, for those who can afford it, there exists a primary school system which almost guarantees a place in a secondary school.

Such is the competition for these places that alongside the dual system of government-maintained schools in Kenya, there has emerged a third system of secondary schools built by communities for themselves in the wake of exhortations from national leaders to be self-reliant. These Harambee schools (so-called from the Swahili word for self-help effort) constituted a kind of 'pre-emptive development' process, 'a bid for, rather than a substitute for, Government resources' (Godfrey and Mutizo, 1974:271), because Government was to provide the recurrent costs of schools which the community had capitalised. These schools, despite their grassroots origins, did little by way of educational innovation, simply plugging themselves into the existing formal system. They produced very poor results. Somerset has shown that while the élite national schools achieved an average school certificate mark close to the twentieth national percentile, the Harambee schools typically equalled the eightieth (Dore, 1976:70).

The Kenyan experience exemplifies an inefficient and inequitable education system of the kind the World Bank had in mind as long ago as 1974 when they opened the Education Policy Paper:

Education systems have been irrelevant to the needs of developing countries during the last two decades because education policies were often keeping company with overall development strategies which were themselves irrelevant to the societies and conditions of developing countries. Emphasis on the development of the modern economic sector, providing employment to a small and intensively trained élite, leads to the neglect of the 60-80 per cent of the population living in sectors characterised by traditionally lower productivity. Consequently, a large part − often more than 50 per cent − of their resources is devoted to secondary and higher education, although the student enrolment at those levels is generally less than 20 per cent of the total. (World Bank, 1974a:269)

AT WHOSE EXPENSE? AT WHAT EXPENSE?

Over these decades, public expenditure on education has grown at double or even triple the rate of growth in GNP of the economies which support them. Virtually all of it, as we have seen, has gone into formal education. Within that system the higher level of education, the greater its unit costs. Simmons produces figures which, for all their generality, suggest that a typical country might have 80 per cent of all its enrolments in primary schools, but spends only half the total budget on them, whereas approaching 20 per cent of the budget is spent on the 3 per cent who benefit from higher education. As we have seen, much of that primary expenditure is wasted due to dropping out, while the lucky 3 per cent receive substantial public funding to enable them to obtain disproportionately high life-time earnings. Moreover, in so far as the dividends from an investment in education are intended to go to the student's parents and other kin as well as his own family-to-be, the families obtaining the greatest benefit are likely to be those already relatively well off. The dice are loaded against the sacrificial investment of poor families.

To describe the situation in these stark terms is to suggest a plausible answer to the question why such a situation has proved so resistant to change; as does a look at those countries where reforms have been achieved, however imperfectly. Successful reform in a direction which both increases the rate of economic growth and reduces social inequality has best been achieved in countries where it is part of a wider distribution of power and economic opportunities.

In an unlikely, non-socialist, never-never land where the existing power structure could be persuaded, without bribes, to surrender their privileged position, what would a reforming minister of education attempt to do? If he listened to the consensus of educational planners and economists he would be urged to stimulate economic growth by transferring much of his departmental funds from higher and later secondary education to primary schooling and vocational training for rural employment. He would have to persuade his finance minister to follow policies which did not use the rural areas to subsidise urban living and wage standards. If he were part of a government whose policy was to improve the quality of life of the poor and to redistribute incomes more equitably, he would be prepared to permit a substantial proportion of his funds to be spent on adult education, but within a programme for rural development which integrated the contributions of health, transport, agriculture and community development. He would be subjected to critics who would claim that the academic standards of the few destined for higher education would suffer by his reductions in their unit costs. His response would be to argue that better value for money is obtained by investment in the pre-school environment and improved nutrition. He would probably want to impose quotas on selection for further education in favour of girls, because it is through mothers that child health can best be improved and the birth rate, partly in consequence, can be controlled. He would introduce an element of work-study into all schools. In setting the criteria for determining admission into further education, he would reduce the significance of achievement in exams by taking into account the results of locally-produced aptitude tests and assessments of motivation in the work component of schooling.

But unless he could carry his ministerial colleagues and the country with him in making all his efforts part of a greater reconstruction of society and the economy, most of his reforms would probably fail.

Thus the question 'At whose expense?' can be answered in two ways: reforms will be at the expense of the privileged, for they will no longer be able to dominate access to education. Which groups actually fund educational expenditure is a question beyond the scope of this chapter.

But even if our minister of education succeeds in some measure, he will be criticised by those who argue that his diversion of funds and effort towards non-formal education have reinforced a dual system, streaming the poorer into manual jobs and inibiting social mobility (Simmons, 1980:9). He will probably have to endure attacks from both political wings: those who say his policies make it more difficult to produce the top level manpower a modern economy must have, and those who say he has betrayed his ideals by supporting a dual system. He will have to have a lot of faith that education is the answer to changing society.

4

Health

The medicine of tomorrow will be shaped by the people for the people, because the people themselves will determine their own condition, their own destiny.' (Dr Madiou Toure, Director of Hygiene and Health Protection, Ministry of Public Health, Republic of Senegal, 1979:10)

The majority of Third World populations are rural. This chapter is focused on health policy issues which affect those populations most directly, in particular the emergence of the primary health care approach and its implementation. Rural health cannot be considered in isolation, however, and it will become clear that the health sector as a whole must be considered if change is to be possible and effective. Furthermore, it will become apparent that the determinants of the state of health lie as much outside the organised health services as within them. Health must be considered as part of the total development effort. In social policy terms health policy is of major significance for two basic reasons; first, because the state of health of the population is fundamental to any concept of development rooted in notions of improvement in the well-being of the mass of people; and second, because health services characteristically take a massive share of expenditure in Third World countries (Sorkin, 1976). In terms of resource use this is true both of those countries which have adopted policies of public provision of health services − the overwhelming majority − and those which have until relatively recently had only modest public services and considerable private sectors in health care provision.

HEALTH CONDITIONS IN DEVELOPING COUNTRIES

In the developed regions, life expectancy at birth is over seventy years. In those countries classified by the World Bank as 'developing' it is about fifty-three years (World Bank, 1979b). At this most general level there are glaring contrasts between rich and poor countries, and the rich and poor within those countries. Although life expectancy in the poorer countries increased dramatically between the 1940s and the 1970s, this trend has been slowing since the late 1960s (World Bank, 1980a). Furthermore, the available evidence suggests that

unemployment, under-employment, malnutrition, bad housing, an unhealthy environment, and lack of minimum education persist on an enormous scale after a period of some thirty years during which planning for development has become increasingly accepted. While the expectation of life in developing countries has improved considerably over this period, there is little other evidence that the basic needs of the poor are being met in any greater extent than they were thirty years ago. (Abel-Smith and Leiserson, 1978:18)

Despite a dramatic lowering of infant mortality rates, it remains the case that the low life expectancy in developing countries is largely due to the death of children, and particularly young children. Michanek (1975) uses the term 'the passing generation' to emphasise the scale of death among young children in the developing countries. In these countries children between the ages of one and five years are twelve to fifteen times more likely to die than children born in the developed countries (World Bank, 1980a:10). For those surviving beyond five years, life expectancy is only six to eight years less than in developed countries, but morbidity rates are high; there is widespread suffering from non-fatal but frequently debilitating illness and disease. Data on health conditions are available for only a small proportion of the populations of developing countries and are generally of dubious reliability (Benyoussef and Christian, 1977; Gish, 1977; Abel-Smith and Leiserson, 1978). However, within the constraints of the information available, it is clear that there is marked variation *among* developing countries. For example, for those countries as a group, life expectancy at birth may be about fifty-three years, but regional differences are significant – life expectancy in Africa is about forty-six years, in South Asia about fifty-one years, and in Latin America about sixty-three years. The range is from just over forty years in Mali and Upper Volta to around seventy years in Sri Lanka, Singapore and Argentina (World Bank, 1980b). Some correlation may be observed between life expectancy and *per capita* income, but both these measures are subject to gross distortions in very many cases, and within countries often mask more than they reveal. However, previously dominant notions of the generally beneficent effects of economic development may seem to be supported by the correlation. But, 'the high levels of health in a few very poor areas (Sri Lanka and the Indian state of Kerala, for example) and the low life expectancy in a smaller number of relatively wealthy areas (Brazil and Nigeria) demonstrate that the relationship is neither simple nor inescapable' (Golladay, 1980:1-2). In addition, of course, there are enormous variations within countries in both mortality and morbidity levels.

Relatively little information has been collected on the impact of ill-health on economic and social activities (Sorkin, 1976; Turshen, 1977a) and what there is must, given the combination of conceptual and practical difficulties involved, be treated cautiously (Jazairi, 1976). An indication of the impact of ill-health is offered by the World Bank:

The few detailed studies that are available suggest that illness disrupts normal activities for roughly one-tenth of people's time in most developing countries. Many of the illnesses are intermittent with recurrent acute episodes; these illnesses disrupt economic activity, often at critical times, such as the planting and harvesting seasons in the case of malaria. Chronic and debilitating diseases impair people's ability to concentrate, students' ability to learn, and adults' productivity. (World Bank, 1980a:11)

It has long been recognised that the diseases of the developing countries are the diseases of poverty; poor environmental conditions, lack of clean water, inadequate nutrition and rapid population growth allow the most widespread diseases to flourish (King, 1966; Bryant, 1969; Gish, 1977). The most common diseases in developing countries are those transmitted by human faeces – the intestinal parasitic and infectious diarrhoeal diseases, but also poliomyelitis, typhoid and cholera (Van Zijl, 1966). Among children, severe diarrhoeal disease is frequently fatal, alone and in combination with other infections. Intestinal parasites are frequently chronic and debilitating rather than causes of acute illness or death. Massive infestations may result in a loss of 30 per cent of the nutritional value of ingested food (George, 1976). The incidence of intestinal parasites is often very high in developing countries:

WHO estimates that in 1971 there were 650 million people in the world with ascariasis, 450 million people with ancylostomiasis, 350 million people with amoebiasis, and 350 million people with trichuriasis . . . A World Bank case study of the labour force engaged in civil construction at three sites in West Java, Indonesia, found 85 per cent infected with hookworm. (World Bank, 1980a:13)

It has been estimated that a quarter of the world's population is infested with roundworms; studies in many countries have found infection rates in excess of 90 per cent, particularly among young children (Van Zijl, 1966; Feachem, *et al.* 1977).

The second major group of diseases are those spread by air-borne transmission, and includes pneumonia, influenza, bronchitis, measles, whooping cough, meningitis, diphtheria, tuberculosis and chicken pox. The eradication of smallpox from this group has been achieved during the 1970s (World Health Organisation, 1979).

Malnutrition may appear less often in official statistics as the 'primary cause of death', but has been identified as the 'biggest single contributor to child mortality in developing countries' (Food and Agricultural Organisation, 1970:7). The impact of inadequate nutrition on young children is massive; very many of the deaths from disease are of children weakened by malnutrition, and nutritional deficiencies are the source of blindness, physical and intellectual impairment and disease (Kraut and Cremer, 1971; Puffer and Serano, 1973; Transnational Institute, 1974; George, 1976; Dumont and Cohen, 1980).

Despite the considerable variation within and between developing countries both in patterns of disease and levels of ill-health it is accepted that the health conditions of *the poor* in developing countries are basically similar everywhere in the world:

Their core disease pattern consists of the faecally related and air-borne diseases and malnutrition. These three disease groups account for the majority of deaths among the poorest people in developing countries. Malnutrition is the primary cause of death among children in the developing world and also a major contributor to the virulence of infectious diseases by impairing normal body responses to the disease, thereby reducing immunity levels. (Benyoussef and Christian, 1977:402)

These then are the conditions common throughout the developing countries. In addition there are major health problems which vary considerably in their impact. Among the diseases which are related to particular geographical areas or particular life-styles the waterborne diseases are the most important (Feacham, *et al*, 1977). Diseases transmitted by direct contact, such as leprosy and venereal disease, are major problems in particular areas although of relatively minor significance in overall morbidity and mortality. In many parts of the world, however, rapid social change and especially population movement with urbanisation have brought increasing levels of sexually-transmitted disease (World Health Organisation, 1975a). Similarly, the vector-borne diseases are less widespread and contribute less to overall figures than the three disease groups discussed earlier. However, they have a devastating impact in affected areas and their incidence has been increasing in recent years. Sleeping sickness (trypanosomiasis) spread through Africa as the movement of people was stimulated by colonialism. By the 1950s the disease was being brought under control in most areas, but since the 1960s it has again become a serious problem (Hughes and Hunter, 1970). Bilharzia (schistosomiasis) is a debilitating disease transmitted via water snails. The vector needs areas of slow-moving water, and the disease is now spreading rapidly with the development of irrigated agriculture and hydro-electricity schemes (Choudrey, 1975). Malaria is the most wide-spread of the vector-borne diseases. World Health Organisation estimates are that about 850 million people live in areas where malaria continues to be transmitted despite activities to control it. An additional 345 million people reside in areas with little or no active malaria control efforts (World Health Organisation, 1976). There was some success in malaria eradication during the 1960s (Weller, 1974), but more recently its incidence has increased dramatically (Cleaver, 1977). The number of new malaria cases increased by over 230 per cent between 1972 and 1976 (World Bank, 1980a).

Although life expectancy has been increasing, and mortality rates have fallen, 'Throughout the world, for lack of even the simplest measures of health care, vast numbers of people are dying of preventable and curable diseases, often associated with mal-nutrition, or survive with impaired bodies and intellects'. (Djukanovic and Mach, 1975) Furthermore, evidence of mortality, even if reliable, tells us very little about the extent of illness, and even less about the health of populations. The point was powerfully made by Myrdal:

> Mortality data alone do not tell us much about the frequency, duration, and after-effects even of diseases that are usually fatal. They tell us next to nothing about many other important health deficiencies: physical infirmities like blindness, incipient illnesses, and more generally, physical and mental weakness caused by malnutrition, intestinal worms, and other infestations and diseases that are usually not fatal in themselves. It is conceivable that a large part of a population may be diseased, or at least lacking in normal vigour, all or most of the time, even though rates of mortality are decreasing and life expectancy is increasing. It is even conceivable that people live longer only to suffer debilitating conditions of ill-health to a greater extent than before. (Myrdal, 1968: Vol.3, 1554)

The patterns of both mortality and morbidity in developing countries are known. Both are overwhelmingly the result of malnutrition, gastro-intestinal diseases, respiratory diseases and vector-borne diseases. The knowledge needed to deal with these is widely available, 'the health problems of developing countries can be controlled or treated with presently known technologies'. (World Bank, 1980a:16)

HEALTH RESOURCES

If health services are to serve the mass of people they must be developed in accordance with the dominant disease patterns. Despite major problems with the collection and analysis of disease statistics in developing countries, the broad patterns of morbidity and mortality are now sufficiently well established to enable relevant health services to be developed. As Gish argues, 'health service development operates within two constraints: one is economic — the availability of resources to carry out planned developments; the other is political — the determination to provide health services capable of providing national coverage, even if only at the simplest level'. (1977:11) Until relatively recently, considerable effort had been made to produce more and better disease statistics but much less with regard to economic, financial, health manpower data, and questions of utilisation of health service facilities by different sections of the population. In addition to basic demographic features and patterns of morbidity and mortality any consideration of health development must be based on knowledge of the level of health resources and their distribution.

There is substantial variation between Third World countries in both the level of health resources and the distribution of those resources between different types of facility and manpower category. Consistently, however, there are marked inequalities within countries with regard to the distribution of health resources, particularly between urban and rural areas. Given such internal maldistributions, and significant variations in the nature and utilisation of resources in different areas, any national indicators can give only a crude relative measure of health resource status. However, as will be seen from the following brief summary, a number of clear themes emerge, despite the inherent difficulties of using such data.

Most Third World countries have three basic levels of health facility: the hospital, the health centre and the sub-centre (called by a variety of names – dispensary, village health post, aid post, etc.). In general, the sub-centre is intended to serve an essentially local population, within easy access. The health centre will deal with more difficult cases, and in theory serves an area with a radius perhaps twice that of the sub-centre. Hospitals may vary from relatively small district hospitals through regional or provincial hospitals to those which are intended to serve as national referral hospitals. In theory each of these types of facility has specific and different tasks to perform, and particular catchment areas to serve; in virtually all cases there is intended to be a hierarchical relationship between the different levels – 'a pyramid of health facilities'. In practice, there is frequently little if any relationship between the scale of the facility and the population it actually serves. The differences in cost at these different levels of facility are typically very great indeed; 'the cost of building and running the different institutions may be in the ratio of £1 to £10 to £100 [sub-centres, health centres and regional hospitals] for capital costs and £1 to £5 to £50 for recurrent costs' (Gish, 1977:39).

A recent analysis of health resources noted major variations between the various regions of the Third World; Latin America has the most developed health infrastructure, South-East Asia is relatively well developed, the Middle East contains enormous variation due to the presence of the oil-exporting states, South Asia has considerably lower levels of facility development and the countries of Africa are poorest on virtually all measures (Golladay, 1980). In most countries, however, there is a consistent maldistribution of facilities; rural areas are poorly served relative to urban areas. In Nigeria, for example, there are only 233 persons per dispensary in the peri-urban areas round the capital, whereas in the rural areas there are between 25,000 and 60,000 persons per dispensary (Nigeria, Ministry of Health, 1978). In Syria, 45 per cent of the health clinics are in Damascus and Alleppo; the population per hospital bed in Damascus is 10 per cent that in the rural provinces (Ueber and Susan, 1978). In general terms a clear picture emerges when health facilities are examined. There is bias, in virtually every case, towards the upper parts of the hierarchy and towards the urban areas. As will be seen later, the bulk of limited resources available for health goes to maintain expensive, relatively well-equipped facilities staffed by more highly trained, and more highly paid staff. These facilities tend to concentrate in urban areas, and even within those areas tend to be inaccessible to the poorer populations.

About half of most health budgets in the Third World are taken by personnel costs, about half to three-quarters of these costs being required for the employment of health workers and the rest for other staff. With regard to health workers a crucially important factor is the considerable variation in training and recurrent costs between different types of worker. 'For example, in African countries the cost of training one university medical doctor is at least fifteen to twenty times greater than the cost of training one medical assistant, and a rural medical aid might be trained for half the cost of a medical assistant.' (Gish, 1977:29) Thus, forty medical auxilliaries may be trained for the cost of training one university medical doctor. Such massive differences will be seen to be of major importance in proposals which attempt to ensure more effective and equitable health policies. As with consideration of health facilities, there are obvious problems with generalisations across the whole range of Third World countries. Not all countries have the same categories of health worker and the levels of training and range of responsibilities may vary considerably; 'nurses' for example may be quite different in different systems (Hall and Mejia, 1978). Nonetheless, a pyramidical, hierarchical structure is characteristic as with health facilities, with medical doctors at the top and medical auxilliaries at the bottom. At this point only those workers employed full-time in health service work are considered. There is enormous variation in the degree to which unpaid or part-time village healthworkers are used in health programmes (World Health Organisation, 1977; 1979). Similarly, the nature of the formal health services, the kind of health policies adopted, and the nature of traditional systems will dramatically affect the extent to which traditional healers are involved in national health care systems (World Health Organisation, 1978).

As with health facilities, it is typical that the poorest populations, generally those with the worst state of health, have the poorest access to health personnel. Again, the pattern tends to be that the poorest countries are worst off and the poorest populations within countries are disadvantaged. The urban bias noted in relation to facilities is similarly found for healthworkers. Overall, there are generally very poor absolute levels of staffing in Third World countries, compounded to tragic levels by gross maldistribution. National figures again can only give a crude relative indication; for medical doctors, for example, most counts are of all registered doctors whether engaged in medical practice or not — and many spend a large part of their time in administration, teaching, research and private practice. This is stressed to underline once more the gulf between presence, access and utilisation. It is only the last of these which has real meaning for the health of people; the first two may be manipulated to improve the third, but there is not any simple relationship between them.

In global terms, it is again Africa which has the poorest provision, with between 20,000 and 40,000 persons per doctor. The distribution of doctors between urban and rural areas is appallingly bad; the overwhelming majority of doctors practise in urban areas where 10 to 20 per cent of the population live, while rural areas are very poorly served (Etten, 1976; Abel-Smith and Leiserson, 1978; IDS Health Group, 1978). In Senegal, for example, 76 per cent of the country's doctors are in the capital, where only 17 per cent of the population lives (Nenes, 1977). In India, which has a greater supply of doctors than many other developing countries, population/ doctor ratios are about 2,000:1 in urban areas and 12,000:1 in rural (Ahluwalia, 1978). Nepal has an overall population/doctor ratio of more than 36,000:1 (World Bank, 1980a). In Latin America, which has relatively high levels of qualified medical manpower, the distribution of doctors is again biased in favour of urban areas – two-thirds of doctors are in large cities, where only one-third of the population lives (Pan-American Health Organisation, 1978). Even more severe maldistribution is characteristic of many of the countries of the Middle East, compounded in many cases by critical shortages of female personnel. 'In Syria, 65 per cent of midwives practise in Damascus leaving only 300 midwives to serve the rest of the country. In the PDRY, 73 per cent of physicians practise in Aden, and in Jordan, 76 per cent practise in Amman.' (Golladay, 1980:11) In Papua New Guinea, the national population/doctor ratio in 1977 was 13,500:1, but within the country this ratio varied from 3000:1 in the province, which includes the capital, to 55,000:1 in the worst served of the nineteen provinces. Population/nurse ratios were similarly skewed; 1504:1 nationally, 630:1 in the best off province and 8800:1 in the worst off (MacPherson, 1980).

These examples serve to illustrate the pattern characteristic of Third World countries; very poor levels of staffing overall marked by extremely uneven distribution. For the vast majority of Third World populations access to qualified medical staff remains slight, and in very many cases is non-existent. It is against this background of health conditions and health resources that contemporary health policy issues must be seen.

HEALTH POLICIES IN DEVELOPING COUNTRIES — THE EMERGENCE OF PRIMARY HEALTH CARE

Health services in the developing countries, the majority of which are former colonial territories, must be seen as reflecting dominant societal relationships (Segall, 1972; Sharpston, 1973; Frankenberg, 1974; Navarro, 1974; Heller and Elliott, 1977; Turshen, 1977a; Doyal and Pennell, 1979; Gish, 1979). Contemporary patterns of underdevelopment have their roots in colonialism; underdeveloped health services have grown out of colonial medical care systems. The metropolitan powers introduced their own health systems into their overseas territories at an early stage of colonial penetration. In many cases, as discussed earlier, this period was dominated by the military and the missions. As Gish states, 'Typically the pattern of "modern" medical care during the colonial era had three major components: the urban hospital, the rural dispensary – often Christian church related, and the hygiene or public health element. In essence, this remains the pattern in the Third World right up to the present.' (1979:205) Colonial administration hospitals were built initially to meet the needs of Europeans and their families; they might have some minor provision for non-European in-patient care, but this was more likely to be provided by mission hospitals (Beck, 1970; Schram, 1971; MacPherson, 1980). As in Papua New Guinea, characteristically hospital provision was in the major centres of European settlement and economic activity (Gershenberg, 1970; Doherty, 1973; Gish, 1973; Benyoussef, 1977). Rural dispensaries, where these existed, were more commonly run by missions and other voluntary organisations; they were essentially curative institutions, dispensing drugs to out-patients, but with very limited in-patient facilities (Titmuss *et al*, 1964). In terms of public health, the essential objective of colonial policy was to provide a 'safer' environment for the Europeans, both in residential areas and areas of economic activity such as estates and plantations (Brown, 1976; Doyal and Pennell, 1979). To the extent that colonial services were extended to the indigenous population their distribution was again generally determined by patterns of economic activity, notably in primary export production. As for their style, the dominant theme was most often the desire to spread the 'scientific and orderly' methods of Western medicine to peoples considered to be backward and lacking in awareness of 'proper' medical practice. 'It was generally assumed that the administered people would prosper to the degree they became like those who administered them.' (Gish, 1979:205) Turshen (1977b) argues that the spread of the clinical medical model was inextricably linked to the spread of the capitalist mode of production; the values and underlying paradigm of the clinical model are connected to the forms of economic organisation that characterise capitalist social life. Many of those who have attempted to analyse the development of health systems in developing countries, without perhaps agreeing with all the views represented by Turshen, accept the importance of the proposition that 'medicine's failure to develop a positive definition of health results from the individualistic and ideological bias that pervades medical research and medical practice, structures relations between practitioners and patients, shapes the approaches selected for treatment (e.g. chemical or surgical intervention) and the technology employed, and rejects the initiation of collective social action by communities'. (Turshen, 1977b:49) Thus the legacy of colonialism was not simply inadequate services, maldistributed and generally irrelevant to the needs of the majority, but an approach to health itself which was to a very great extent inimical to the development of an appropriate health system.

Political independence, gained by most of the colonies in the twenty years after the Second World War, in general made little difference to health policies. As Leys suggests, the change was most often:

The replacement of direct colonial administration by independent governments representing local strata and classes with an interest in sustaining the colonial economic relationships. To the extent that the state in the metropolitan countries was a committee for managing the common affairs of the whole bourgeoisie, the state which emerged in the periphery country was a sort of sub-committee. (Leys, 1975:9-10)

The nature and effects of neo-colonialism have been extensively documented. Studies of neo-colonialism and health have stressed both the continuing injustice of health care systems in the developing countries, and the crucial inter-relationships between those systems and those of the former colonial powers (Gish, 1971; Lall and Bibile, 1977; Doyal and Pennell, 1979). Most newly independent states attempted expansion of their health provision, but essentially in the form developed under colonialism. Despite stated objectives to the contrary, in most countries post-independence health allocations were biased as much, or more, in the direction of emerging élite and urban groups than had been the case before political independence (Cliffe, 1973; Lipton, 1977; Mburu, 1979). The rhetoric of post-independence health plans was almost always contradicted by actual expenditures and programmes; 'the rhetoric emphasised preventive and rural priorities at the same time that expenditures were overwhelmingly curative and urban'. (Gish, 1979:206)

Although the fundamental nature of health provision changed little there was considerable expansion, most notably in the rapid growth of hospital provision and the drive to produce medical graduates. This provision was almost always in urban areas and widened the gulf between rural and urban populations. While in general rural services expanded less than urban, there were some significant developments, in particular the rural health centre concept was developed, especially in East Africa, and elaborated in King's widely influential book (King, 1966). There can be little doubt that King's work had considerable impact, not just in Africa but throughout the developing countries. In contrast with many developing countries, however, the countries of East Africa relied heavily on the medical assistant at the rural health centres (Fendall, 1963; 1965; 1968). However, the emphasis in Fendall's concept of medical auxilliaries was very much on relatively highly-trained healthworkers working in health systems which still had the medical doctor as the lynchpin of a strictly hierarchical system (Fendall, 1972).

Despite such developments and the more profound changes which were beginning to take place in certain newly independent countries, for example Tanzania (Kilama *et al,* 1974; Gish, 1975), most countries continued to emphasise 'growth' and health policies matched the dominant economic ideology. It was not until the 1970s that emphasis on 'growth' and 'gross national product' as the measures of development began to give way to alternative views informed by the realities of conditions for the mass of people in developing countries.

As outlined earlier, at the beginning of the 1970s those arguing for new approaches to development were a minority, for example President Nyerere of Tanzania, whose lucid and compelling writing on his country's attempt to develop on the basis of equality and the needs of the mass of the rural population was profoundly in-fluential. By the end of the 1970s it is possible to say, albeit with some qualifications, that: 'The emergence of a new majority view of development focused upon the needs of the most impoverished, including perhaps especially their nutritional and health requirements, has more or less "swept the development boards".' (Gish, 1979:208) International concern with health in developing countries began to reflect this new view of development. There was more attention paid to the problems and issues of basic health services in rural areas (World Health Organisation, 1973a and b; 1974). The principles of the primary health approach care were enunciated by the Director-General of the World Health Organisation in 1975, and these have been the focus of attention by the international agencies ever since (World Health Organisation, 1975b; 1979).

The major background study for the World Health Organisation primary health care programme resulted from the joint WHO/UNICEF effort (Djukanovic and Mach, 1975). This study was unequivocal in its criticism of existing approaches to health policy and the need for a shift of emphasis to basic health services:

Despite great efforts by government and international organisations, the basic health needs of vast numbers of the world's people remain unsatisfied. In many countries less than 15 per cent of the rural population and other unprivileged groups have access to health services . . . The strategy adopted . . . by many developing countries has been modelled on that of the industrialised countries, but as a strategy it has been a failure . . . In sum, history and experience show that conventional health services, organised along Western or other centralised lines, are unlikely to expand to meet the basic health needs of all people . . . Clearly the time has come to take a fresh look at the world's priority health problems and at alternative approaches to their solution. (Djukanovic and Mach, 1975:7)

Their conclusions, based on an analysis of the failure of conventional health services and the example of countries with successful, or potentially successful, basic health programmes emphasised the need for clear national health policies, the relationship between health and development strategies, the need for massive redistribution of resources and, fundamentally, the reorientation of health systems around community-based primary health workers. They were aware that their proposals implied 'a virtual revolution in most health service systems. It will bring about changes in the distribution of power, in the pattern of political decision-making, in the attitude and commitment of the health professionals and adminstrators, ministries of health and universities, and in people's awareness of what they are entitled to'. (Djukanovic and Mach, 1975: 104-05)

Although several types of primary healthworker were identified all were seen as needing 'a wider social outlook'. Whatever the specific form of health service, it was argued that the basis of such services was the group of trained primary health workers chosen by the people from their own community and controlled by them. Such workers were contrasted with 'a reluctant, alienated, frustrated group of bureaucrats "parachuted" into the community'. (Djukanovic and Mach, 1975:105)

It was further argued that the entire health service system would have to be mobilised to support these new primary healthworkers. From their examination of country case studies, Djukanovic and Mach suggested that whereas the existence of appropriate national development goals and overall development strategies facilitated the adoption of such an approach to health, some significant advances were possible on a regional or sectional basis. However, although they argued that the systems they studied could be adapted for application in 'many political, social, economic and environmental situations' (1975:104), quite clearly the most successful programmes in terms of the development of equitable national systems of health were in those countries where health had been integrated into a general development programme. Of the countries discussed by Djukanovic and Mach, Cuba, China and Tanzania were those which provided the most dramatic results from the application of the 'primary health care approach'.

The Djukanovic and Mach study very clearly established the primary healthworker as the foundation of health systems in developing countries. In doing so, major emphasis was put on the involvement of the community which the health worker served. This was examined in a further World Health Organisation publication which suggested that basic health should be 'health by the people' (Newell, 1975). Again, a series of case studies was used as the basis of an exploration of the issues, problems and possibilities of community organisation for health. As Benyoussef and Christian note, 'health by the people' is both a philosophical and a pragmatic idea (1977:401). Philosophically it may be believed that organised communities, representing the basic unit of a functioning democracy, should be the starting-point of health services. On a practical level, since resources are almost invariably too limited to consider any other course of action, community organisation has to be the starting-point. Newell's study was concerned with successful community organisation for health and although drawing examples from countries with very different social, economic and political characteristics he was able to identify common themes. The first was again the crucial importance of the community-based primary healthworkers: 'Author after author describes the primary healthworker as one of the keys to success, not only on the grounds of cheapness but because he or she is accepted and can deal with many of the local problems better than anyone has done before and because he or she is *there*.' (Newell, 1975:193) In all the examples presented by Newell the new systems of primary health care were either linked with pre-existing indigenous health systems or attempted to function in ways which were qualitatively similar to such systems; 'in this sense the new did not win over or destroy the old, but achieved an adjustment that had some new qualities and techniques and provided a link between the present and the past'. (1975:193) Closely related to this is the further common feature that in no case was there a separation of promotional, preventive and curative health action at the primary health care level. As Newell states, 'the arguments for linking curative, promotive and preventive actions appear to be overwhelming'. (1975:195) However, the key similarity between the successful examples discussed lay in community organisations:

Each area or country started with the formation, reinforcement or recognition of a local community organisation. This appeared to have five relevant functions. It laid down the priorities; it organised community action for problems that could not be resolved by individuals (e.g. water supply or basic sanitation); it controlled the primary health care service by selecting, appointing or legitimising the primary health worker; it assisted in financing services; and it linked health actions with wider community goals. (Newell, 1975:193)

Successful local community organisation was thus identified as the basis of success in primary health care. However, Newell acknowledges the major dilemmas of a 'community development' approach in widely different developmental contexts. Three types were described, national change (China, Cuba, Tanzania), extensions of the existing system (Iran, Nigeria, Venezuela), and local community development (Guatemala, India, Indonesia). Where there was national change considerable advantages could be seen, not least that:

Even though these were poor countries, the clear statement of national decision and national will mobilised effort, gave recognition to health as something that was not imprisoned within the sectoral confines of a health ministry, and plucked health out of the directing hands of the health industry . . . The biggest benefit of this change appeared to be an increased ability to reorient resources quickly in direct relation to national goals, which in each case underlined the needs of the underserved rural populations. (Newell, 1975:199)

In those countries which had extended their existing systems there was a desire to bring services to those presently without them, but no assumption that the methods necessary to do this would demand changes in the society as a whole or in the pattern of existing health services, 'it was even considered possible that the rural primary health care methods adopted might be temporary or interim ones, and that at some future time the country would be served by a single system with characteristics approaching those at present existing in the cities' (Newell, 1975:199).

The third group of examples, those dealing with local community development projects, did not involve any changes, political or administrative, outside the local area. The projects, although successful in themselves, showed few signs of replication even to neighbouring areas and had not influenced national policies in the countries concerned. In view of the widespread adoption of the primary health care approach which has taken place in recent years, Newell's conclusions regarding those countries which had extended existing systems are of importance. Although there were connections with national decisions in these cases, local strengths were less, and their main thrust was seen to be more in relation to the health service itself and less towards overall rural development. These projects did not seem to link local community organisation and national change but were seen as solutions in themselves. In so far as such approaches do not therefore demand significant change outside the health system, it may be, as Newell suggests, that:

They would appear to be of relevance to countries with widely differing political systems and to be a step that could be taken to expand a local effort to the provincial and later to the national level. The weaknesses are mainly the dangers of bureaucracy, lack of contact between sectors of government, and the reactionary forces within the health professions that could organise at this level of national endeavour to stop change. (1975:201)

Thus the proponents of primary health care argued that some significant advances could be made, whatever the social context. Benyoussef and Christian expressed a pragmatic view in asking whether primary health care is the best approach to providing health care in developing countries. 'It is at least an attempt to provide some health care where none exists now. Present medical care systems are clearly inadequate, so if the choice is between offering primary health care or no health care at all, then the choice is obvious'. (1977:407) Others have placed much greater emphasis on the relationship between developments in health and social, economic and political forces. In particular, it has been argued that if genuine progress towards justice and the strengthening of communities is to be made this can only occur where there is a fundamental shift of power (Navarro, 1972; Rifkin and Kaplinsky, 1973; Sidel and Sidel, 1974, 1977; Feuerstein, 1976).

In September 1978, the Alma-Ata International Conference on Primary Health Care, 'probably the largest single-theme conference ever held' (Bennett 1979:505), clearly established primary health care as the model of health development in the majority of developing countries (WHO/UNICEF, 1978; World Health Organisation, 1978a). The Declaration of Alma-Ata stressed the 'existing gross inequality' in health status, and argued that health should be a main focus of overall social and economic development. The definition of primary health care offered at Alma-Ata is one which many countries have adopted, and many more will undoubtedly do so:

Primary Health Care:
1.   reflects and evolves from the economic conditions and socio-cultural and political characteristics of the country and its communities and is based on the application of the relevant results of social, bio-medical and health services research and public health experience;
2.   addresses the main health problems in the community, providing promotive, preventive, curative and rehabilitative services accordingly;
3.   includes at least: education concerning prevailing health problems and the methods of preventing and controlling them; promotion of food supply and proper nutrition; an adequate supply of safe water and basic sanitation; maternal and child health care, including family planning; immunisation against the major infectious diseases; prevention and control of locally endemic diseases; appropriate treatment of common diseases and injuries; and provision of essential drugs;
4.   involves, in addition to the health sector, all related sectors and aspects of national and community development, in particular agriculture, animal husbandry, food, industry, education, housing, public works, com-

munications, and other sectors; and demands the co-ordinated efforts of all those sectors;

5. requires and promotes maximum community and individual self-reliance and participation in the planning, organisation, operation and control of primary health care, making fullest use of local, national and other available resources; and to this end develops through appropriate education the ability of communities to participate;

6. should be sustained by integrated, functional and mutually supportive referral systems, leading to the progressive improvement of comprehensive health care for all, and giving priority to those most in need;

7. relies, at local and referral levels, on healthworkers, including physicians, nurses, midwives, auxilliaries and community workers as applicable, as well as traditional practitioners as needed, suitably trained socially and technically to work as a health team and to respond to the expressed health needs of the community. (World Health Organisation, 1979:VIII-IX)

Bennett, in a full discussion of the development of the primary health concept, identified a number of important aspects. Although careful to elaborate the deficiences of existing health systems and the obstacles to be overcome, he was essentially optimistic: 'Primary health care is the outcome of collective human conscience – a recent awareness that there has been inequality in the distribution of health which is a human right . . . Primary health care programmes aim at changing this situation and the achievement of health for all by [the year] 2000 has now become a feasible proposition.' (Bennett, 1979:513)

For the international health agencies and many others, the primary health care approach is seen to offer a solution to the health problems of the majority of people in developing countries. The extent to which these ideas have come to dominate in recent years may be seen in the significant difference between recent policy statements on health produced by the World Bank (1975b; 1980). In marked contrast to the 1975 policy document, that produced in 1980 stressed the role of community-level healthworkers and announced a major change in policy – the World Bank would begin direct lending for health projects. It was argued that for technical, social and economic reasons the adoption or extension of simplified systems of health care was imperative. The World Bank expressed the intention of supporting health projects which were aimed at strengthening the planning and budgeting capacities of Third World countries in addition to direct improvements of their primary health care systems. However, optimism is by no means universal. Gish, for example, suggests that the discussion on primary health care has demonstrated wishful thinking at best and cynicism at worst. In his view there has been far too little hard analysis of the real issues involved: 'The discussion appears to have moved in remarkably short order from almost total rejection of the traditional practitioner, the village healthworkers or even other types of "medical practitioners" than those with university degrees to idyllic glorification of these types of cadres.' (Gish, 1979:209) He points out that there has been a failure to examine sufficiently the context of health programmes in countries such as Cuba, China and Tanzania. Rifkin develops this argument in relation to China, whose health care system has consistently been held up as a model for primary health care development. Rifkin argues that although the primary health care approach adopted at Alma-Ata drew heavily on the Chinese experience, the problems which have arisen in attempts to implement this approach arise in part from fundamental misinterpretations of the Chinese model itself. Identifying political will and community participation as the key features of the model, Rifkin argues these have been misunderstood by many of those attempting to build primary health care systems on these principles elsewhere. Political will, she argues, cannot be taken to mean simply a commitment to allocate resources to the health sector, in China political will is concerned with the total transformation of society. 'In health, political will means that health care *follows, does not create* the strategy of total development. Changes in the health sector reflect changes in the national approach to development. They cannot create, support or maintain changes which are divorced from other social changes.' (Rifkin, 1981:4) Similarly, community participation may be seen simply as another component of the health care delivery system with little or no appreciation of its nature in the Chinese system. In Rifkin's view it is essential to recognise that the Chinese health care model is not a model for improvement in health care delivery, but a model for social change. Health improvements in China came as a result of a strategy of total development not as a result of changes in the health services alone. The health care system 'reflects, not leads, political commitment to improve health by changing the social, political and economic structures and by educating the masses, through participation, to accept these changes'. (Rifkin, 1981:5) Others have pointed to the impossibility of taking health practice out of its social, economic and political context and attempting to transfer it elsewhere (Doyal and Pennell, 1979). Even those countries where the appropriate conditions for success appear to be more likely have experienced serious difficulties in attempting radical reform of their health systems. In Tanzania for example, despite major advances, rural health workers have been found to be careerist, deferential to the established medical hierarchy, and unsympathetic to the people among whom they worked (Gish 1975; Etten, 1976); similar attitudes have been found among rural healthworkers in Papua New Guinea (MacPherson, 1980). Genuine primary health care will only be extensively developed if there are fundamental reforms of the more conventional health delivery systems. There is as yet little evidence even of significant shifts in the resource allocations for health in most developing countries despite the espousal of primary health care (Mburu, 1979). To be successful, primary health care cannot simply be a matter of 'projects' grafted on to existing systems; the nature of health systems must be changed. If they are so changed, from being inequitably distributed, urban and hospital-oriented to being part of a just, overall social and economic development, the evidence is that such a change will demand major social transformation (Frankenberg and Leeson, 1973; New, 1974; Sidel and Sidel, 1974; Aziz, 1978). 'It must be stressed that the major obstacle to more just and efficient health care systems (whether "by", "for" or "with" the people) are not the usually cited ones of limited resources, poor communications, or lack of technological knowledge and data, but rather social systems that place a low value on the health care needs of the poor.' (Gish, 1979:209)

SUMMARY

Primary health care has emerged as the dominant approach to the health problems of developing countries. It has clearly developed out of the realisation that existing health systems have failed the majority of people in developing countries. Concern for basic health needs may be seen as part of a more general trend in perceptions of development and national economic criteria have to some extent been displaced by social and distributional criteria. Alternative approaches to meeting basic health needs have drawn to a considerable extent on the experiences of such countries as Cuba, China and Tanzania, where attempts to achieve massive social transformations in which health is part of overall national change have been made. Primary health care has rapidly emerged as the dominant model for health service development in the 1970s, and its approach focuses on the basic health needs of the majority of people, attempts to integrate promotional, preventive and curative health, stresses the use of low-level manpower and relies heavily on community organisation.

Doubts regarding its real long-term success stem essentially from explanations of the existing patterns of inequality in health conditions and access to health resources. To the extent that these are the product of the 'development of underdevelopment', significant changes in health will depend not simply on health policies but on changes in the pattern of social, economic and political forces in developing countries. From this perspective, improved health is not simply, or even primarily, a matter of medical systems, but a much more complex question of the relationship between health and underdevelopment, and the nature of the underdevelopment. As Gish argues:

All activities concerned with health must begin with the specifics of underdevelopment in particular circumstances. Only from this background will it be possible to come to grips with the issues of improved health status as well as more relevant health and medical services in the Third World. As long as it remains essentially impossible to deal seriously with existing social and property relations, so long will it remain impossible to alter significantly the health status of the world's poorest, say, one billion people. (Gish, 1979:210)

5

Urbanisation and Housing

'The settlers' town is a strongly built town, all made of stone and steel. It is a brightly lit town; the streets are covered with asphalt, and the garbage cans swallow all the leavings, unseen, unknown and hardly thought about . . . The settlers' town is a well-fed town, an easy-going town; its belly is always full of good things. The settlers' town is a town of white people, of foreigners. . . .

The town belonging to the coloured people, or at least the native town, the Negro village, the medina, the reservation, is a place of ill fame, peopled by men of evil repute. They are born there, it matters little where or how; they die there, it matters not where, nor how. It is a world without spaciousness; men live there on top of each other, and their huts are built one on top of the other. The native town is a hungry town, starved of bread, of meat, of shoes, of coal, of light. The native town is a crouching village, a town on its knees, a town wallowing in the mire.' (Fanon, 1967:39)

Previous chapters have stressed the overwhelming importance of rural populations in the countries of the Third World and the need for social policy to be oriented to the rural populations, and in so doing to redress the characteristic urban bias in the distribution of resources. This chapter is concerned with urban areas, and in particular with the provision of housing in those areas. In common with discussion of other areas of policy, attention is focused on the conditions and needs of the poorest groups. As will become clear, the relationships between urban and rural areas, and the formulation and implementation of social policies for the former, throw up many profound dilemmas for Third World countries.

There are three major justifications for this examination of urban housing issues. First, rates of urban growth are very high in most Third World countries; social policy, if it is to be effective, must attempt to provide for predictable future conditions. Second, there are complex patterns of linkage between urban and rural areas; earlier discussion of underdevelopment has indicated that these areas may develop unevenly, but they do not develop separately. At all levels, from macro-economic patterns of resource exploitation and resource flows, through to the systems of individual migratory movement and kinship support networks, these linkages are of profound significance. Third, it must be recognised that urban housing policy is a critical factor in determining the nature and extent of urban privilege on the one hand, and extreme urban poverty on the other. The dominance of élite urban populations has already been noted. As will be seen, the role of the state is crucial in housing provision both for the poor and for those primarily urban-based groups earlier identified as pivotal in the class formation of underdeveloped societies. Urban development, and the gross inequalities characteristic of that development, epitomise the social dilemmas of underdevelopment.

The lack of attention paid here to problems of rural housing reflects the reality of the majority of Third World countries, although some reference to rural housing improvement will be found in later discussions of community development programmes. This chapter is concentrated on the urban situation, and in particular on those features of housing provision susceptible to policy initiatives.

URBANISATION IN THE THIRD WORLD

As with so many other aspects of social conditions in the Third World, the available statistical information on urbanisation is marked by serious flaws. There is considerable variation in levels of accuracy and reliability, together with basic differences in the definitions used (Hardoy and Satterthwaite, 1981). With regard to the latter, the definition of 'urban' adopted in a particular country may depend on differences in the historical experience — where recognised non-agricultural settlements of some size have existed for a considerable time, definitions may favour the legal status of such settlements as the basic criterion. In Tunisia, for example, urban refers to all those settlements with commune status. In the Philippines, similar criteria are adopted in so far as only settlements which are 'chartered cities' or 'municipalities' may be urban, and here an additional factor is introduced — only settlements with population densities in excess of 1000 per square kilometre are defined as urban.

Brazil has a seemingly very large urban population — over 65 per cent — which is partly explained by the fact that all administrative centres are counted as urban, regardless of size. The majority of Third World countries use, whether alone or in conjunction with other factors, some measure of population size in their definition of urban areas. This is also true of the international agencies, such as the World Bank, which attempt to produce standardised information in order that international comparisons may be made. For the UN and the World Bank 'urban' covers settlements of at least 20,000 inhabitants, while 'city' is used to describe an urban agglomeration of more than 100,000 people. But Third World countries themselves are quite inconsistent in the size of settlement chosen to mark what is urban. Colombia records an urban population of 70 per cent, but has a definition of 1500 person settlements. Nigeria, in contrast, adopts a figure of 20,000 and a national population which is 75 per cent rural. Mexico, with 67 per cent of its total population in urban areas, contains the most populous city in the world — Mexico City has 14 million inhabitants — its definition of urban areas, however, is any settlement of more than 2500 people, and quite clearly is an extreme example of the enormous variation found in very many parts of the world in the environments classified as urban. Kenya and Tanzania, neighbours in East Africa, differ widely in the size of settlement they define as urban — the former takes 2000, the later 5000.

India, with a massive share of the total Third World population, has only 22 per cent of its population in urban areas using its own definition. Their definition is of interest in that it uses three criteria — settlements must be of more then 5000 people, have a population density of more than 1000 per square kilometre; and have more than 75 per cent of people 'non-agricultural'. With this definition we can begin to see, even at this level, the complexities of the urban concept. The Indian attempt to define in terms of density and economic character is suggestive of the difficulties which arise when settlements are defined as urban with reference only to administrative boundaries, and without reference to their socio-economic characteristics and functions. In practice, of course, such definitions will be difficult to apply in many cases. Nonetheless, not many countries have adopted definitions as loose as that used in Indonesia (80 per cent rural) which defines urban areas as 'places with urban characteristics' (Hardoy and Satterthwaite, 1981:62). Whatever the difficulties involved in administering a system which uses such a definition, there is an important message in the Indonesian example.

It would be unproductive to illustrate the worldwide variation in definitions at any greater length; what is important is that 'urban' has for many purposes related to social policy questions a meaning derived from the particular society in question. Enough has also been said to make it clear that extreme caution is necessary when statistics are encountered which divide populations between urban and rural, and that considerable care must be taken to ensure that the bases of such divisions are known.

Despite all the difficulties inherent in the information available, several major features of urbanisation are clear. First, 'it is the astonishing speed of urbanisation in the Third World that is so startling'. (Mountjoy, 1978:103) Contemporary urban growth in developing countries is of such a massive absolute scale as to distinguish it from nineteenth-century trends in Europe and America with which it is frequently compared. 'Between 1800 and 1900 the total city population of Europe [including Russia] increased by some 4.3 million, whereas in the less developed countries of Asia the urban population has risen by 160 million in just the last twenty-five years.' (Drakakis-Smith, 1981:3) Second, urban growth is likely to accelerate during the next twenty years as many of the countries in Asia and Africa have not yet reached their forecast maximum rates of urban growth. Third, although there is considerable confusion as to the pattern of urban growth in smaller urban centres of the Third World, particularly outside capitals, it is clear that the larger cities are expanding very rapidly. Cities of a million or more inhabitants are growing faster than smaller cities, and the huge cities of more than five million are growing even faster (World Bank, 1979a). The degree of variation in city size, rates of urban growth, and the patterns of urban settlement outside primary cities, is so great that generalisations about patterns of urbanisation in the Third World as a whole are impossible. In what follows, much will apply only to particular urban formations; such formations will be characterised less by their absolute then their relative size, less by their scale than by their nature and less by the enormous differences in physical context and more by the depressing continuity in the experience of their poorest inhabitants.

CAUSES OF URBAN GROWTH

There are two major components of urban growth — natural urban population growth and rural-urban migration. The relative importance of these is of major significance to policy makers, but it is unfortunately the case that precise information is generally lacking. Generalisations are unhelpful in this regard. Drakakis-Smith, for example, suggests that 'about half of the population growth in Third World cities is the result of natural increase — rather more than half in Asia, rather less in Africa'. (1981:6) This tends to understate the very wide variations between countries and regions. Recent World Bank estimates for the period 1970–5 show that in fact the rate of rural-urban migration in urban growth is generally quite significant, and is particularly high at low levels of urbanisation, and at very high levels of urbanisation (World Bank, 1979a). The most striking contrasts were between the recently independent, primarily agricultural countries of Africa, the Middle East and the South Pacific and the countries of Latin America. In the former, natural growth accounted for only about a quarter to a third of urban growth, whereas in the latter about two-thirds to three-quarters of urban growth resulted from natural urban population growth. In the present discussion, however, the focus of attention is on those underdeveloped countries with relatively low total levels of urbanisation but high rates of urban growth where migration is of major significance.

Attempts to influence rates of natural population increase in towns and cities are not considered here. The use of birth control programmes and other measures as part of overall national population policies is discussed later in relation to social policy and social planning. At this stage, however, it is appropriate to consider briefly the relationship between fertility and urbanisation itself. A number of factors have been identified as associated with the current downward trend in Third World fertility rates. The first is improved health, particularly of infants, since greater rates of survival may lead parents to consider the restriction of family size. Urban areas may offer the possibility of better health, partly through greater access to health services but also, in some circumstances, to clean water, more reliable food supplies and reduced exposure to major vector-borne diseases. Against these possibilities however, must be put the major health risks of urbanisation, for the poorer groups conditions may be very much worse than those in the rural areas. In addition to the appalling squalor characteristic of many Third World cities must be added the new risks of urban living. As an example, the widespread use of powdered milk for infants in urban areas has been conclusively shown to constitute a major health risk (Chetley, 1980).

A second factor, partly linked with greater access to health services, is the possibility that urban families may make greater use of family planning services where these are available. Here, greater exposure to family planning propaganda and education may be relevant. Perhaps most relevant of all may be the changing position of women in urban areas. In general, then, given the uneven distribution of services in favour of urban areas, it may be suggested that the possibility exists that urban families will make relatively greater use of birth control programmes thus affecting population growth rates. However, there are serious qualifications which must be made at this point. It is clear that expectations of rising living standards are linked with declining birth rates, which raises fundamental questions about the distribution of resources, even in situations where overall economic growth rates are high (Haq, 1976). But economic development in the majority of Third World countries has most often been extremely unequal in terms of distribution. For the majority of urban populations the higher costs of urban living and the greater demands on income − for education and housing in particular − mean that both objectively and subjectively families do not have expectations of rising living standards. However, levels of fertility are associated with specific features of development rather than with overall levels of economic development (McNamara, 1977). Despite changing attitudes to family size and function among urban residents, the likelihood of dramatic falls in fertility rates is problematic (Davis, 1972).

As noted above, migration to towns and cities is a major cause of urban growth, 'indeed, the problems of Third World cities have often been attributed to the prevalence within them of large numbers of persons who are only lately acquainted with the demands of urban life'. (Abu-Lughod and Hay, 1979:195). Why this migration occurs, why people migrate, and what the consequences are for the migrants themselves, the development of the society as a whole and for the class structure in urban areas are important questions for social policy in underdeveloped countries. Very many attempts have been made in the past to analyse the migration phenomenon and many of the traditional theories have been subject to recent criticism. Essentially much earlier work has been attacked as simplistic, determinist and tending to mono-casual explanations. The complexity of rural-urban migration is expressed by Lloyd:

Who emigrates to the cities, and from what areas do they come? The quick and simple answer is that migration involves most categories of people, rich and poor, educated and illiterate, and that they come from all parts of the state, its advanced and its backward regions, and even in some cases from beyond the national frontiers. (1979:111)

In general, movement of rural populations to the towns and cities has been seen as the result of increasing population pressure on resources, and exacerbated by 'uneven development' by which the urban areas become increasingly attractive as rural areas are increasingly unable to fulfil rising expectations. In attempts to interpret differences in rate, incidence and paths of migration, 'push' and 'pull' factors have typically been identified. Mountjoy, for example, suggests that 'it is against a background of chronic rural poverty, of a stagnating country, that the economic and social attractions of the town may appear so alluring'. (1978:106) Thus poverty and lack of opportunity operate to expel migrants from rural areas, and the towns and cities attract migrants with the promise of wage employment, better services and by the apparent glamour, pace and excitement of city life. Critics of the 'push-pull' approach have not so much attacked the relevance of these factors but rather the implied dichotomy between unrelated factors. More persuasive theories stress the essential common roots of rural emiseration and urban growth. As noted earlier particular forms of economic development are marked by the establishment and extension of unequal, exploitative relationships between urban and rural areas.

Similarly, attempts to reduce explanations of migration to economic models which are based on differentials between rural and urban rewards (Todaro, 1971) ignore the complexities of the decisions which migrants actually make. In particular, such explanations fail to account for movements which are essentially non-economic in motivation. For example, it has been noted in many areas that temporary urban residence may be regarded by rural populations as an important stage through which young adults, usually male, should pass. (Little, 1974; Levine, 1979; Lloyd, 1979).

Only a few aspects of Third World urban migration have been touched on here, as the intention is simply to indicate the complexity of the migratory process. Earlier discussion of underdevelopment has indicated that the economic situations to which migrants are reacting is determined by broad national and international socio-economic forces. There is no doubt that, as Mehmet argues, population movement is primarily due to the poverty of rural areas relative to the urban areas; the contrast results directly from urban bias in economic and social policies (Mehmet, 1978).

However, explanations of population movement in general are not necessarily sufficient for comprehension of specific patterns of migration in particular. Several issues are important for later discussion of housing policy. Social and economic links may be maintained or developed between migrants and their home communities and new urban dwellers and urban groups with whom the new arrival has kinship or cultural ties. Numerous studies in all parts of the Third World have examined the nature and extent of these links. In general, two conclusions emerge: first, an enormous variation, and second the relatively greater importance of links within the urban situation than with the rural areas. Nonetheless, rural-urban links are important, and in Africa the maintenance of kinship ties and rural land rights by urban Africans, their patterns of visiting, plans to retire to the village and attempts to give primacy to ethnicity over class in certain situations are common themes. Similar features have been noted in Papua New Guinea where urbanisation is relatively recent. There, townsmen have been characterised as 'ambivalent' and it is suggested that as 'a generation comes of age in the towns, they may (despite continuing ideological ties to rural areas) come to identify more strongly with urban life-styles' (Levine and Levine, 1979:138).

The second sort of link is of major significance, and closely related to the first. Throughout the towns and cities of the Third World, the migrant is likely to be assisted by some social group with which he has ties. These groups, whether formal or informal, will be of crucial importance in providing both material and social support, together with the contacts and the information which assist the new arrival in establishing a new life in the town. The great variation in such groupings would appear to be related to the size of the urban area, the strength of traditional systems with which such groups are associated, and the homogeneity of the urban group as a whole. Where such groups are to be found, however, their role is of great importance. In many areas the dominant feature of the social structure of urban communities may be these networks of relationships based on community of origin (Lloyd, 1979). Thus the patterns of migration are complex, and generalisations are not simply difficult but dangerous. Lloyd again provides a useful summary:

The ties of the immigrant to his co-villagers and to his home community not only needs to be stressed but also needs to be examined closely so that these differences in the nature of the relationships, their intensity and the differential involvement of persons of high and low socio-economic status, is fully explored. We must distinguish clearly between the personal links which bind the migrant to his family in the rural area, and those which unite co-villagers in the city; and between associational activities which serve to develop the home area and those which are for the benefit of the city immigrants themselves. (Lloyd, 1979:140)

THE HOUSING PROBLEM

The nature of Third World towns and cities can only be understood in the context of underdevelopment. It is only recently that the crucial difference between 'dependent urbanisation' (Castells, 1977) and urbanisation in the metropolitan countries has begun to be recognised. Many analyses of urban growth, however, still see slums and unemployment as undesirable but inevitable consequences of economic development and ultimate modernisation. Given the nature of contemporary underdevelopment, as discussed earlier, work which has been done on colonial urbanisation and the naure of colonial cities is of major relevance. Many of the features of the colonial period have remained beyond independence to influence contemporary urban structures. There is increasing recognition that colonial relationships and those of underdevelopment, constitute a significant force in the generation of urban settlement patterns which have specific historical functions (Balandier, 1966; Horvath, 1972; King, 1976; Payne, 1977).

Of course, within the period of colonialism and beyond the particular form of urban settlement has varied enormously in different parts of the world. It is not possible to identify a 'colonial city' in physical terms. Some grew from nothing as trading centres for channelling the products of expanding primary production to world markets and imported manufactures from the metropolitan countries. Others were administrative centres, military bases or centres of transport and communication networks, such as railway towns. However, despite such variation, all colonial settlements were essentially there to facilitate the economic exploitation of the rural areas, whether directly or indirectly. Weeks (1972) relates the impact of colonialism to the forms of urban growth in West Africa. Two basic forms are identified – 'colonial urban transformation' and 'European urban creation'. The former, with Lagos, Mombasa, Zanzibar and many of the cities of North Africa as examples, was defined as a situation in which foreign systems were imposed on pre-existing urban formations and through their control transformed the process of urbanisation. The latter, of which there are very many examples including Nairobi, Lusaka, Dar-es-Salaam and Port Harcourt, were urban centres established in areas with little or no significant urbanisation prior to colonialism. Weeks argues that in the case of the 'transformed' urban areas, urbanisation took place in a situation where the indigenous population possessed traditions of urban craftsmanship, commercial activity and entrepreneurial skill. This brought direct conflict with the colonisers, particularly in trade. Weeks suggests that where this was the case the advantages enjoyed by European-controlled enterprises restricted the expansion of indigenous areas of economic activity except for some production geared to the increasing low-income population. In many of the created settlements, the lack of local industries and services frequently led to the importation of other ethnic groups from different regions, and in some cases from outside the country. One effect of this was that unskilled indigenous migrants were unable to fill significant economic positions and these were occupied by separate social groups. In East Africa, the Asian community became established in this way (Weeks, 1972:6).

The disruption of existing patterns of urbanisation has also been described in the case of the Indian sub-continent. Nilsson (1973) shows that Lahore was reduced sevenfold in area as overland trading patterns were replaced by new maritime routes. But most of the colonial urban settlements in India were newly created; Bombay, Madras and Calcutta were all built up from the 'residency towns' established in the early period of colonialism (Payne, 1977). Only Delhi may be considered as an example or urban transformation, and while that city is clearly not typical of the majority of Third World cities, the analysis produced by King (1976) based on Delhi is useful. King identifies several distinct but inter-related elements in this form of urban settlement. First, there is the area of indigenous settlement which may pre-date colonialism and may either have been a pre-industrial urban settlement with the characteristics noted earlier, or may, in some cases, have been a small settlement which grew as a result of its position in relation to the incoming colonial centre. The second element is that of the 'modern' Western or European sector, which King calls the 'colonial urban settlement'. A third element of particular importance in many parts of the world is the sector which accommodates migrants brought in by the colonial administration from other regions to provide labour from the growing urban area. In King's analysis the impact of colonialism on levels and forms of urban development is made very clear – spatial distributions, transport systems, housing types and systems of town planning and administration are shown to reflect, to an extreme degree, the rigid socio-economic structures which were developed to reinforce the colonial order. Relationships between the social, economic and political characteristics of colonialism and the nature of Third World towns and cities are fundamental.

The consistency of basic features may be underlined by a brief examination of urbanisation in Papua New Guinea, which offers a considerable contrast, in terms of scale, with the vast urban agglomeration referred to by King. In Papua New Guinea, no urban settlements existed prior to the establishment of colonial rule at the end of the nineteenth century, although there were substantial permanent villages in many parts of the country. The basis for the establishment of urban centres was clear: towns were established to service the growth of the colonial economy, directly or indirectly. In

New Guinea towns served plantation interests, and acted as collection points for plantation products and for the import of equipment and supplies. As Jackson suggests:

Whilst the explicit motivation for the foundation of urban centres in Papua was less clearly economic, the growth or decline of such centres depended, as in New Guinea, upon the prosperity of that aspect of the colonial economy each centre served. Such towns did not serve and were not designed to serve indigenous rural interests; they were distinct appendages of the metropolitan urban hierarchy. (Jackson, 1978:172)

A feature of colonial urbanisation in Papua New Guinea was the explicit nature of control. As elsewhere, considerable efforts were made to ensure that the newly-established towns grew in ways suited to the interests of the metropolitan powers. To this end a considerable body of rules and regulations were enacted which closely defined the nature of the towns, the vast majority of which were directed at the indigenous population and prescribed the type of economic activity, housing and systems of society which could or could not be practised or exist. Severe restrictions were placed on ndigenous people, including the denial of the right to residence for migrants, the imposition of curfews, and the enforcement of temporary labour contracts (Oram, 1976). For those indigenous people who were allowed to settle in or near the towns as a source of labour, strict regulations ensured separate development of housing areas for Europeans and Papua New Guineans. In addition to the legislation which excluded Papua New Guineans from towns, 'a whole web of indirect regulations were enacted governing health, building, zoning, trade and recreation, the chief purpose of which was to deliberately eradicate the slightest trace of anything Papuan or New Guinean from the urban areas'. (Jackson, 1978:173)

In practice, the pressures of the expanding colonial economy forced deviations from the strict intentions of legislation. Certain classes of workers, particularly domestic servants, were allowed to live within the towns. As demands for labour grew so too did the need to have workers housed in the towns. Legislation required employers to provide accommodation, but this was for workers only, not their families — a system of barrack provision for single males was established. However, as Oram points out, for the largest town, Port Moresby, the regulations could only be applied in

practice on public land. As the boundaries of the town grew out-
wards they embraced areas of land which were not under the control
of the colonial administration. Port Moresby included substantial
areas of customary-owned land by the 1950s, and on this land
migrants settled who would otherwise be denied urban residence by
the law. By 1960 there were three groups of urban housing in Papua
New Guinea (Jackson, 1978): first, expatriate housing of high
quality, with extensive services and associated quarters for
domestic servants; second, barracks and hostels which, together
with the vast majority of expatriate housing, were on government
land within the towns; third, informal migrant settlements located
either immediately outside the existing urban legal boundaries, or
enclosed within the towns on plots of customary land. In addition
there were some illegal migrant settlements on unused government
land and there were also the settlements which had existed prior to
the establishment of colonial rule (Norwood, 1979). Thus in Papua
New Guinea colonialism quite clearly created the towns, and
furthermore did so in ways which produced a particular pattern of
urban settlement characterised by segregation, inequality and, for
the poorest groups, marginality marked by lack of security and a
precarious, semi-legal existence. Both the spatial distribution of
housing and its quality reflected very clearly and quite deliberately
the unequal power of socio-economic groups. The degree to which
colonial patterns are carried through beyond independence is
demonstrated very clearly indeed by consideration of access to high
quality housing. For a small group in the colonial period, high
income employment was associated with high quality subsidised
housing. This situation came about, as in very many other colonial
territories, because the administration provided housing to virtually
all its European employees. This housing was heavily subsidised on
the grounds that cheap housing was a vital incentive to the recruitment of expatriate staff (Stretton, 1979a). The association between
public service employment and subsidised housing continued as the
administration began to localise before and after independence.
Jackson argues that the link has in fact become even stronger as
'localisation has entrenched the association through the growing
strength of the public servants' union and through the development
of vested interests amongst the local bureaucracy which are no less
strong than those of the formerly dominant (and still important)

expatriate administrators' (Jackson, 1978:174).

The example of Papua New Guinea serves to illustrate what has been noted as a pattern typical of very many underdeveloped societies. As Castells (1977) has shown, urban form is a function of the economic, social and political forces operating in the city. In the majority of Third World countries those forces are to a considerable extent determined by the continuing process of underdevelopment, 'without doubt, the overwhelming influence on the socio-spatial structure of cities in the Third World is continuing capitalist exploitation' (Drakakis-Smith, 1981:20). As discussed elsewhere, the dominant features of underdevelopment are poverty, inequality and unemployment which produce the appalling housing problems characteristic of the rapidly growing urban areas, and the problem is compounded by population growth and urban structures inherited from colonialism. The present discussion is concerned with social policy and the housing problems of the urban poor.

Drakakis-Smith (1981) points out the fundamental problems inherent in attempts to quantify the housing problem. Assessment of housing need generally involves demographic data and assessments of the current housing in terms of number, condition, size and facilities. However, data in these areas are of extremely dubious reliability and subject to wide variation in the definitions used in different countries. Drakakis-Smith is undoubtedly correct to resist the almost meaningless statistics produced by conventional analyses of housing need. Nonetheless such statistics are commonly encountered, and in this context it is worth noting some of the problems associated with them in more detail. The World Bank (1975c) discussed the poorest developing countries in two distinct groups. The first were Asian countries – Bangladesh, India, Indonesia and Pakistan – which have very large cities and extreme housing problems. 'Squatters and slum dwellers in Calcutta (1,720,000), Jakarta (1,125,000) and Karachi (811,500), for example, outnumber the total populations of some countries.' (World Bank, 1975:13) The second group identified were primarily the less urbanised African countries which generally had relatively small cities of less than 100,000, but very high rates of urban population growth. The proportion of the urban populations in these countries living in slums and uncontrolled settlements was reported as 'very high'. Thus the World Bank used the traditional approach to indicate the scale of urban housing problems. In doing so, however, an important qualification was made:

Traditional housing 'deficit' estimates, which use data on slum and squatter housing as indicators of inappropriate housing . . . tend to overstate the seriousness of the housing problem. Although such housing may be illegal, built from traditional materials, or both, it is not necessarily of an unacceptably low standard. Much of this housing, in most cities, provides both adequate shelter and good access to employment. Some is quite substantial. (World Bank, 1975c:13)

There have been many studies of Third World cities which have described not just the extreme levels of deprivation experienced by the poor but the glaring contrast between conditions of considerable luxury for the few and abject squalor for the many (Breese, 1972; Dwyer, 1975; Ward, 1976). Given that the poor are the majority in all urban areas of the Third World, the amount of bad urban housing is increasing faster than any other part of urban development, however that housing is defined. Payne (1977) summarises a number of studies which have attempted to indicate the scale of the problem. In Malaysia, unofficial estimates show more than a third of the population of Kuala Lumpur in squatter settlements, and in Zambia half the population of Lusaka live as squatters. In Bombay, over 600,000 people live in 'hutments' and even more in multi-storey tenements. Calcutta represents the extreme of a spectrum on which, whatever the absolute numbers, every part produces conditions of deprivation for the poorest:

In Calcutta occupancy rates for housing indicate that more than two-thirds of the families live in one room *or less* . . . approximately 200,000 people live part, if not all, of their lives on public pavements without any shelter or public services such as water or sewerage, and an estimated 1.75-2 million people (equivalent to 25 per cent of the population) live in one-storey hutments called *bustees*. (Payne, 1977:52)

Hardoy and Satterthwaite (1981) reviewed conditions in seventeen Third World countries and concluded that all share similar housing and settlement problems. Urban centres were found to be growing faster than housing, services and infrastructure. 'It is not uncommon to find half or more of a major city's population inadequately served by potable water and sanitary waste disposal.' (Hardoy and Satterthwaite, 1981:203) Only a small minority of these urban populations were served by formal housing, and cities with more than a million people in squatter settlements were becoming increasingly common. Among the countries studied by Hardoy and Satterthwaite the majority of people were found to be badly housed and lacking in direct access to the most basic services. Employing the frequently criticised housing deficit approach, and drawing on both official and unofficial sources, this study indicated both the scale of the problem and the gap between urban housing needs and the production of adequate housing. By 1975, the quantitative urban housing deficit was estimated at more than 1.5 million dwellings; urban housing needs were growing by 150,000 units each year, while total annual production in the formal sector was only just over 60,000 units. In the Philippines the urban housing deficit was estimated at a little under one million units in 1977, the figure for Nigeria in the mid-1970s was about the same. In Kenya, where urban housing needs grew by 160,000 units between 1974 and 1978, the Government aimed to meet half of these needs through publicly funded low cost housing and site and service schemes. Hardoy and Satterthwaite suggest that the Kenyan government 'probably met no more than 5 per cent of these needs' (1981:204). Finally, Colombia was reported as having a quantitative urban deficit of three-quarters of a million units by 1974 – in Bogota, close to 70 per cent of the housing was categorised as sub-standard. It is important to stress that these figures cannot be compared as different definitions were used to define sub-standard housing in each case. Furthermore, as suggested earlier, the housing deficit approach itself is extremely suspect as an indication of the scale of the housing problem, not least because, as Drakakis-Smith suggests, 'the estimates produced are so daunting in relation to the physical and fiscal capacities of most developing countries, that housing investment is discouraged rather than encouraged' (Drakakis-Smith, 1981:28).

Hardroy and Satterthwaite conclude, in common with the majority of studies of urban housing in the Third World, that the fundamental constraint on government attempts to improve housing conditions is the inability of a very large and growing proportion of the urban populations to pay for housing and services. But basic settlement problems, they argue, are compounded by the generally low priority given to the housing problems of the mass of urban people in Third World social policy. Furthermore:

The major multilateral lending agencies have also given little support to housing and basic service projects. Up to 1978, fifteen major multilateral agencies had committed only 1.8 per cent of their loans and grants to housing, site and services slum upgrading, urban development and urban transport in their entire history. Only 5.2 per cent had gone to building material projects. And the trend is for much of this multilateral aid to be concentrated in the larger urban agglomerations. (Hardoy and Satterthwaite, 1981:205)

Thus some indication of the scale of urban housing problems can be gained from existing studies. However as Drakakis-Smith (1981) points out, the disadvantages of calculations based on need have given impetus to a tendency to shift to assessments related to effective demand, that is, to the ability to pay. Where such calculations are used to identify priorities for more equitable resource distribution they may have considerable utility. In practice, however, it would seem that 'effective demand is more often used as a justification for directing government housing programmes towards the middle-income groups in order to avoid rental deficits' (Drakakis-Smith, 1981:28). This point, which will be explored in more detail later, underlines the need to examine housing provision in the specific conditions of individual countries, and in particular to focus attention on the distribution of housing, and housing-related, resources between socio-economic groups. In doing so it is clear that the issues involved cannot be reduced to quantifiable statistical forms. The inequalities of resource distribution are essentially determined by the structural relationships of urban systems and the linkages of those systems with wider social, political and economic forces (Nelson, 1979).

TYPES OF HOUSING

Two main forms of urban housing have generally been identified and are most often characterised as formal and informal. Whether these terms are used, or as Drakakis-Smith (1981) suggests, conventional and non-conventional are to be preferred, what is found in practice is a spectrum of housing types with several basic criteria determining the place of a particular housing type on the continuum. Three factors may be considered to be of particular importance – involvement of the formal economy in construction, legality and standards. Housing will be regarded as formal where it is constructed and used through recognised formal institutions, such as planning authorities, banks and the formal building industry, and in accordance with local legal rules and housing standards. Non-formal housing is that which does not meet one, or a number, of the prevailing legal and housing standard requirements. 'It is usually constructed outside the institutions of the building industry, is frequently in contravention of existing legislation and is almost always unacceptable in terms of prevailing bourgeois *mores*.' (Drakakis-Smith, 1981:241) As suggested earlier, much urban housing falls between these two extremes. Houses which meet legal requirements may be built by individuals or small groups; otherwise conventional housing may be illegally sited; housing which meets all legal rules may then be illegally rented, and so on. The crucially important issue of housing standards will be examined, following a brief examination of several of the most common types of both informal and formal housing.

Squatter settlements are perhaps the most obvious form of informal housing in Third World towns and cities. Considerable debate has centred on the terminology to be employed to describe these areas. Oram (1978) for example objects, quite correctly, to the implications for practice of the use of certain terms:

The image which most of those concerned with the administration of towns in developing countries have is still the western town. This is often coupled with a nationalistic pride in ostentatious buildings. Their attitudes also give rise to the use of such pejorative terms as 'slums', 'squatters' and 'shanty towns' without definition or analysis. (Oram, 1978:45)

A number of other terms have been employed to describe these areas of housing outside the formal system. 'Shanty-town' is still used (Lloyd, 1979), while 'uncontrolled settlements' and 'spontaneous settlements' both attempt to convey particular features and avoid the labelling criticised by Oram. The use of particular terminology may indicate either the particular characteristics of settlements in a specific context or, more usually, indicate a focus on certain characteristics. Drakakis-Smith uses squatters in preference to what he sees as alternative euphemisms. There is some strength in his argument that overall the use of this term, which has general legal meaning, emphasises a major feature of these settlements, certainly crucial in relation to social policy – their essential illegality. While the enormous variation in squatter settlements must be recognised, they are characterised by predominantly makeshift dwellings, are frequently overcrowded, virtually always lack even basic services, and marked by high levels of insecurity given the ever-present threat of eviction and demolition. This does not necessarily mean that squatter settlements are short-lived, many have existed for considerable periods of time, gaining *de facto* if not *de jure* recognition from controlling authorities. This indeed is perhaps one of the most important features of such settlements. They are neither temporary in themselves nor for specific residents but are permanent features of the urban system, maintained outside the law by administrations which are incapable of providing adequate services to their populations within contemporary patterns of resource distribution. Numerous accounts have stressed the crucial economic function of these settlements in providing cheap labour and informal economic activities which support exploitative economic systems.

Santos (1979), analysing the political economy of Third World urban systems, identifies two 'circuits', in which the squatter settlements form a major part of the 'lower circuit', and it is the interaction of the two circuits of the urban economy, dominated by underdevelopment and dependency, which for Santos generates patterns of growth, forms of state intervention, and forms of spatial organisation:

The lower circuit constitutes a permanent integrative mechanism, involving for the most part the mass of insolvent and unskilled migrants to be found in all Third World cities. It supplies maximum employment for a minimum capital outlay, responds both to changes in consumption patterns and to the general conditions of employment and capital. (Santos, 1979:136)

In terms of relationships within the urban political economy, slums may also be considered as part of the lower circuit in many cases. As areas of housing, however, they differ from squatter settlements in ways which are significant for social policy. Essentially, the slums are distinguished by their condition and pattern of use, rather than the legality of their existence as buildings. Thus the slums are legal, permanent dwellings which have become sub-standard in a variety of ways. Immediately, of course, the use of the term sub-standard raises the question of definition, and as before, realistic definitions are only possible within a particular context. Having said that, it is very often the case that locally applied criteria are derived almost entirely from imported conceptions of acceptable housing, with little regard for local conditions. However, to whatever extent slums may be redefined, their existence cannot be denied. Massive numbers of the poorest people in Third World urban areas are housed in slums (Hardoy and Satterthwaite, 1981), which are created by a more or less gradual process of deterioration, ever-increasing sub-division and multi-occupation, lack of maintenance and repair, and the operation of exploitative rental systems. For social policy, particularly intractable problems are created by the permanence of structures which are generally operated in the private sector.

The basic factor in the housing problems of the urban poor is their inability to pay for housing which is constructed, maintained and rented at standards considered necessary in Western countries, and thus required by law. The fact is that in very many Third World countries those same standards are enshrined in laws governing formal housing:

Many governments have insisted on maintaining high standards which raise the cost of housing and prohibit self-help construction by low-income households. Prohibitive building codes, costly land acquisition procedures and other barriers prevent the poor from building permanent legal houses where they can earn a living. The sentiment 'construct big, beautiful and forever' is not unusual. The poor, who are frequently described as 'marginal' by those who resent slum and squatter areas, are thus 'marginalised' by policy failure. (World Bank, 1975c:15)

Income levels for the majority of people in urban areas are extremely low and urban populations are expanding very rapidly. The cost of providing housing to 'modern' standards by conventional means and by the use of subsidies is beyond the means of Third World governments. Examination of these two features of the contemporary housing dilemma will illustrate the nature of that dilemma. First, the great majority of Third World countries do operate extensive systems of housing subsidy. As noted earlier, underdevelopment is characterised by the inheritance of privilege by a relatively small minority, primarily in the urban areas. Particularly in those countries which have gained independence more recently, relatively high-cost housing with significant subsidy has been a common feature of employment in the public sector. As discussed earlier, the public sector has been dominant in providing wage employment and the upper echelons of the public service form a significant part of emerging class formations. Zambia, where urbanisation has proceeded somewhat further than in many other countries, provides a good example of the nature of subsidisation of high-cost housing. There, Simons argues, housing inequalities 'stem from the colonial system of racial discrimination and residential segregation' (1979:19). With localisation following independence, new élite groups took the place of expatriates in high-cost suburbs. As elsewhere, the subsidisation of housing for public service employees dates from the colonial period and enables the subsidised tenants to enjoy a far higher standard of housing than they could otherwise afford.

An officer occupying a government house in a low density area pays 12½ per cent of his salary in rent, and this amount is well below the market rate for housing of a comparable standard. To encourage home ownership, the government pays a housing allowance to officers who occupy their own homes. The allowances were doubled in 1975 and currently range from K40 a month for a house valued at K5000 or less to K150 for one valued at K30,000 and above. It is doubtful whether the allowance is sufficient in most cases to bridge the gap between subsidised rents and the monthly cost to the owner of a mortgaged house . . . Most officers and parastatal employees consequently prefer to live in rented houses, and expect employers to supply these by building new houses if old ones are not available. (Simons, 1979:19)

This analysis of subsidisation is quoted at length because it illustrates very well the elements of what is always a complex pattern of inter-related factors. First, the proportion of income demanded of public servants as rent is frequently quite low, and bears little relation to economic rent. In Papua New Guinea for example, those in the most expensive houses pay less than 8 per cent of their salary in rent, those in slightly less expensive houses between 4 and 14 per cent, whereas the majority, around 70 per cent of public employees who are housed in purpose-built low-cost housing, pay around 20 per cent (Stretton, 1979a). The provision of superior housing, therefore, represents a major additional income benefit. Second, as in Zambia, attempts to remove employees from heavily subsidised, rented houses by encouraging house purchase also involve very heavy subsidies, and even then are generally unsuccessful. State intervention in the provision of finance is generally necessary given the lack of commercial sources providing funds on terms which purchasers can afford. A variety of methods may be used – individual subsidy as in Zambia, state-controlled loan funds, or subsidised co-operative housing purchase schemes. Whatever the method, the result is the same – the purchasers of property are given major benefits from the allocation of state-controlled resources. Hardoy and Satterthwaite (1981) report on the operation of the Brazilian National Housing Bank, which, from 1967, has resorted to a compulsory savings programme to guarantee the supply of funds for housing loans. Every 'registered worker' in Brazil in both the private and public sectors had to contribute to the fund, which could be drawn on for income maintenance requirements as well as housing loans:

But an analysis of the income groups that benefitted from the Housing Bank's programmes up to 1974 shows lower-income groups contributing far more to the Bank through the forced savings than they actually received in housing loans. In effect, the whole programme used money drawn from lower-income groups to help fund housing loans for middle and upper-income groups. (Hardoy and Satterthwaite, 1981:260)

This last point is absolutely fundamental. Any system of subsidisation of housing for upper-income groups is ultimately a vertical transfer of resources from the poor to the rich.

The third major point to emerge from the Zambian case is that privileged employees, preferring in general to rent subsidised property, expect new property to be built to satisfy their demands:

Expensive houses built for the emergent élite swallow up the bulk of urban housing investments. Thus the construction of 1710 high- and medium-cost dwellings and 1307 servants' quarters absorbed 77.2 per cent of the amount spent on urban housing in 1974. Another 13.4 per cent went into the building of 1266 low-cost units, 4.7 per cent into 2000 houses on serviced plots, and the remaining 4.7 per cent into 9905 shanty houses. (Simons, 1979:19)

The massive bias of state-controlled finance in favour of high-quality housing for a privileged minority is common in Third World countries. The social policies which embody this bias are the result of social forces which determine the allocation of resources and the determination of priorities. However, the gap between incomes and the cost of conventional housing is so great for the majority of even those with wage employment, that the construction of unsubsidised low-cost conventional housing is virtually impossible (Oram, 1978). Numerous studies have reported attempts to 'build down' to the ability to pay, but where these have employed conventional building methods in low-income market economies standards have been so low that the final product is of very little use (Payne, 1977). Thus, the governments of Third World countries are faced with a fundamental dilemma; conventional housing must be subsidised, but subsidies take a massive share of the total resources available for housing, benefit the rich rather than the poor, and fuel continuing high expectations from those receiving them. But they maintain substantial numbers of subsidised dwellings, those who live in them are a major political force, and current demands for housing from these groups are for housing at similar or better standards. Thus gross inequality in housing is one of the most visible manifestations of underdevelopment. That the most rational way to proceed would frequently be to demolish high-quality houses rather than squatter settlements to break the vicious circle only underlines the depths of the dilemma.

The second major theme in contemporary housing policies is the development of 'serviced-site schemes'. As a relatively low-cost answer to some of the housing problems of Third World urban areas, this approach has received considerable attention in recent years. Essentially, there is a recognition that larger numbers of people may be housed more satisfactorily by this means than by any conventional means. Mabogunjie *et al.* express the fundamentally pragmatic arguments for aided self-help in housing:

First is that in virtually none of the countries can the government afford to provide shelter for all its people, especially the poorer ones, and therefore it must be accepted that most shelter will have to be self-provided. Secondly, such self-provision takes place initially in a poor way but is maintained by continuous efforts at improvement. (Mabogunjie, *et al.*, 1978:3)

The basis of self-help housing is that people themselves take a significant role in the provision of their own housing, participating in construction through their own labour or the payment of others, rather than having to rely on renting or buying conventional housing. It has already been seen that informal housing provides the largest single amount of urban accommodation; the 'squatter settlements' are a response to the inadequacies of formal housing provision. One of the squatters' major achievements is that they do build an enormous number of houses; by themselves, with little or no government assistance in most cases, and frequently with varying degrees of government hindrance. Until relatively recently urban housing policies were dominated by constant attempts to demolish informal housing and build formal housing; there is now more awareness of the potential of alternative approaches. A considerable part of this results from acknowledgement of the resources which already exist within informal settlements. The United Nations argued over a decade ago that there were previously unacknowledged resources of physical organisation, technical skill and labour in poor urban communities (United Nations, 1971c). The recognition of these strengths may be embodied in upgrading schemes which attempt to improve conditions in squatter settlements by the granting of tenure, reduction in density, provision of basic services, and relaxation of formal building standards. Such schemes were heavily endorsed by the Habitat Conference, 1976, and Hardoy and Satterthwaite report that 'in the last ten years, slum and squatter upgrading programmes have generally replaced slum demolition and squatter "resettlement" (although there are notable exceptions . . .)' (Hardoy and Satterthwaite, 1981:225).

Despite the variation in experience in Third World urban areas, it is consistently the case that security of tenure is fundamental to improvement in housing conditions. The skill and desire to build, of the mass of people can be utilised, and legally-secure owner-occupation can provide the incentive for improvement over an indefinite period. The basic principles which inform upgrading programmes are shared by site and service schemes (World Bank, 1974b) but there are fundamental differences in practice. Such schemes, of necessity, generally involve entirely new developments on vacant land, which will most often mean that sites are on the periphery of urban areas. The site is physically prepared and basic services such as drainage, water supply, roads and footpaths, electricity supply are provided, although the extent of such provision may vary. Sites for individual dwellings are demarcated, and are then sold or leased to new residents who may either build houses themselves individually or in groups of varying size and composition, or contract all or part of the work to others. In some cases, government subsidies may be extended to cover the provision of building materials directly or as loans (World Bank, 1974b). Given the variety of forms it is clear that site and service schemes have considerable operational flexibility, allowing response to local needs and resources. 'From the resident's point of view the primary attraction of site and service housing is undoubtedly the security of tenure it offers, together with adequate infrastructure and the freedom to build at one's own pace.' (Drakakis-Smith, 1981:141)

Hardoy and Satterthwaite suggest that 'the first sign of governments moving away from exclusive concentration on public housing programmes is usually the support of serviced-site schemes' (1981:254). Their review of seventeen Third World countries concludes that serviced lots are usually accessible to a far wider proportion of the population, though very often not the very poorest. Although a significant number of the countries they studied had adopted this approach as part of their national shelter policies, only in two – Sudan and Tanzania – have they become 'the central part of urban housing policies'.

As noted earlier, site and service schemes have begun to figure extensively in Third World social policy. There can be little doubt that the approach has considerable advantages over conventional approaches to housing for the urban poor, and that significant achievements have been made using the approach in many parts of the world. However, a closer examination of some of the more critical analyses of the approach will demonstrate that here, as elsewhere, there is a complex relationship between social policy and ongoing underdevelopment. Comparisons with existing policies may overstate the benefits of site and service schemes to a considerable extent.

Hardoy and Satterthwaite point out that although these schemes can reach far more people and 'do represent a step towards more widely based housing programmes which support informal sector construction activities . . . they also suffer from some of the disadvantages of public housing programmes' (1981:254). Of particular importance is the fact that such schemes maintain, or extend, control over where the poorer groups can live. Many studies have demonstrated that the needs of the poor are not met by the decisions which are made (Rew, 1977). For many reasons, sites are often developed at the periphery of urban areas. This frequently means both high travelling costs and the loss of access to central urban economic activity, particularly informal activity. Furthermore, practice frequently negates the purpose of the site and service approach:

Many government officials still regard serviced-site schemes as no more than officially sponsored slum or squatter settlement construction. There is also a tendency for government agencies to make standards too high – so unit costs are beyond the reach of the lower-income groups – or even to begin constructing core houses or 'low-cost' houses which again defeats the intention of minimising unit costs. (Hardoy and Satterthwaite, 1981:255)

Others have directed more fundamental criticism to this approach. It is not the concept itself which is attacked, however, but rather a perceived failure to view the approach in the context of underdevelopment. A number of authors have criticised what is seen as a dogmatic position which argues for aided self-help as a universal panacea (Lea, 1979; Ward, 1979; Drakakis-Smith, 1981). Much of this attack is focused on the work of Turner (1969; 1972; 1980) who has had enormous influence on the development of the self-help approach. There are basically two forms of criticism – theoretical critics attack the failure to analyse the position of the poor in relation to the socio-economic formations of underdevelopment; and empiral investigators query the specific process of settlement development advocated by Turner. Lea (1979), in a useful discussion of these debates, concludes that three broad issues must be faced. First, too much should not be expected of self-help solutions: 'greater levels of autonomy imply political and societal transformation of a kind which transcends the debate on housing' (1979:53). Second, the possibilities of success are conditioned by the wider economic context in which they operate. Third, the urbanisation process is reflected in patterns of urban migration and the nature of urban settlement, particularly the extent of commitment to permanent urban residence. Housing policies are both influenced by, and to an extent influence these factors. However, although clearly aware of the major problems inherent in this

approach to urban housing, Lea finally adopts what he acknowledges to be a cynical position: 'Few governments in the LDCs
have any real alternatives to the use and promotion of self-help
strategies if real progress is to be made to overcome present housing
deficits' (Lea, 1979:53).

It is of course precisely in the hard reality of Third World policy
choices that the dilemmas of underdevelopment become most
visible. Site and service schemes are a fundamentally sound
approach to the massive problem of housing in urban areas; living
conditions can undoubtedly be improved by government supple-
mentation of the energies and skills of ordinary people; conventional housing is simply not capable of providing adequate
shelter. But what are the costs of pursuing such policies? and where
do they fall? To what extent does increasing support for these
approaches represent a desire on the part of governments to extend
and deepen their control of otherwise potentially threatening uncontrolled growth? If inequitable social and economic structures
remain, and the processes of underdevelopment continue, to what
extent do such policies simply incorporate the poorest more firmly
into those structures? Is it, in fact, the case that the energies of the
poorest are exploited in order to provide barely adequate shelter at
very low cost in support of the capitalist economy? As Drakakis-
Smith suggests:

In this context it is possible to interpret the increased availability of World
Bank funds for self-help projects, and their eager acceptance by many Third
World governments, as a concerted effort by the capitalist sector to short-
circuit the aspirations of the urban poor, thereby averting a possible threat
to the present unequal economic system. (Drakakis-Smith, 1981:146)

The dynamics of class formation and political action in urban
areas are exceedingly complex, and the relationship between
improvements in material living conditions and social change are
equally so (Nelson, 1979). In terms of social policy the desires may
ultimately be only pragmatic ones, made as far as possible with
regard to the wider context. In these terms, the two aspects of
housing policy examined here clearly interact and underline again
the dilemmas facing Third World governments. Any attempts to
improve conditions for the poorer groups – the majority of the
population – demand a redistribution of resources. As discussed

earlier, most contemporary systems are dominated by massive sub-sidisation of high-cost housing for a minority. That subsidisation is, in the majority of cases, rooted firmly in the social fabric of Third World societies and perpetuated by the forces of emerging class formations. Part, at least, of the solution must lie in switching funds from high-cost housing to low-cost housing, and to aided self- help in particular. But the groups who must organise that transfer are precisely those who benefit most from the present arrangements. Furthermore, opposition to dramatic improvements in housing for the poor may support this case by the argument that improved conditions may encourage yet more urban migration. Unless urban housing policy is genuinely part of an overall development strategy which is concerned with the needs of the mass of the people, it cannot succeed. There are better or worse policy choices which may be made, but patterns of underdevelopement impose massive constraints.

6
Social Services

'Social welfare, conscious of its role as a fundamental component of the social development process, will respond to the needs of the 1970s through consideration of its new functions, the elaboration of more scientific processes and their incorporation into multi-disciplinary development work.' (Junqueira, 1971:68)

'The findings of this study contrast sharply with the idealised accounts of social work practice in developing countries which pervade the profession's literature.' (Midgley, 1981:126)

Social services are here defined as provision which is aimed at the individual and is concerned, in principle, with the welfare of the individual. Considerable problems are encountered with drawing boundaries between social services and other aspects of social welfare, and these have been extensively discussed in the predominantly Western literature (Madison, 1980). As previously discussed, the institutions and practices of Third World social services were largely established in periods of colonial administration; the dominant theme in any discussion of contemporary social services in the Third World must be that of the irrelevance of existing forms to contemporary needs. Services for children will be examined, in order to illustrate the nature of that irrelevance and the dilemmas of social services in the context of underdevelopment. This follows a brief outline of the nature of social services in general, and their relationship to development.

We are here concerned with organised systems of social service provision provided by both government and non-government organisations. As will become clear, there are a number of serious problems which arise from the general dominance of non-government organisations in this area. Ultimately, the responsibility for the reform and development of social services must fall on governments.

Historically, organised social services emerge with the

destruction of traditional societies (Friedlander, 1955), and two particular factors are important in periods of rapid social change – the generation of greater numbers of more extreme, individual social problems, and the progressive inability of traditional forms of social support to cope with the new demands placed on them. Prior to the penetration of colonialism, the majority of Third World societies were small, scattered local communities which were basically self-sufficient and self-reliant. Community solidarity and mutual aid were an unplanned and essentially unconscious feature of communities of people marked by a relatively high degree of equality and cohesiveness. At low levels of production, solidarity and services from people to people within communities has been seen as characteristic (Shanin, 1971), and it has been argued that in pre-colonial societies, people faced with common problems supported each other. However, this notion has been subject to considerable criticism, perhaps particularly in terms of the nature of that support, the levels of tolerance, and the degree of repressive social control in traditional systems (Goldthorpe, 1975). What is important for the present discussion is the emergence of deliberately planned, organised systems of service to deal with individual needs which have emerged to supplant traditional forms.

The typical pattern, seen in the development of feudal society in the West and colonial society in the Third World was the rapid emergence of economic social and political inequalities with an attendant erosion of traditional patterns of obligation and social support. Individualism becomes the predominant motif of social life, and responses to need are determined accordingly. The fundamental point here is that by the time Western forms were beginning to be imposed on the majority of Third World societies, the responsibility for social welfare was that of churches and often related private charitable organisations. The nature of the relationship between those in need and those providing services was no longer part of a system of mutual obligation and reciprocity, but one in which the rich, through compassion, assisted those who 'through no fault of their own' were in need (Romanyshyn, 1971). The crucial point here is that social welfare is privatised, and individual responsibility more and more emphasised; this is of course consonant with the values of the capitalist market economy. Social welfare then is increasingly perceived, not as the responsibility of the organised community as a whole, but as the task of private groups, whether religiously or otherwise inspired. As was seen in earlier discussions of colonial history, colonial administrations were generally reluctant to take responsibility for welfare activity and left this to non-government organisations, and principally missions. However, as was also seen, the primary aim of colonial administration was the maintenance of order; the continuing growth of the money economy demanded more extensive systems of control both to ensure its operation and cope with its consequences. In a perverted reflection of trends within the metropolitan countries, the colonial state began to take over more of the functions of private groups and agencies, as the threat to social order posed by the ever-increasing social problems obliged the state to expand its services. Thus, the functional necessity of social welfare in general was to counteract the marginalising effects of uneven economic growth and the destruction of existing social systems:

In the pre-colonial Philippine communities, although they were characterised by a low level of development of the productive forces (small-scale organisation, minimal differentiation of functions, primitive technology), there was neither poverty nor starvation, although there was a certain degree of differentiation in status, control and possession. The maintenance of the well-being and welfare of all was a responsibility of all and mutual aid was a 'natural' feature of community life. (Kuitenbrower, 1977:20)

Although certain common themes have been suggested in the emergence of organised social welfare in both the metropolitan countries themselves and, later, in the colonies, there are profound dangers in drawing the comparison at all closely. Indeed, assumptions regarding the proper responses to conditions which appear similar to those which have been encountered elsewhere, are important in the emergence of inappropriate social services. As we have seen with respect to other areas of social policy, there are fundamental differences in the nature of Third World societies. There are superficial similarities – population growth, urbanisation, industrialisation, the growth of formal social control – but contemporary Third World societies must contend with underdevelopment. As a British writer argues:

In fact, although the mirror of the Third World does show us ourselves it is as the authors of their predicament, rather than as we were in the past . . . The present–day developing country has to contend with our earlier activities within it, as imperial rulers and exploiters, and also with our present commercial activities, and the pattern of economic and cultural dependence which these have imposed upon them. (Jones, 1981:148)

The replication of inappropriate social policies, imported into Third World countries from the metropolitan countries, is not simply a side-effect of continuing underdevelopment, but is a crucial part of the process of underdevelopment.

Social services may be seen to have a number of functions in any society. In the context of development, these functions are related to the problems of the mass of the people who are all, to a greater or lesser extent, involved in the process of change and are affected by the consequences of change. The relationship between the provision of social services and the political economy is not the subject of the present discussion, and other chapters will examine the nature of social policy in these terms.

Three general aims have been identified for organised social services (United Nations, 1968): reducing the stresses of social and economic change; forestalling adverse social consequences of change; and creating social conditions for improved well-being. In terms of the more specific nature of social services, four main types may be identified, with, of course, considerable overlap – remedial, preventive, developmental and supportive.

Remedial services are the most common, representing the assumption that individuals, families and social groups are unable to fulfil the roles necessary to meet needs. When services are primarily remedial they aim at either supplementing existing systems of support or, in many cases, substituting for those systems entirely. Such services may be short-term, for example the provision of temporary care for children at a time of family crisis, or long-term as in the case of institutional care for children without family support. The latter is an example of substitute care, which is of particular significance in the provision of social services in Third World countries. Dominated by residential, institutional forms, this approach has been used in many parts of the world for a wide variety of purposes. Children, the old, the handicapped and the destitute have all been provided for by such provision. To some extent this illustrates the carry-over of practices, now subject to widespread criticism, from the metropolitan countries. Of more importance perhaps is the fact that as services have, until relatively recently, been managed by outsiders they were necessarily divorced from the social context in which they operated. Indeed, it may be argued that the physical separation of certain groups, often for substantial periods of time, was necessary in order that alien solutions could be imposed on the problems created by rapid social change and the strains more easily contained. This may certainly be seen in relation to provision for the mentally ill in Third World countries, which has been marked by institutional responses and a lack of regard for pre-existing systems of care and treatment (MacPherson, 1982). Thus, assumptions regarding the inability of informal systems of support to cope, and indeed their continuing disintegration, may, in many cases, become a self-fulfilling prophecy. This will be discussed further in relation to the specific services examined later. The complex relationship between formal and informal systems was suggested by a conference of ministers of social welfare in 1968:

Substitutive assistance . . . is a remedial function which takes on particular importance in societies at the stage of development where traditional social organisation is breaking down and the institutions of the modern state are only gradually being established. In a number of developing countries, social welfare services in the rapidly growing cities or changing countryside are actively engaged in substituting for the traditional family or tribal laws and customs and, at the same time, in providing services in areas of need which should be met at a later stage by a nation-wide network of social services in the broad sense or by structural change. (United Nations, 1968:36)

Several important points are well illustrated by this statement: an acceptance of the inevitability of traditional social organisation breaking down, active substitution of organised services for informal support, and the assumption that progress is to be measured in terms of the establishment of more and more organised social services.

Where it is the individual's disability which is the immediate focus of remedial action, social services may be rehabilitative. Put simply, this means the provision of services which will enable the individual to overcome the disabling condition to the extent that 'normal' life becomes possible. For example, in the case of a victim of polio-myelitis such services may include the provision of mobility aids, training and assistance with employment. In the case of certain forms of physical disability the concept of rehabilitation may appear to cause few problems. However in practice, and particularly where the notion is applied more widely to those suffering from mental disorder or judged to have deviant behaviour patterns, there are serious difficulties (Bean, 1976). Perhaps the most fundamental of these is that rehabilitation necessarily involves judgements regarding what is normal. The relationship between rehabilitation and control is extremely complex.

At present, there can be little doubt that services in Third World countries have been dominated by remedial approaches which have generally been small-scale and have responded to the most extreme cases with methods imported from outside. In virtually every country, access is extremely uneven with the urban bias characteristic of all areas of social policy (Thursz and Vigilante, 1975; 1976; Madison, 1980).

In principle, it should perhaps be the case that social services could act to prevent social distress. However, there is a major dilemma: emphasis on remedial action to meet problems at the individual level is inherently contradictory with those forms of action which might successfully reduce the extent of need. In their patterns of organisation, staffing, types of training and underlying philosophy, social service agencies in the Third World, in common with those in the metropolitan countries, are biased against preventive action (Midgley, 1981). Most often poorly staffed and badly financed, agencies are under pressure to deal with the individual cases their existence defines and brings forward, and preventive work is very often given low priority simply because it is less visible, and does not meet the demands put on social service agencies from elsewhere. The processing of juvenile offenders is a good example. In very many countries even the minimal amount of work done by social service agencies is in relation to the legal requirements of probation or detention systems, despite the recognition that more generalised work with families and communities may be more successful in the long term. It is not simply the conflict between visible, short-term results and less tangible long-term results which produces this bias, the dynamics of underdevelopment produce social distress which is not preventable by social service intervention, even where this is wholly committed to preventive strategies. Within a context of commitment to national development, however, it is possible that preventive action can be successful. In many cases this will be closely linked with community development activity, discussed in a later chapter.

Related to this, it is possible to see social services as having a positive role in development. In a number of countries, social service agencies are involved in activities which contribute directly to the improvement of living conditions but which may, conventionally, be the responsibility of other agencies. Perhaps the most important theme of such activity is that the people themselves are directly involved in finding and implementing solutions to their own problems. Nutrition programmes, adult literacy schemes, recreational programmes, and housing improvement initiatives are examples of situations in which social services may be involved in mass development work (Tanzania, 1974). In general, however, social services do not adopt a developmental approach. There is a widespread tendency for functions to be rigidly demarcated between the various sectoral government departments, with little or no co-ordination between them.

Although the distinction may frequently be somewhat blurred in practice, a fourth dimension of social service provision is suggested. Social services may be seen as supportive when a major reason for their existence is to facilitate the achievement of some other objectives. The most common example of this is the large-scale development project, which may involve very rapid and very extensive social disruption. Such projects, both in urban and rural areas, have characteristically resulted in the disruption of families, increased rates of alcoholism, juvenile delinquency and child welfare problems (Valentine and Valentine, 1979). It is increasingly common for the planning of such projects to include an anticipation of these consequences and thus the building-in of services to minimise their impact on the successful outcome of the project (United Nations, 1970; 1971a). This is not preventive but anticipatory social service. There is frequently little willingness to compromise the needs of large-scale economic development projects in favour of the people affected by them. Such social services are distinguished from developmental activity because although such schemes may have a significant national development impact, they rarely improve conditions for those in the immediate locality. This may appear to be a cynical position, and if it is, then it is taken consciously, for such activity is in direct line of descent from the very deliberate siting and operation of welfare services to facilitate economic activity in the colonial period.

However, more positive aspects of supportive services should also be stressed. Day care centres for children, for example, may be provided both for the benefit of children themselves, but also as a crucial part of support for policies which aim to increase the degree of participation by women in social and economic activity (United Nations, 1980).

In summary, the major types of social service may be seen first as providing assistance to those individuals 'with problems' – essentially the remedial approach. Secondly, services may attempt to analyse social problems, predict their emergence and take measures to reduce their occurrence – the preventive approach. Thirdly, services may aim to help in creating the conditions for 'real development' – the developmental approach. And, fourthly, the fundamental aim of services may be in contributing to the achievement of other objectives. In this supportive approach, the specific social service objectives may be important in themselves but are not ultimately dominant.

Organised social services in the Third World have most often concentrated on remedial activity with some emphasis on the supportive, but in general they have done little in terms of the preventive or developmental (Madison, 1980). This is mainly because these services, inherited from colonial administrations, have been dominated by the need to deal with problems and to patch up when the changes wrought by underdevelopment have damaged individuals and communities. The 'Band-aid approach' is recognised everywhere, but is particularly visible in Third World countries with massive problems and minimal resources. For social services to be positive and contribute to development, there must be a clear national commitment to a particular development path and the principles of this should inform the work of all social services (International Council on Social Welfare, 1973). As with health care, the most innovative and successful social service programmes in the Third World have emerged from those countries where there is commitment to social transformation for the benefit of the mass of people and an attempt to escape from underdevelopment.

Considerable space has been devoted to the question of the nature of social services; the importance of the issue is much greater than simply that of an analytical exercise. In very many Third World countries, the priority given to social services is very largely affected by confusion as to what the role of social services is supposed to be. The lack of a clear and consistent conception is well illustrated by the Tanzanian example. From 1946 onwards, social welfare was moved from ministry to ministry as various notions of the role of social services in development were dominant. Social services were, at different times, administered from the ministries of education, rural development, health and labour among others. With each move the influence of the host department was apparent. During the period from 1969 to 1973, for example, when social services were part of the Ministry of Health, particular emphasis was put on development activities related to contraception, maternal and child health services (Tanzania, NCSWS, 1974). This frequent shifting of responsibility illustrates a common ambivalence regarding the role of social services in development. In many countries this problem remains unresolved and social service agencies still attempt to carry two very different sets of tasks − first to provide Western-style social services primarily in the urban areas, and second to contribute to social development in the widest sense (Midgley, 1981).

SERVICES FOR CHILDREN

Given the low priority accorded to social services in general, and the remedial approach which has dominated social services in the majority of Third World countries, it is hardly surprising that organised social services for children are generally minimal. Non-government organisations tend to dominate this aspect of social service provision even more than others, with very many charitable organisations having a long history of child welfare activity stretching back into the colonial period. For the most part, services have been urban-centred and have directly imported Western

Social Services

methods. Furthermore, legal provisions which enable these imported institutions to function have been incorporated into the legislation of developing countries (Mwambene, 1970; Nyerinda, 1972). Thus, many developing countries have inherited, and continue to operate, child welfare services which are focused on the provision of residential care, supplemented wih the use of foster care and adoption procedures (United Nations, 1980). It is essentially the inappropriateness of these responses to child welfare needs, and the more recent emergence of alternative strategies, which forms the basis of the discussion which follows.

Nyerinda, in a discussion of social services in Zambia, provides an example of the pattern of provision inherited from the colonial period. With respect to adoption, it was noted that in the years following independence there was a sharp decline in the number of children being adopted through the formal adoption system. This decline was attributed to the departure of expatriate civil servants and other Europeans who provided the main source of both adoptive parents and of infants placed for adoption! (Nyerinda, 1972:31). Thus adoption at least may be seen very obviously as a service introduced by the colonial administration and operated by non-government organisations for the direct benefit of the expatriate population. Furthermore, the service was quite irrelevant to the Zambian population. 'Although the Zambian family is undergoing rapid changes, it seems there is still a great deal of resistance towards adoption. In many Zambian tribes, adoption – even foster care – is equated with buying or selling of children.' (Nyerinda, 1972:31) This example serves to illustrate a fundamental common theme – introduced provisions were based, inevitably, on alien conceptions. With independence, the developing countries generally continued to operate services in more or less the way they had been operated under colonialism; very often the same expatriate staff continued in post, or were replaced by local staff trained to do the same jobs in the same way (Midgley, 1981). The services provided were therefore not simply influenced by Western theory and practice, they were very often carbon copies of services in the West. Drawing again on the Zambian case, Nyerinda summarised the dilemma of these services in the context of an independent developing country with a particularly apposite phrase: 'The potential recipients resist them, and the people charged with the task of delivering them have difficulty in interpreting them and the net result is that such services turn into the proverbial "White Elephants".' (Nyerinda, 1972:41)

In terms of residential provision for children in need, Uganda provides a typical example of the pattern commonly found in the years following independence. A review of services available in 1972 (Farrant, *et al.,* 1972) ten years after independence found that virtually all provision for children was made through non-government organisations, apart from that which dealt with children convicted of offences. The voluntary organisations were loosely federated into a National Council of Social Services which was supported by government funds by means of annual subventions. Control of both management of facilities and general policy thus remained with the non-government organisations. Many of these had connections with religious organisations, some were part of international organisations, others were local but in receipt of donations from overseas. The Ugandan government saw the majority of social welfare activities remaining in the hands of the voluntary agencies for many years (Farrant, *et al.,* 1972:28). Virtually all the services provided by these agencies were located in the capital, Kampala, and three agencies were responsible for deserted, motherless or destitute children. One was Protestant, another Catholic, and the third was the unaffiliated Save the Children Fund, a British-based relief-agency. All three operated children's homes in Kampala, accommodating between twenty and forty children each, with some demarcation between the homes with respect to the ages of children taken. In addition, there were five smaller cottage homes run by the same agencies. Finally, there were about one hundred children placed in foster homes through these agencies, and less than ten adopted each year. The report concluded that the efforts of voluntary organisations were largely unco-ordinated, and even competitive, and although representing an enormous degree of effort and commitment on the part of those who staffed them, largely irrelevant to the needs of the majority of children. This example illustrates a common pattern – small-scale provision by voluntary agencies adopting conventional Western approaches.

The provision of substitute care for children, in the form of residential homes or through organised foster care and adoption,

represents a fundamental dilemma for developing countries. On the
one hand, there can be no denial of the need for provision to assist
those children who, as victims of social disruption, are without
family support of any kind, or who are seriously deprived and
threatened within their families. The pressure to provide alternative care is thus enormous. In the urban areas alone, 'some 156
million children below fifteen years of age live . . . in overcrowded
slums, shanty towns and makeshift pavement dwellings in major
cities of developing countries. By the year 2000, their number will
have grown to an estimated 7000 million'. (Hollnsteiner, 1978:21)
There must be no easy assumption of links between urban poverty
and family breakdown, as the earlier discussion of urbanisation
emphasised, nonetheless the problems of Third World urban areas
are such as to produce child welfare problems to a massive degree.
On the other hand, policies and programmes for children cannot be
dominated by the provision of substitute care as has so often been
the case. Such provision can only, at best, remedy the problems of a
handful of children. What of the great mass of children in need?
Surely services must be geared primarily to them? We are here
concerned with formal social policy initiatives, for the evidence of
recent years quite clearly points to the need for policies which more
fully meet the needs of children. Narrowly based remedial programmes do not.

A UNICEF-sponsored publication in 1963 dealt with the
problems of children in developing countries and represented a
significant shift in approaches to their needs (Sicault, 1963). Within
a comprehensive review of the needs of children, the report argued
for 'the fundamental importance of assisting in the improvement,
extension, and establishment of comprehensive national systems of
social services and related programs to strengthen the family,
improve levels of living and provide children with needed care and
protection'. (Sicault, 1963:134). Significantly, the report gave
major emphasis to the wider social causes of children's welfare
needs, particularly poverty and urbanisation. Although to use the
notions elaborated earlier, there was still a substantial remedial
element in the proposed social service objectives, there was considerably more emphasis on preventive measures. There was not,
however, a particularly marked emphasis on developmental roles
for social service, indicated in part by the preoccupation with

problems of family functioning. What was clear from the survey was that serious deficiencies existed in the organisation and administration of social services for children, which were found to be fragmented and largely unplanned, and that rural areas were neglected and the vast majority of resources devoted to the provision of substitute care. In 1964, the first United Nations conference devoted to planning for the needs of children endorsed the theme of the UNICEF report: there should be comprehensive child welfare policies which recognised the whole range of needs of all children (Stein, 1964). Again, however, the major emphasis was still on preventive action directed at families under attack from rapid social change. As in other areas of social policy, assumptions regarding the inevitable consequence of modernisation continued to predominate.

By 1971 it was possible to detect some slight shift in the direction of a developmental perspective. The United Nations, '*Report on Children*' of that year put more emphasis on the national and international context of the problems affecting children, and somewhat more emphasis on positive programmes:

The underlying emphasis of this report is on the right of the child to adequate protection and effective preparation for a useful life. Attention has been directed to sectoral and intersectoral problems, programmes and prospects. The report considers the following main headings: demographic trends and social changes in relation to the needs of the child; the child's protection − including his health and nutrition and the necessary physical, social, psychological and economic prerequisites; preparation for life − including education and the process of socialisation and modernisation; and appraisal of action aimed at the child. (United Nations, 1971:3)

The 1971 report examined the development plans of forty-six countries, most of which placed policies for children in three sectors − education, health and social welfare. The degree of co-operation and co-ordination between these sectors was generally found to be weak, and provision in social welfare itself ranged 'from reformatories for juvenile delinquents to youth vacation resorts and children's clubs'. (United Nations, 1971a:7) In practice, things had changed very little − social services for children were still predominantly concerned with the provision of substitute care, and the control of young offenders. The report did not have a separate section on social services, and there was recognition of the need for services to assist children 'needing special attention', but little specific discussion of the developmental role of social services. There was some discussion of the role of day care centres for children of working mothers, but this was still largely in terms of remedial and preventive action, based primarily on the loss suffered by children due to the increased employment of women; it was not seen as a positive developmental policy.

Thus by the 1970s, at the international level at least, there was a recognition that policies for children must be very different from those adopted during the colonial period. There was, however, only a very tentative acceptance of the developmental role of social services within the overall pattern of policies. As with health care, the rhetoric of international discussion was not matched by practice in developing countries; almost everywhere social services continued to operate as they had done for many years.

As with health again, the most significant advances in the provision of developmental services may be seen in those countries which have adopted development strategies based on the needs of the majority. Many of the more recent discussions of child care services have drawn, directly and indirectly, on the experiences of China, Cuba and Tanzania (Leiner and Ubell, 1974; Sidel, 1974). The Tanzanian case provides an interesting example of the attempt to develop appropriate policies. A major study of the needs of young children was conducted in 1972 as part of a world-wide UNICEF programme (Tanzania National Scientific Research Council:1973). Tanzania was chosen because of its particular development strategy, and the study formed the basis for the planning of services. The neglect of social welfare during the colonial period and in the years immediately following independence was starkly recorded in the foreword:

There is at present, no clear-cut policy on the mother and the young child, both of whom as this study has clearly shown, are inextricably intertwined. We would all be terribly shocked if by some natural catastrophe or by some man-made accident 150,000 children were to die, yet this is what is quietly happening around us. Furthermore, a sizeable number of children to whom we are going to bequeath this land when we are all gone, are starting life with a life-long mental handicap due to protein and calorie malnutrition. It will not be their fault that they cannot perform well mentally and physically in a global competition for survival. The fault will be ours. (Tanzania, NSRC, 1973:foreword)

Although the whole report was of major significance, it is the section on day care centres which is of particular interest here. The provision of these facilities may be seen to represent a potentially positive, developmental role for social services, and one which has more recently gained considerable ground in many parts of the world. In the report, a good deal of emphasis was put on the destructive effects of modernisation and urbanisation:

The growth of towns has affected the traditional structures of the Tanzania society. Communal customs, habits and values have been disrupted by modern technologies and industrialisation. The idea of the extended family is almost becoming a myth, especially in towns. Consequently, the grandparents and relatives who could take care of children while other members of the family were in some economically productive activities are not available to all families any more. (Tanzania, NSRC:113)

However, it was not simply the failure of traditional family systems to cope with new demands which formed the basis of the need for child care provision. Significantly, emphasis was put on the emergence within Tanzania of a new political ideology. It was argued that under the national policy of socialism and self-reliance women and men were equal members of the society; this was especially true in the new Ujamaa villages, established on socialist principles. 'Women and men have to fully participate in economic work of the village. Consequently the mothers cannot be left at home looking after children.' (Tanzania, NSRC:113) Thus, the Tanzanian government approved a day care centre programme for Ujamaa village children, not because mothers were not available for proper child care, but because of the necessity for women to be engaged in economic, social and political activity.

This particular argument illustrates a very different approach to the provision of social services for children from those which have almost exclusively dominated this aspect of social policy. There were additional justifications for the widespread provision of day care facilities – they have general relevance in Third World countries. Traditionally, child rearing in Tanzanian families was shared between parents, older children, virtually always girls, and grandparents. Given that families may be large, and that women have a huge burden of work in addition to that connected with domestic and child care roles, siblings have a major part in infant care. With increased school attendance, the availability of siblings for child care is reduced. The more effort put into the enrolment of children in school, the greater the burden on families with young children. 'So if parents are to be free to move around for economic and social endeavours, demands for collective child care facilities are likely to increase.' (Tanzania, NSRC:114) Furthermore, it was suggested that this demand was likely to be even more inflated by the involvement of parents in adult education programmes. In Tanzania, the numbers were increasing very rapidly. By the end of 1972 nearly three million adults out of an adult population of seven million were attending adult education classes; the number of women attending classes was increasing particularly rapidly. Thus again, there was an argument for child care facilities which only partly rested on the needs of the child as such, these services were seen as part of a total development effort.

A final explanation for the growth of day care centres introduces a somewhat disturbing note, however. Again, the phenomenon is common in Third World countries. The report stresses the increased employment of women in urban, white-collar work after independence, together with a rise in industrial employment for urban women. It was no accident, the report suggested, that many day care centres were under the management of employment agencies and were in urban areas. Indeed, at the end of 1972 nearly 150 of the 367 day care centres in the country were in urban areas, furthermore, most rural centres were located on tea and sisal estates. Prior to 1969, nearly all day care facilities were run by non-government organisations, and there was no defined government policy in this area. Not only was there urban bias in the distribution of these facilities, but class bias in terms of those who had access to them. Furthermore, the largely urban, non-government facilities tended to have more and better-trained staff and greater emphasis on educational goals. A profoundly important point is made by the report with respect to the growth of these facilities:

A small but influential group of educated Tanzanian adults is starting to realize that pre-school education for their children is good preparation for formal schooling. Selection for secondary education being competitive as it is, parents will do whatever is possible to place their children in secondary schools. One of the ways for achieving this is through pre-school education.

Consequently, demand for nursery schools, kindergartens and Day Care facilities will be increasing from among this group of people (Tanzania, NSRC:114)

Thus, yet again, the impact of underdevelopment can be seen even in the area of day care facilities for children: unequal distribution of facilities, uneven standards, the use of this provision to entrench and consolidate positions of relative privilege and the familiar bias towards urban areas, may penetrate social service provision as they penetrate other aspects of social policy. Although the Tanzanian government was opposed to the growth of pre-school facilities with educational rather than social service orientation, very little was, or could be done to prevent their establishment or use. Their existence was seen to undermine the growth of development-oriented social service-based day care centres. As with other areas of social policy, the 'demonstration effect' of facilities used by a relatively privileged minority gave a second-rate appearance to those provided for the majority. Parents demanded more education for their children, the employment of teachers, study rather than play, and so on. The lack of faith in rural day care centres was compounded by poor organisation, lack of funds, and inconsistent objectives at the local level.

Despite these serious problems the Tanzanian day care centres, in common with numerous programmes elsewhere (Palmer, 1977; McSweeney, 1980; Zenderstein, 1980) represented a major shift in conceptions of social service provision. In terms of the approaches to social services discussed earlier there was at least the potential for developmental objectives to be translated into action. Not only can day care centres provide a point of contact for a whole range of services to meet the needs of children, but they could, if part of a national development strategy, enable communities to participate more fully in their own development. This is of crucial importance to women, the vast majority of whom have little or no influence on the systems which exploit them.

By 1979 – designated by the United Nations as the 'Year of the Child' – approaches to social policy in respect to children had moved much more clearly in the direction of that represented by the Tanzanian example. In a review of that year, it was argued that 'Since 1964 . . . substantial improvements have been made in taking account of children in planning and programming.

Furthermore both development theories and the conception of the role of children have changed.' (Mandl, 1979:9) Major emphasis was put on poverty and inequality as the fundamental causes of social problems and in terms of policy two approaches now dominated discussion – community-based services and basic needs strategies. The scale of the shift in approaches to the provision of services was even more strongly put in a more recent statement by a senior UNICEF officer:

UNICEF was trying to be a development agency before the basic services strategy evolved, but according to a model we now believe was wrong . . . Over the years it had become clear that merely extending the conventional pattern of services – the pattern familiar in the industrialised world – could not resolve the problem, at least within any reasonable time frame. (Haywood, 1981:29)

The essential feature of the basic services approach is community involvement, and, following the typology established earlier, the establishment of developmental services in rural areas as opposed to remedial services largely in towns is a characteristic of initiatives which have emerged from community-based programmes.

In a review of Peruvian experiences of community-organised programmes, Cano (1979) concludes that communities must cut the ties of their dependency on traditional services and begin a process of self-development. 'The development of programmes for children begins with small, simple experiments, which may eventually offer the government viable alternatives which differ from the traditional approaches that have done so little to solve the problems of poverty.' (Cano, 1979:164)

The relationship between the provision of day care centres and the role of women in development now receives attention in discussions of such programmes in very many developing countries. For example, Bashizi (1979) reported on one area of Senegal in which fifty-eight day care centres have been created from initiatives by rural women themselves, beginning in 1962. In 1978 the centres catered for 6004 children. Initially the day care centre scheme was begun by the women in order to deal with the problem of caring for their young children while they and their older daughters were planting out rice. From an early stage, however, the functions of the centre were widened:

The day care center has in fact become the focal point for the pooled efforts of the community, the authorities, and several outside aid agencies who, together, provide a balanced diet for every child who attends. The day care center also opened up wide-ranging opportunities for socialisation and early stimulation through the children's contact with each other and with the adults in the village. (Bashizi, 1979:167)

Although the Senegal example appears to represent a major achievement of community organisation in a country with a long history of rural community development activity, there were a number of problems reported which may be seen as typical of schemes of this kind. First, it was the case in some parts of the area that parents were too poor to contribute at all to the maintenance of the centres; there were no funds available from the state to supplement those provided from within the community. Second, there were no trained staff made available by government agencies, and many communities found extreme difficulty in recruiting a sufficient number of workers themselves who were required for other work. Thus, although the scheme represents a major success for the communities concerned, it also illustrates very clearly the serious limitations of basic services which are based only on the resources which poor communities have within themselves. Those communities have very few, if any, excess resources, and without some outside support even the most highly organised and determined community initiative faces enormous difficulties.

The present discussion has been limited to only one aspect of social service provision – services for children; and even within that limited area very few issues have been examined. But the contrast between institutional-based programmes inherited from colonialism and more recent community based, developmental programmes illustrates a fundamental dilemma for social services in the Third World. Not only are resources low, and policies inappropriate, but there is resistance to new approaches from within the social welfare professions themselves:

Many governments in the Third World have not only retained the residual social policies of colonialism, but have also relegated social welfare services to a level where they enjoy less priority than tourism and sport. Social workers are not provided with resources which are sufficient to help the destitute, or house the homeless, or even to place neglected children, or the handicapped and abandoned old people in suitable residential institutions . . . the profession has been remarkably uncritical of the problem of inadequate resources and it has not campaigned vociferously for the provision of more extensive, basic welfare services. Indeed this pressing issue is hardly mentioned in the profession's literature. (Midgley, 1981: 154-5)

Lack of interest in new approaches may in part be the response of groups with only a tenuous hold on professional status: 'Much of the resistance to basic services is generated by the professionals and stems from their disinclination to believe that non-professionals are capable of performing certain functions. They fear that their role is being usurped.' (Haywood, 1981:31) Social welfare professionals in the Third World, in common with those in other fields, have been trained in Western methods, and have imbued Western conceptions of social service provision. The structures within which they work encourage and sustain these. The reality in Third World countries is that remedial services are stretched to their limits and the social consequences of contemporary change continue to increase the demands put on them. The urban bias, characteristic of all social policies, ensures that attention is focused on a minority of the population; the progressive inability of traditional family and community support to cope forces organised welfare to provide services, if only to maintain a minimum level of social order and stability. As with health care, the situation demands radical reform, and a shift to policies and programmes which serve the mass of people. At the level of international rhetoric, this has happened. There is little evidence, however, that it has made a major impact on social service provision in very many developing countries.

However, it is naïve to assume that a change of emphasis to community-based basic services necessarily brings real progress. Without external assistance, poor communities, whether in urban or rural areas, cannot significantly alter the conditions of their existence; the problems which beset them are not the result of their own ignorance or lack of motivation. Furthermore, grave doubts may be cast on the real developmental effect of even 'successful' programmes of this kind. For example, day care centres may not be of real benefit to rural women – the opposite may often be the case. Rogers (1980) points out that Western ideologies which legitimise the domestication of women have been 'extremely influential in determining the view that women should be confined to a domestic role, as full-time "mothers", and that this would automatically exclude them from mainstream development'. (Rogers, 1980:91) Thus, Rogers argues, child care projects most often reinforce the 'mothering' role to the exclusion of others; women do not need to be taught how to be mothers but need the means to feed and maintain children. Another aspect of projects involving women is the common assumption that they will work for nothing. This is generally quite impractical in poor communities, and one of its effects is 'an increase in the involvement of female dependents of the male élite'. (Rogers, 1980:100) As Rogers concludes, the crucial element in projects which attempt to mobilise women is their relationship with the total development strategy. Programmes which successfully train women for more efficient domestic subservience and exploitation are not developmental:

Women can be an important resource for development, and women's groups an effective channel for funds aimed at meeting the needs of the poorest people in rural areas of the Third World. Their potential can best be realised if they are integrated into the whole spectrum of development programs, and not relegated to the marginal sector currently reserved for women. (Rogers, 1980:107)

Social services can be organised in ways which maximise their preventive and developmental potential, but only if they are seen as part of an overall development strategy which is concerned to maximise the welfare of the mass of people, and not as the means by which society minimises, at as low a cost as possible, only the worst effects of social disruption and individual distress.

7

Community Development

The Seven Phases of a Project:

1. uncritical acceptance
2. wild enthusiasm
3. dejected disillusionment
4. escape of the clever
5. search for the guilty
6. punishment of the innocent
7. promotion of the non-participants.`

(Ideas in Action, 122(3):21)

Throughout earlier chapters, the trend towards community-based, participatory policies has been noted in relation to the whole range of social programmes. To reduce costs, achieve more equitable distribution, and develop basic services which meet the real needs of the mass of people, stress is now put on development from below. This chapter examines briefly the central features of such an approach — the theory and practice of community development.

Although recent enthusiasm for this approach may tend to obscure the fact, we find that the term was adopted by the British Colonial Office as long ago as 1948. The Conference on African Administration defined it as

a movement designed to promote better living for the whole community with the active participation and if possible on the initiative of the community but if this initiative is not forthcoming spontaneously by the use of techniques for arousing and stimulating it in order to secure its active and enthusiastic response to the movement. Community Development embraces all forms of betterment. (Great Britain, Colonial Office, 1958:2)

The fact that this definition embraces so many of the themes characteristic of all later approaches gives some warning of the dangers and difficulties ahead; this was a concept elaborated in order to maximise the extension and growth of colonial penetration and control.

During the 1950s, community development was promoted to a

large extent by the colonial administrators in the British colonies, by the United Nations, and by the governments of a few independent Third World countries. The trends in thinking about community development during this period were outlined in a United Nations' document published in 1955. Perhaps the key feature of the definition offered was the emphasis on communtiy development as a method which would be used in a wide variety of political contexts; there was virtually no attempt to relate the approach to overall patterns of social, economic and political change or, more significantly, the realities of the distribution of power in Third World societies. There was an assumption of harmony of interests between the mass of people and those in control:

The term community development has come into international usage to connote the processes by which the efforts of the people themselves are united with those of governmental authorities to improve the economic, social and cultural conditions of communities, to integrate these communities into the life of the nation, and to enable them to contribute fully to national progress. This complex of processes is then made up of two essential elements: the participation by the people themselves in efforts to improve their level of living with as much reliance as possible on their own initiative; and the provision of technical and other services in ways which encourage initiative, self-help and mutual help and make these more effective. It is expressed in programmes designed to achieve a wide variety of specific improvements. (United Nations, 1971b:2)

Such an approach, in the context of colonial underdevelopment, was at best paternalistic, but more generally a cynical device by which people could, by their own efforts, be more fully incorporated into the new social and economic formations of externally-oriented economic growth. To the extent that it was used as a channel for services, which it was in many cases, two points must be made. First, as we have seen elsewhere, services which benefitted the mass of rural people were minimal and 'community development' allowed the burden on colonial administrations to be kept very low. Second, the bulk of services were in fact those related most closely to the encouragement of cash crop production and other economic activity necessary for economic growth. The degree to which these contributed to the improvement of levels of living for the majority will be discussed further below.

The most influential writer on community development in the 1950s and 1960s, whose work continues to influence training in many Third World countries, was T.R. Batten (1957; 1962). Batten's concern was with community development techniques, which could be used by external agents working in specific communities. His basic premise 'was that the colonised people had to identify and overcome obstacles which prevented the attainment of responsible self-government. The obstacles were to be found inside the colonies themselves and among the dependent people'. (Yeates, 1979:15) Batten had identified three problems which had .to be overcome by the colonial administration and the emergent ruling élite if development was to be achieved – lack of statistical knowledge, unwillingness of colonised people to make drastic changes from existing custom, and a lack of manpower willing to co-operate with the colonial government (Batten, 1954). Thus external agents were to persuade people, through local leaders, to participate in projects directed at increasing the rate of social and economic change. For Batten, the completion of specific projects was less important than an emphasis on community development technique and changing attitudes among the people. Du Sautoy, who based his work on experience as a colonial officer in Ghana, saw community development as dealing 'with simple things and unsophisticated people' (Du Sautoy, 1958:1). The paternalism of community development in the colonial context was clear in his discussions of the administrative problems of such programmes (Du Sautoy, 1962). In Ghana, community development was concerned with a wide range of activities including literacy programmes, health extension, agricultural extension, 'women's activities' – especially home economics – and youth work. The administrative system, widely adopted in the British colonies was one in which 'The decision making process was top-down. The policy and plans originated at the national level filtered down to the people via the technical activities of the community development officer'. (Yeates, 1979:18) Such approaches underline the realities of power in colonial societies; vague references to participation and the development of self-reliant communities could not disguise those realities.

In all colonies, major decisions in government were made by officials of the metropolitan power . . . The fact that there was, particularly in later years some degree of consultation with indigenous inhabitants does not alter this fundamental locus of power . . . power ultimately remained in the hands of the metropolitan country. Consequently there was some sort of paternalism, benevolent or otherwise, in decision making. (Brokensha and Hodge, 1969:149-50)

Thus one strand in the evolution of community development was the attempt by British colonial administrations, particularly in Africa, to 'educate' rural populations and encourage them to take responsibility for their own development. In essence, however, what this meant was the encouragement and stimulation of economic and social formations conducive to the transition to self-government and political independence; the fundamental process of underdevelopment was untouched, indeed it was crucially supported by such programmes. Although participation was stressed, it was participation within a system very firmly administered from the top, which did not begin to challenge the distribution of political power.

Another important strand in the history of community development was the emergence of what has been called the 'Ghandian approach to rural development' in India (Shah, 1978; Juyal and Vikashbai, 1979; Gaikwad, 1981). India became independent in 1947 and the non-violent revolution against British colonialism was largely inspired by Ghandi, one of the earliest exponents of village development as the basis for national development. Citizen participation, self-reliance and democracy were the central concerns of an approach which centred on the village as the basic unit of organisation. In marked contrast with the concept elaborated by colonial administrations, Ghandi's conception was potentially revolutionary. The stress on non-material objectives as the ultimate goal, with economic development for the satisfaction of basic needs, would, if it had been carried through into practice, have demanded a reordering of Indian society, politically, economically and socially. However, the application of Ghandi's community development was far from the ideals he originally expressed (Jain, 1967). Under Nehru, the essential elements of Ghandi's approach were lost in the adoption of a programme of community development projects which stressed dependence on outside sources for economic development, thus undermining the basic principle of self-reliance. The fifty-two projects launched in 1952 were sponsored through an aid agreement with the Ford Foundation in the United States. Shorn of its most fundamental principles, community development practice in India, became, as in colonial administrations, a means by which the national government could transmit its policies more effectively downwards and stimulate rapid economic development. As Juyal and Vikashbai have recently suggested:

There is a real danger that the 'modernising' of Ghandi's approach, with its diminishing emphasis on village self-sufficiency, self-reliant development, resistance against city exploitation as well as foreign economic domination, will rob Ghandi's approach to rural reconstruction of its specific qualities. Shorn of these and other basic ideas, Ghandism can become a tool for *status quo*, even revivalist forces. (Juyal and Vikashbai, 1979:23)

Despite the difficulties encountered in attempts to implement what may be seen as more genuine approaches to community development, as a technique community development was increasingly used during the 1960s. Yeates (1979) identifies four major trends in this period. First, the use of community development techniques by Western powers as part of their aid programmes in newly independent nations. Second, the application of community development ideas in urban areas, particularly 'slums'. Third, the extension of community development to embrace other forms of social action in urban areas, and fourth, growing criticism of community development programmes. Some aspects of the extension of these approaches to urban areas have been discussed earlier, for the present discussion it is the fourth trend which is of particular importance.

The criticisms of community development came with the growing awareness that the development strategies imposed on Third World countries were not bringing 'development', but were entrenching the process of underdevelopment. From the 1960s, community development was criticised on both theoretical and practical grounds (Stavenhagen, 1964; Freire, 1972; Coombs and Ahmed, 1974; Mayo, 1975; Alldred, 1976; Manghezi, 1976).

A large part of the explanation for mounting criticism was, as with many other areas of social policy, the example of the relatively few developing countries which were attempting forms of socialist development. These embodied community organisation and community participation in ways which highlighted the deficiencies of prevailing community development programmes in most developing countries. Again the principal examples were China, Cuba and Tanzania.

One critique in particular may be taken to express the general thrust of this questioning of community development. Andre G. Frank, in a profoundly influential book published in 1969, outlined the basic reasons for the failure of these programmes (Frank, 1969). According to him, prevailing community development theory was based on three false assumptions: first, that in conditions of continuing underdevelopment and rapid social and economic change, small rural communities were viable social units; second, that deprived and disadvantaged communities, in both rural and urban areas, were not yet integrated into the national society and economy; third, that there was a community of interests among all the members of specific communities. He pointed out that in reality solutions to the problem of material improvement were not viable if restricted to action within local communities, such solutions demanded action at regional and national levels. He stressed that in the Latin American case, the conquest of that continent by European colonisers and the patterns of underdevelopment subsequently established had integrated the vast majority of people into society, but on social and economic terms which were against their interests and supported the dominant, ruling-class interests. Earlier chapters have underlined this crucially important point; both rural communities and poor urban communities have funda-mentally important relationships with the economic systems which dominate the societies of which they are a part.

A recent study of the Brazilian North-east illustrates this point. Brazil is a country where 'the élite are fabulously rich; the majority have children suffering from malnutrition'. (Mitchell, 1981:1) The misery of the North-east is not that of an area suffering because it has no part in the wider society, its poverty is a direct consequence of the part it plays.

The region experienced four centuries of an agriculturally-based export economy in which capitalist and pre-capitalist sectors evolved, the two existing symbiotically, with the former feeding off the latter. The type of industrialisation which has developed in more recent times has permitted these two sectors to continue in being, the pre-capitalist sector providing cheap food and a reserve labour army for the capitalist sector. Moreover, the North-east is a quasi-colony within Brazil, a region dependent upon the more developed Centre-South of the country, and a victim of capitalist forces controlled by the Centre-South and by multi-national companies operating in Brazil. (Mitchell, 1981:7)

North-east Brazil may be an extreme case, but it is not a special case.

The third point made by Frank was that communities were in fact ridden with conflict, and did not have the harmony of interests assumed by the majority of community development theorists, to the extent that communities were penetrated by wider economic systems, then they contained elements of exploitative class structures. Again, earlier chapters have stressed this point; class formation in rural areas extends and deepens patterns of inequality and intensifies competition for scarce resources of all kinds. The emergence of wage labour means that there is no longer a fundamental community of interests among all members of the rural population. Furthermore, there is considerable evidence that for half the population, the women, there never was such a communtiy of interests: the pattern of relationships between men and women in pre-capitalist systems was marked hy exploitation (Caplan and Bujra, 1979).

With such an analysis of the context in which community development programmes actually operate, Frank views such programmes rather differently from the way in which they had been conventionally conceived:

Community development programmes must aid peasants and mobilise them to confront the landowners, merchants, and political-military authorities that exploit and oppress them . . . this involves *participation popular* not so much in the productive sense but in the economic and political processes. Ultimately, of course, community development can only proceed through a change in the class structure of the community and the society as a whole. (Frank, 1969:248)

This conception of community development was, in sharp distinction to those outlined earlier, fundamentally concerned with power. The emphasis was on the organisation of communities in a struggle against exploitation. During the 1970s such approaches were widely adopted, although perhaps more widely in theoretical expositions than practical action. In terms of social policy, however, awareness of the deficiencies of conventional approaches, and indeed the ultimately repressive character of programmes which were concerned with attitudinal change and the more complete integration of poor communities into exploitative systems, gives rise to profound dilemmas. Put simply, how can it be possible for organised community development programmes to challenge the systems of which they are so clearly a part? In practice, the several approaches to community development practice continue to operate, frequently at one and the same time. Programmes are used to encourage self-help, deliver services, and stimulate the political mobilisation of communities.

Some of the fundamental dilemmas of community development as social policy will be discussed in more detail following a brief examination of two contrasting examples of attempts to use some of its principles. Long (1977) discusses the types of approach used by Third World governments for initiating economic development and social change, and focuses on two different approaches – the 'improvement approach' and the 'transformation approach'. The first is essentially that used in conventional community development and is dominated by an emphasis on extension – the transmission downwards of policies, resources and technical advice and assistance, with the purpose of increasing production within existing political and economic systems. Although extension may be used for a wide variety of social functions, emphasis is on production. This approach attempts to establish new forms of organisation and to break with existing systems. Long suggests that the improvement approach has been successful in increasing levels of production but has two fundamental shortcomings:

In the first place, it leads to the reinforcement or development of socio-economic inequality in the countryside, sometimes resulting in a widening of the gap between the commercial farmer and the poor peasant or landless categories. And second, it is a slow-moving process which cannot be expected to produce quick returns. (Long,1977:148)

The community development programme in India, already referred to, is examined by Long as an example of this approach. The programme had two broad aims – improvement in conditions, and the promotion of 'a process of integrated culture change aimed at transforming the social and economic life of the villages'. (Dube, 1958:8) The intention of the planners was to engender in the people a 'burning desire for change', but this was to be achieved through 'progressive improvement of the existing socio-economic system'. (Long, 1977:149) Each of the projects begun in 1952 covered around one hundred villages with a population of 50,000; each group of villages had a multi-purpose extension agent working at village level. The second Five-Year Plan extended the programme, with the intention of incorporating every village in India, and an exceedingly complex bureaucratic structure was developed to administer this massive programme. Long, drawing largely on Dube's study (1958), quotes a number of examples of the problems of the programmes in practice. For example, the plan to introduce production-related co-operatives encountered problems found in many similar projects elsewhere:

As Dube shows, many people were hostile to this idea as they regarded these co-operatives as official organisations imposed from outside. Moreover, when they were set up, membership, and especially the leadership positions, were monopolised by persons of high social and economic status. The general population found the complex rules and administrative procedures tiresome and feared getting involved in complicated legal issues. (Long, 1977:153)

Another example – the introduction of adult literacy classes – illustrates some of the problems encountered by programmes introduced from the outside without regard for the prevailing customs of the community. Although the value of education was generally accepted, two particular problems arose: first, there was a perceived incompatibility between adult status and attendances at classes which were run in similar ways to those for school children; second, there were special difficulties encountered by women. A daughter-in-law was expected by custom to remain in her mother-in-law's household and not to leave frequently until she had achieved responsible status by having children. 'Thus, so long as she remained subordinate in the mother-in-law's household, she was prevented from participating in public activities and in mixed classes; and, on the other hand, later, when adult with children, she faced additional responsbilities and found it equally difficult to get away.' (Long, 1977:154)

A third important example was the mobilisation of 'voluntary' labour for community projects. In Uttar Pradesh, village councils were empowered to compel five days' labour every year from residents. The use of legal compulsion was similarly found with respect to the enforcement of public health improvements, and is common in community development schemes throughout the world. In the Uttar Pradesh case, according to Dube, the voluntary labour concept was welcomed by the higher-status, upper-income groups since the labour was used primarily for the improvement of roads to be used by carts. These groups were both assisted in the transportation of their export crops and afforded 'the opportunity of reinforcing their positions of power through the organisation of work parties, since it was the lower castes who did the manual work. Those of higher status assumed supervisory roles'. (Long, 1977:154) The poorer sections of the community received little gain from this aspect of the programme, and the organisation of work parties gave the already dominant upper castes a means by which they could assert their authority over others in ways very similar to traditional practices which had been prohibited by law.

These examples serve to show how the community development programme failed to meet its basic stated objectives. Long concludes that in general the programme, in terms of successful projects, was heavily biased to agricultural extension. But not all producers benefitted, most benefits going to the most affluent farmers. In addition, the programme ignored completely the needs of those without land. The deficiencies of the programme intensified conflict between poor and wealthy members of communities, which was made worse by the increased unemployment caused by the adoption of agricultural improvements – particularly machinery.

In Long's view, the Indian case exemplifies the effects of an improvement approach. First, the approach tends 'to reinforce existing economic differentiation or leads to the emergence of more marked patterns of stratification based on differential access to the new technology and facilities'. (Long, 1977:156) As Long points out, a basic feature of the improvement approach is that it does not affect any prevailing maldistribution of productive resources. Although agricultural extension may result in substantial increases in productivity and production, there is 'not necessarily any qualitative change in the socio-economic and power structure of rural areas'. (Long, 1977:157) As will be discussed below, the improvement approach continues to be widely used for a variety of purposes. In health, education, housing and social service provision the use of extension agents in the transmission of ideas, techniques and resources had, and continues to have, significant impact on living conditions. The fundamental dilemma remains however: real improvements at the local level are always contained by external forces. The power of those forces will vary in practice, and thus the impact of community-level improvement approaches will similarly vary. The relationship between local, national and international forces is complex. Recent analyses have stressed the need to avoid deterministic views of socio-economic change and to examine the interplay of forces at all levels (Long, 1977; Coombs, 1981; Dore and Mars, 1981).

The second approach to community development, frequently contrasted with improvement, is transformation. The Tanzanian experience provides a useful and instructive case study of this form. The focus of any discussion of community development in Tanzania must be the Ujamaa village programme, which has been in operation since 1967. Mushi (1981) outlines three models of community development which have operated in Tanzania — the 'liberal-incremental', the 'revolutionary-change' and the 'guided evolutionary'. The first 'is rooted in the basic values of Western liberal democracy'; for advocates of this model 'progress is measured by two criteria: economic growth — with little concern with the distribution of the proceeds of growth — and stability of the polity and the class structure upon which it rests'. (Mushi, 1981:151-2)

The revolutionary-change model is the product of very different, socialist theories of social change. It 'sees a fundamental revolutionary change of the pre-existing socio-political and socio-economic system, not just change *within* the system, as necessary for development' (Mushi, 1981:152). In this model there is a major role for the state and politicised cadres as agents of change and mobilisation. Emphasis is on groups, not individuals, and particularly on the achievement, through redistribution, of more equality in income, wealth and power.

According to Mushi, the guided-evolutionary model is 'unstable' and lies somewhere between the other two. While still dependent on mobilisation:

It is essentially a 'mixed economy' model, relying on a mixture of group and individual incentives and action of coercion and persuasion . . . and seeking a balance between material and normative goals, and a redistribution of wealth consonant with political stability and continued economic growth. Planning, an essential feature of this model, seeks to achieve a balance between bureaucratic action and mass or popular action. (Mushi, 1981: 152-3)

Until independence in 1961, community development in Tanzania, as in India, was dominated by the liberal-incremental model as it operated in the context of colonialism. In the early period of independence, 1961-7, essentially the same form of community development approach was pursued, though with increased vigour and on a wider scale. As has been seen from earlier discussions of other areas of social policy, this is a typical pattern – the carry-over of colonial policies within the context of a prevailing approach to development which stressed the overwhelming importance of modernisation and economic growth. Nevertheless, some important changes did take place during this period: on a practical level more emphasis was given to co-operative and self-help groups, at the ideological level, 'the central leadership sought to reactivate the traditional norms of behaviour which were expected to create a sense of community in the villages'. (Mushi, 1981:237) Perhaps the most significant example of this was Nyerere's early essay on the principles of Ujamaa, a statement of ideals which was used as the basis for the policies which flowed from the Arusha Declaration of 1967 (Nyerere, 1966).

At the ideological level, the Declaration marked a major and widely influential break with prevailing development models. At the practical level, the post-1967 development programmes brought significant changes – state control of the major means of production and exchange, resettlement and collectivisation of the rural population into Ujamaa villages, and decentralisation and the creation of participatory organisations. These changes, together with other developments in the early 1970s, 'showed clearly that Tanzania was moving away from the liberal-incremental model and closer to the revolutionary model'. (Mushi, 1981:237) However, as numerous studies began to point out, there were contradictions in the implementation of Tanzanian socialism, which began to emerge more clearly during the 1970s (Saul and Arrighi, 1973; Shivji, 1973;

Freyhold, 1979; Mwansasu and Pratt, 1979; Hyden, 1980). First, there was a clear tendency in the reform of administrative organisation for the mobilising role of the party and the genuine participation of the mass of people to be neglected, while the powers of bureaucracy were extended and strengthened. Second, the principles of self-reliance were undermined by continuing and even increasing dependence on foreign aid, much of it from traditional Western sources. Third, the ideals of collective, socialist production were compromised by the trend to individual farming which was characteristic of the villages established after 1974 in a period of 'mass villagisation'. This programme itself, has, for many observers, undermined almost completely the principles of collective, community-based, self-reliant development. The imposition of 'villagisation' on a frequently unwilling population dramatically underlines the power of the bureaucracy and the failure of voluntary programmes (Hyden, 1980).

Mushi concludes that: 'From about 1972, therefore, there appears to be tendencies towards a reversion to the liberal-incremental model; emphasis having shifted from communal to individual or *bloc* farming; from aid from socialist countries (as observers had expected) to aid from the West; from equity to productivity.' (Mushi, 1981:238)

An examination of some of the causes of this apparent failure of a community development approach which was hailed as the basis for 'revolution by evolution', is instructive for the issues it raises which are of more general relevance in Third World countries. There were, of course, specific factors: from 1973 to 1976, and again in the past several years, there were serious food shortages, due largely to natural disasters and massive inflationary pressures from international price fluctuations, particularly huge oil price increases. Pressures such as these must, in any developing country, bring demands for emphasis on productivity, even at the expense of greater equity.

But, as Mushi suggests, 'The most important lesson to be learnt from Tanzania's CD approach is the instability of the guided-evolutionary model itself'. (1981:239) The most important feature of this instability is the opportunity for those with power to use the programmes for their own interests. The Tanzanian approach has been one which has been based on 'class collaboration' not 'class struggle', and this minimises the possibilities of real development from below. Despite the open acknowledgement of these problems, which is in itself of major importance, it would appear that opportunism, individualism and reversion to the liberal model have continued (Freyhold, 1979). This is a complex issue, which cannot be fully discussed here, but the lesson is of profound significance. Without the mobilisation of genuine mass consciousness and participation, community development programmes which aim at social transformation may be seriously diverted in practice.

Another lesson which has been noted in many other studies is that community development may be slower in producing results than leaderships demand. If too much is expected too soon, the outcome may be very poor programme performance. In Tanzania, the pressure for rapid change has meant the introduction of

Too many projects, programmes, operations and campaigns at the same time, often without elaborate implementation guidelines or timetables. Although this impatience is really the result of a genuine desire by the central leadership to improve the lot of the peasants, it has led to a number of problems. The main ones include: unfinished projects; little attention paid to the utility and maintenance of projects after completion; little time left to the peasants and local leaders to do feasibility studies or to evaluate their own successes and failures and draw appropriate lessons; and premature winding up of projects and programmes without examining the reasons for poor outcome. (Mushi, 1981:240)

A third lesson to be drawn from the Tanzanian case is one which lies at the heart of community development as part of social policy in developing countries. This is that, whatever the specific focus of particular programmes, development is more than the provision of funds or the establishment of services. In all areas of social policy it is about the mobilisation of people. Such mobilisation must mean more than just the use of unpaid labour or the use of resources generated within communities, it means the progressive attainment by people themselves of control over the conditions in which they live. Not only must mobilisation entail broadly-defined educational programmes which give people awareness, knowledge and self-confidence but it must, if it is to be successful in the longer term, be concerned with the power which people have to translate ideas into action. This demands administrative and political systems which recognise and genuinely accommodate the imperatives of community development. Furthermore, it demands that social policy as a whole is formulated and implemented with a close regard to community development as part of the strategy of overall development. Very often, in health, education, housing and social services community development methods and techniques are used to entrench patterns of resource distribution and forms of service, which are based on fundamentally different principles from those which inform the concept of community development. This is not to say they are ineffective, but they should not be confused with a strategy which is concerned with the genuine achievement of development from below. The point is made by Dore and Mars in relation to the tension between equality and efficiency in assistance to different communities:

Which of the two principles predominates, of course, will depend a great deal on the way the community development movement is perceived by central policy-makers – whether it is a welfare measure to keep the villagers happy while the industrialisers get on with the *real* job of building a modern economy, or whether substantial productive contributions from agriculture are counted as an important part of, and springboard for further stages of a comprehensive strategy of economic growth. (Dore and Mars, 1981:29)

Consideration of community development thus highlights the relationship between social policy and underdevelopment; community-based initiatives for real progress must operate within a wider socio-economic framework which militates against the interests of the majority of poor people. In a discussion of large-scale, government-sponsored settlement and land reform schemes, Long and Winder conclude that 'unless the state adopts a determined effort to favour the rural poor in its rural development programmes there is little likelihood of the rural poor themselves being able to strengthen their own collective position *vis-a-vis* other opposing interest groups'. (1981:86) They argue that the role of non-government organisations of all kinds is therefore crucial to the development of more effective organisations of the poor. For social policy, this raises difficult problems – support for non-government organisations may frequently mean support for groups which are actively hostile to government policies. Lack of support may mean that such organisations are simply not viable. For the organisations themselves, acceptance of government assistance may involve compromises which effectively undermine their objectives and freedom of action.

As Dore and Mars argue, in the real conditions of Third World societies it is of little value to debate whether 'community development *tout court* is a good or bad thing'. (1981:16) Their review of bureaucratically organised programmes in several countries with very different approaches to development was intended to identify 'what sort of methods achieve what sort of improvement goals under what sets of initial conditions'. (1981:16) In doing so, several common features were identified.

They all required imaginative initiative, and a distributional honesty on the part of salaried officials, for instance; they all required some kind of group, if not whole-community, action for mutual benefits; they all showed a preference for egalitarian improvements over improvements that increased income disparities, and so on.' (1981:18)

Thus, while the constraints of particular national contexts are real and of major significance in limiting the success of community development in practice, it is possible for considerable progress to be made in a wide variety of circumstances.

In relation to organised community development, the role of staff is obviously important. As noted earlier, social service departments in the majority of Third World countries are still dominated by inappropriate methods, largely the result of the colonial legacy and continuing 'professional imperialism' (Midgley, 1981). Alldred (1976), in a discussion of the contradictions inherent in professional community development, emphasises that community development cannot be viewed simply as a method which can be applied in any context. One suggestion he makes is 'that Governments' position as employers of CD workers must be usurped – not by well-meaning and efficient voluntary agencies, but by the communities themselves'. (1976:138) At the same time, 'rather than blindly condemning Government action, whilst simultaneously offering naïve panegyrics in favour of the grassroots, it seems more prudent to welcome the positive role Government can play in development'. (1976:139-40)

A similar recognition of the situation in most developing countries, the majority of which are not infused with the dedication to social transformation found in Tanzania, Mozambique and Cuba, lies behind Midgley's argument for a 'pragmatic approach' to the role of social workers in the Third World:

There can be no quarrel with the idea that social workers should become involved in rural development, or in community work with urban slum dwellers, or that they should become advocates of the poor and deprived, or that they should take a greater interest in family planning, adult education or nutrition. But if social workers are to adopt these roles, they must do so pragmatically; their implications for social work education must be examined realistically and the profession's potential for becoming involved in these activities must be assessed properly. (Midgley, 1981:168)

A pragmatic approach demands emphasis on real developmental issues, awareness of the wider context in which local problems exist, the replacement of irrelevant methods with more practical skills, and the emergence of groups of community development workers genuinely committed to working with people. But a pragmatic approach which attempts to improve conditions without fundamental political change as a prerequisite faces major obstacles. Harrison, in a review of 'egalitarian and participatory approaches' in many fields argues that 'they have much in common, and together they add up to a coherent strategy which has much to teach Western countries'. (Harrison, 1980:7) His numerous examples of successful projects and programmes give powerful support to the community development approach. But as he points out, 'despite the change in development thinking, actual practice has not changed in very many, perhaps most countries'. (1980:303) As we have seen in earlier chapters, community-based social policies may be pursued across a wide range of needs, but they may only be peripheral; the social policies of underdevelopment may continue to drain the greater part of available resources and negate the effects of relevant, equitable policies. Harrison argues, and the point will be discussed further in the concluding chapter, that 'the new development strategy' in which community development is the focus, 'is not a collection of piecemeal reforms for unconnected sectors . . . to be effective it has to be applied to the whole structure'. (1980:302-3)

Although radical change in the training, deployment and attitudes of community-development workers will make change more possible, if community development is part of a strategy applied only to the poor it will only have very limited potential. It is not as pointed out earlier a method, but must be part of an overall strategy:

In so many countries the élite seems to expect to carry on as before while the masses are uplifting themselves through self-help. In some countries the new development strategy is being used piecemeal to buy off the poor with minimal reforms that do not significantly affect the privileges of the rich . . . If change is really to benefit the poor and the powerless it has to hurt the rich and powerful. (Harrison, 1980:303-4)

The dilemmas of community development, and those engaged in trying to stimulate it, are numerous and frequently appear intractable. The emphasis in the present discussion has been largely in its limitations and the constraints it faces, but this should not be taken to diminish its importance. Conversely, it is precisely because it is of such profound importance that some understanding of its negative features is vital. It is only when these are known that the enormous potential of community development may be realised. Community organisation can be, and has been in very many cases, crucial in the emergence of movements for radical social change. Even the smallest, seemingly most insignificant local programme which involves the people in controlling their own development may increase the solidarity and self-confidence of the mass of people, and contribute to the emergence of those pressures which will achieve development from below.

8

Social Policy and Social Planning

' . . . the desire to maintain the stability of existing patterns of power and privilege may motivate concern with planning to deal primarily with threats to social order.' (Romanyshyn, 1971:379)

Earlier chapters have identified a number of the dilemmas which face developing countries in a variety of social policy fields. Despite the different problems encountered in housing, health, education and social services a number of themes consistently recur. This chapter is concerned with inter-relationships between the components of social policy and the fundamentally similar responses which are demanded of all social policies dedicated to the improvement of living conditions for the mass of people. Social planning, conceived as the process through which the goals and objectives of social policy are implemented, will be discussed very briefly.

All preceding discussion has been dominated by the impact of continuing underdevelopment, on patterns of social and economic change and on the nature of existing policies and programmes. Furthermore, the extent to which underdevelopment constrains and determines the range and nature of policy responses has been illustrated in respect of very many basic social issues. Policies inherited from colonial administrations have been seen to continue, frequently modified very little, after independence, and are dominated by the emergence of new class formations which determine the allocation of resources. The clearest, and most important determinants of living conditions for the poor are the economic relationships of underdevelopment which pervert both relationships between countries and relationships within countries. In all sectors, the emphasis in alternative policies, which attempt to shift the pattern of resource distribution in favour of the poor, is on programmes which are organised from below, and which focus on the basic needs of the majority. Consistently, the theme of community-based policies is repeated in the various sectors.

However, both explicitly and implicitly, the context in which such policies must operate has been seen to demand substantial change if they are to succeed. The Director of the Papua New Guinea National Planning Office identified this dilemma:

Because development planning is concerned with wide-ranging changes and inter-relationships in the whole social and economic fabric of society, within the framework of active external factors in the world political economy, many 'solutions' involve very radical changes [necessitating] the development of a political machinery and mass mobilisation. (Lepani, 1976:17)

Social policies which have been formulated without regard to the wider context of development and underdevelopment have failed to meet the needs of Third World countries, and have imposed alien and irrelevant systems of provision and contributed to the extension and entrenchment of patterns of inequality and privilege. In the development of appropriate policies two features stand out – the enormous gap between rhetoric and reality, and the variation between different sectors. In health, for example, far more progress has been made in the direction of the 'basic needs approach' than in housing or social services. But even in health, the patterns of resource distribution and the nature of health services continue to reflect the imperatives of underdevelopment. It is only relatively recently that discussion of social policies has begun to focus on the relationship between these policies and overall patterns of development, rather than being concerned with more effective implementation of inappropriate programmes derived from external sources. As discussed earlier, a major factor in the emergence of new social policies has been the rejection of development strategies which were primarily based on economic growth and modernisation. The shift to concern with human development and increasing awareness of the realities of continuing underdevelopment have forced reconsideration of policies in all sectors.

Thus, in recent years, there has been a significant shift in the way social welfare has been viewed in Third World countries. Previously, both in theory and practice, the dominant conception was one which saw social policy as being concerned with the formulation and implementation of narrowly specific programmes to meet special social needs. To a very large extent these needs were those created, or made more severe, by the process of rapid economic and social change. The growth of social policy tended to be in terms of crisis intervention, attempting to deal with the worst social consequences of particular economic and social changes. Furthermore, in many cases, the nature of such policies reflected a response to actual or possible threats to social order. To the extent that social policies went beyond this, they were frequently, as in health, education and housing, very clearly determined by the priorities and imperatives of economic development of a particular sort, and not by considerations of national social welfare. In addition, the term social welfare was often reserved for social policies which dealt with needs of particularly vulnerable groups – children, vagrants, the handicapped. This had the effect of diminishing the concept and reinforcing the dominance of materialistic definitions of development.

In the colonial period, social policy as a national concern was relegated to an inferior position. The minor role of social policy reflected both the nature of the relationship between the colonies and the metropolitan powers and, to some extent, the views of social policy dominant in those metropolitan countries.

The most significant shift, therefore, is from the conception of social policy as peripheral, residual and primarily concerned with reacting to the imperatives and ill-effects of externally-determined economic and social change, to one which virtually equates social policy with social development. In this latter view social development may be seen as the set of social goals which a society sets itself. This comprises both ultimate objectives in the terms of the nature of relationships in that society and the dominant social values which should permeate that society. Furthermore, it determines the range of means that society is willing to use to achieve its ultimate objective. Social development, then, must be seen as both a set of objectives and a process for achieving those objectives.

Within this conception, which is profoundly different from the narrow, administrative concept previously dominant, social welfare is a distributive principle, a focus for action and concern with poverty, inequality, and access to resources of all kinds. And within this approach, it has been increasingly recognised that what were conventionally regarded as 'problems of social policy' cannot be examined meaningfully in isolation from the distributive system as a whole. Seen in this way, social policy is concerned with the achievement of social development. Social development is seen as a normative orientation, that is, a way of viewing things based on a specific set of values. The particular set of values which informs the 'social development orientation' is one which is primarily concerned with distribution based on needs. Social policies are concerned with the distribution of social resources. The distinction between such policies and others is essentially arbitrary, as the concerns of social policy touch all areas of activity. In particular, earlier discussions have demonstrated the impossibility of considering social policies in isolation from economic policies; the nature of underdevelopment demands that they be considered together.

Social policy must be seen as essentially based on a set of guiding principles which together generate and sustain the processes of social development. These principles express the goals of development and the basis for the allocation and distribution of social resources of all kinds. In relation to particular kinds of resources specific policies will translate these principles into concrete programmes of action and administration determined by the overall concept of social policy. Thus, although the specific nature of programmes will vary in relation to different needs, and the principles, values and goals which guide decision-making, the ordering of priorities and choices between alternative strategies will be the same. The dilemmas which have been observed in the various sectors discussed arise from fundamental conflicts between the objectives of social policy and the dynamics of underdevelopment. In very many instances, the principles which inform the operation of policies and programmes in particular sectors contradict those which inform overall developmental goals.

In practice, therefore, two major problems face governments which attempt to translate social policy principles into practice. One is the need to ensure that every sector operates on the basis of the principles which inform development objectives, the other is to relate the activity of every sector with every other. As we have seen, the values and principles espoused in statements of intent, both at national and international levels, are very often different from those which actually determine policy formulation in detail and programme design and implementation. There are very many intervening stages during which the initial goals may be compromised or undermined. Not least, the social formations characteristic of underdevelopment produce profound dilemmas for the implementation of social policy. We have seen how the social classes which derive their power from association with international capital and the powerful machinery of state administration place demands on social resources which continue to pull social policies away from basic services and towards the extension of systems of provision which maintain inequality in distribution and access. Furthermore, such groups are generally the most powerful source of demands for Western standards and 'modern facilities'. This is particularly clear in health, housing and education. But if progress is to be made and services efficiently administered, there is a continuing necessity to deploy relatively scarce high-level manpower for these tasks. How then can relevant, appropriate policies, dedicated to a reduction of inequality and privilege, be implemented by those who are seeking to maintain the *status quo*? The earlier discussion of community development illustrated this dilemma; the basic issue in community development approaches is that of power.

Space does not permit a satisfactory discussion of these issues here, and in any case the political realities of specific societies will determine the nature of this fundamental dilemma. But any conscious attempts to bring about real development through social policy must recognise that if the institutional structures and powerful social forces in society are in conflict with the basic philosophy of that development and operate on essentially contradictory principles, the chances of translating statements of social policy into action are severely constrained.

In practice, of course, the cruelty of the dilemma is very real: the several options may be equally unfavourable but action must be taken. Nihilism will certainly not improve the conditions of living for the mass of people, and will almost certainly ensure that they become worse. We may identify what might ideally be done, and we should, but the conditions of the majority demand the best possible be done, in awareness that this falls short of the ideal in the short term.

The essential issues, then, for those concerned with social policy fall into two groups. First, those concerned with bringing about political change which will ensure that policies are formulated and implemented for the real benefit of the majority. Specific social policies may be closely related to this, but ultimately these issues must lie outside the processes of state-directed social policy. They are, as Lepani was earlier quoted as suggesting, concerned with mobilisation and political will. There are obvious and fundamental dilemmas facing those who work within systems which they seek to alter; the relationship between politics and administration is extremely complex and poses great difficulties for those with genuine concern for development.

The second concerns the action which can be taken by those responsible for social policy. Here it is important to reiterate that this will mean virtually everyone involved in administration. The social consequences of change and the impact of almost every policy from whatever sector mean that it is not possible to divide-off social policy concerns from the rest. The essential question then is how to ensure that all stages of policy – formulation, programme design, resource allocation and programme implementation – are rigorously exposed to the application of the fundamental principles of development.

We are brought by this to the question of social planning. The literature on this subject is vast, and no attempt will be made here to discuss it. What can be emphasised is that although the process demands, in any context, a wide range of technical skills and complex organisational and administrative forms, we are fundamentally concerned with its purpose, which may often be lost in a frequently observed concentration on technique:

Whatever definition you give to social planning, whatever technical content it may have, whatever degree of precision it may achieve, social planning will always mean, above all, the affirmation of a will to act, of a will to achieve something, of a will to determine the direction we wish to follow. (ISSA, 1972:55)

Part of any solution to the problem of articulating the will to act will be organisational – the establishment of mechanisms through which policies are generated and proposals scrutinised. In very many administrative systems there is a fundamental problem which arises from the sheer volume of development activity and the inevitable conflict between the need to process current proposals and the need for reflective and wide-ranging policy analysis. Although many countries are attempting to establish systems of directive planning, in many cases planning remains largely reactive. Thus, the planning system nationally can respond to proposals from specific government departments, or other administrative levels, but does not have the capacity or authority to ensure that particular policy proposals are generated in all sectors in line with overall social policy goals. There is often fragmentation and contradiction at the policy level, which to a large extent is political: if it is to be effective, the establishment of clear guidelines for policy demands both fundamental agreement as to the principles of social policy and the political will to carry those principles through into action.

There are several ways in which social policy objectives may be injected more effectively into the reality of social programmes. First, national planning bodies can be established or strengthened to the point where they are able to influence not just the allocation of resources between projects proposed, but the actual pattern of policy-formulation in all sectors. But such a strategy has serious dangers. 'Unless central planning is balanced by and rooted in vigorous democratic self-management and control, the rise of new forms of inequality and domination cannot be avoided.' (Kuitenbrower, 1976:15) Second, the capacity of specific government departments and decentralised administrative units for policy-formulation can be increased. This requires staff who are not simply concerned with issues of plan implementation but are able and willing to examine both existing and proposed policies against the principles which have been established nationally. A major difficulty here is the power of vested interests – professional, social and economic self-interest may determine support for the status quo against any substantial shift in policy. This was clearly seen for example, in relation to health and housing policies. With regard to relationships between national and local planning very serious problems are clearly faced. The devolution of power to lower tiers of administration may be both desirable and administratively more efficient, but without a political system which ensures the implementation of national strategy, the possibilities of uneven development and the further entrenchment of internal inequalities are very great. Given the maldistribution of services and resources characteristic of underdevelopment, this is a major dilemma; the desire for decentralisation may undermine the pursuit of balanced development for the mass of people.

The third approach is closely linked with the first two. The generation of genuine participation in policy formulation achieves both a counter-balance to the dangers of more effective planning, and is itself an expression of a fundamental principle of social policy as discussed in earlier chapters. Discussion of community development in particular emphasised local control, initiative and participation. Thus the most effective means to ensure that policies reflect the principles established for development will be to strive consciously for a widening and deepening of public knowledge of policy issues, together with genuine participation in the implementation of the programmes which are implemented. An informed, involved population with real rather than illusory control over the processes of social development is the surest way to control the direction of policy making and programme implementation. In concrete terms this would argue for, as examples, mass literacy campaigns which focus their materials on development issues, mass campaigns for health education, which emphasise community involvement in health programmes, both curative and preventive; non-formal education and continuing education, which treat education as a life-long activity and not as an instrument for young people alone. It would also mean that workers in particular sectors would have more involvement, more real control, over the sectors in which they work and the formulation of policy in those sectors. Planning must therefore face the dilemma of two imperatives – direction from above and control from below.

While central planning is indispensable to the balanced development between people, regions and sectors (so as to gradually overcome uneven development), such planning can only be sensitive to people's needs and potentialities if it is embedded in a continuous process of consultation from the base upwards. This is particularly important in terms of leader and authorities, who should be chosen, and periodically rotated or confirmed, by the local communities and their direct representatives. Those who plan from the centre and higher units can only be sensitive to the needs and potentialities of the local people if they are accountable to them and to a movement which is trusted and actively supported by most people. (Kuitenbrower, 1976:16)

A final example will illustrate a number of the points raised above – 'population projects'. The issue of population control and the 'family planning solution' to the problems of poverty and deprivation in the Third World have not been discussed in this study. The principal reason for this is that the considerable emphasis on such policies in recent years has been essentially diversionary, and has misconceived the nature of the problems and obscured the real issues of underdevelopment. However, and this is of fundamental importance, policies which aim to give women greater control of their lives through control of fertility are very different from policies of population control. But for this difference to be real, new approaches are needed to formulating planning and implementing policies in this area. It is still the case that 'population programs are planned and organised mainly by men, and aimed almost entirely at women – women as objects whose fertility is to be controlled . . . rather than as people who would wish to control their own fertility. It is assumed that women do not know what is good for them' (Rogers, 1980:107). Where such attitudes prevail, they clearly contradict notions of participation and control from below, and contradict the basic principles of a development philosophy rooted in the value and growth of every individual. The coercive, mechanistic attributes of many population projects may be in part related to the fact that such projects have most often been the responsibility of health administrations dominated by an 'engineering and technological approach to health development' (Gish, 1975:202). Without minimising the crucial relevance of fertility control to the health of women and children, it has been clearly shown that programmes which focus almost entirely on the maximisation of contraceptive acceptance not only fail in their objective but do not provide the basis for genuine development initiatives. As Rogers argues, the more successful projects are those which recognise the complex social and economic patterns which affect the position of women. 'Many of the emerging attempts to reduce the birth-rate by "raising the status of women" are useful because they help to meet the need for women's control over their own fertility.' (Rogers, 1980:114) But such attempts demand policies which involve numerous sectors at the same time: health education, social services, community development and economic development are only a few of those which must be involved. Thus, this example demonstrates the necessity for social policy as an expression of fundamental principles; in this, the need to give women, half the population, equality in development. Social policies 'for women' cannot be restricted to a few programmes of 'women's affairs', but must face the enormous barriers to women across the whole range of social and economic affairs. The embodiment of the fundamental principles of social policy in action for development remains and in conditions of continuing underdevelopment, this may be seen as the most profound dilemma of all. But

The human and material costs of maintaining an established, inegalitarian social order tend to increase exponentially in spite of sporadic patchwork efforts to save that order from collapsing. Sooner or later this process tends to reach levels of massive breakdown. To refer to this self-defeating process as social development is, of course absurd . . . Social development, like human freedom and dignity, is indivisible. It simply cannot be secured for segments of a population at the price of exploiting and oppressing other segments. (Gil, 1976:93)

Bibliography

Abel-Smith, B. and Leiserson, A. 1978. *Poverty, Development and Health Policy*, Public Health Papers No. 69, Geneva, World Health Organisation.

Abu-Lughod, J. and Hay, R. (eds), 1979. *Third World Urbanisation*, London and New York, Methuen.

Adu, A.L., 1969. *The Civil Service in Commonwealth Africa*, London, Allen & Unwin.

Ahluwalia. M.S., 1978. *India: Occasional Papers*, Washington, World Bank.

Allbrook, D.B., 1972. 'Medical care, health and national development in Australia's neighbourhood', *Medical Journal of Australia*, 2: 1045-50.

Alldred, N., 1976. 'Some contradictions in community development', *Community Development Journal*, 11(2): 134-140.

Amarshi, A., Good, K. and Mortimer, R., 1979. *Development and Dependency: The Political Economy of Papua New Guinea*, Melbourne, Oxford University Press.

Amin, S., 1974. *Accumulation on a World Scale: A Critique of the Theory of Underdevelopment*, New York, Monthly Review Press

Anderson, J., 1970. *The Struggle for the School*, London, Longman.

Arnold, G., 1979. *Aid in Africa*, London, Kogan Page; New York, Nicholls Publishing Company.

Aziz, S., 1978. *Rural Development: Learning from China*, London, Macmillan.

Balandier, P., 1966. 'The colonial situation: a theoretical approach,' in Wallerstein, I. (ed.), *Social Change: the Colonial Situation*, London and New York, Wiley.

Baran, P.A., 1957. *The Political Economy of Growth*, New York, Monthly Review Press.

Bashizi, B., 1979. 'Day-care centers in Senegal,' *Assignment Children*, 47-8: 165-71.

Baster, N., 1972. 'Development indicators: an introduction,' *Journal of Development Studies*, 8(3):1-20.

Batten, T.R., 1954. *Problems of African Development*, London, Oxford University Press.

Batten, T.R., 1957. *Communities and Their Development: An Introductory*

Study with Special Reference to the Tropics, London, Oxford University Press.

Batten, T.R., 1962. *Training for Community Development: A Critical Study of Method*, London, Oxford University Press.

Batten, T.R., 1967. *The Non-Directive Approach in Group and Community Work*, London, Oxford University Press.

Bean, P.T., 1976. *Rehabilitation and Deviance*, London, Routledge & Kegan Paul.

Beck, A., 1970. *A History of the British Medical Administration of East Africa*, Cambridge, Harvard University Press.

Bell, C.O., 1972. 'The basis of national health planning in Papua New Guinea — the work of the health planning epidemiology units', *Papua New Guinea Medical Journal*, 15(4):246-8.

Bell, C.O., 1973. *Diseases and Health Services of Papua New Guinea: A Basis for National Health Planning*, Konedobu, Papua New Guinea, Department of Public Health.

Bennett, F.J., 1979. 'Primary health care and developing countries,' *Social Science and Medicine*, 13A:505-14.

Benyoussef, A., 1977. 'Health service delivery in developing countries,' *International Social Science Journal*, 29(3):397-418.

Benyoussef, A. and Christian, B., 1977. 'Health care in developing countries', *Social Science and Medicine*, 11(6/7): 399-408.

Bernstein, H. (ed.), 1973. *Underdevelopment and Development: The Third World Today*, Harmondsworth and Baltimore, Penguin.

Black, R.H., 1959. The health of patrol officers in the Territory of Papua and New Guinea', *Medical Journal of Australia*, 2:428-35.

Blackburn, C.R.B., 1970. 'Medicine in New Guinea: three and a half centuries of change', *Post Graduate Medical Journal*, 46:250-6.

Blowers, A. and Thompson, G. (eds.), 1976. *Inequalities, Conflict and Change*, Milton Keynes, Open University.

Booth, D., 1975. 'Andre Gundar Frank: an introduction and appreciation', in Oxall, I. (ed.) *Beyond the Sociology of Development*, pp. 50-85, London and Boston, Routledge & Kegan Paul.

Bourdieu, C. & Passeron, J.C., 1977. *Reproduction in Education. Society and Culture*, London, Sage Publications.

Bowles, S., 1971. 'Cuban education and the revolutionary ideology', *Harvard Education Review*, 41,iv.

Breese, G. (ed.), 1972. *The City in Newly Developing Countries*, London and Englewood-Cliffs, Prentice-Hall.

Brokensha, D. and Hodge, P., 1969. *Community Development: An Interpretation*, San Fransisco, Chandler Publishing Company.

Brown, E.R., 1976. 'Public health to imperialism,' *American Journal of Public Health*, 66(9):897-903.

Bryant, J., 1969. *Health and the Developing World*, Ithaca, Cornell University Press.

Bussim, L.N., 1972. 'The type of training a doctor, particularly a R.M.O., should have before being posted to an out-station hospital', *Papua New Guinea Medical Journal*, 15(4):247.

Calov. W.L., 1929. 'Some notes on the practice of medicine in Melanesia', *Medical Journal of Australia*, 1:241-4.

Calov, W.L., 1955. 'The medical service of Papua and New Guinea', *Medical Journal of Australia*, 2:304-10.

Cano, M.T., 1979. 'From the child to community participation, *Assignment Children*', 47-8:143-64.

Caplan, P. and Bujra, J.N., (eds) 1979. *Women United, Women Divided, Cross-Cultural Perspectives on Female Solidarity*, London, Tavistock.

Carnoy, M., 1979. *Can Educational Policy Equalise Income Distribution in Latin America?* Farnborough, Saxon House.

Carnoy, M. and Wertheim, J., 1979. 'Cuba: Economic change and education reform', *World Bank Staff Working Paper No. 317.* Washington D.C., World Bank.

Castells, M., 1977. *The Urban Question*, London, Edward Arnold.

Castells, M., 1979. *City, Class and Power*, London, Macmillan.

Chetley, A., 1980. *The Baby Killer Scandal*, London, War on Want.

Chinnery, E.W.P., 1923. 'The care, management and health of native labour in Papua', in *Proceedings of the Pan-Pacific Science Congress, Australia, 1923*, Vol. 2:1408-09.

Choudrey, A.W., 1975. 'Potential effects of irrigation on the spread of bilharziasis in Kenya', *East African Medical Journal*, 53(3):120-6.

Cilento, R.W., 1927. 'Report on the public health of the territory of New Guinea', in *Report to the League of Nations on the Administration of the Territory of New Guinea for 1925-26*, pp. 92-6, Canberra, Government Printer.

Clammer, J., 1975. 'Economic anthropology and the sociology of development', in Oxaal, I., *et al* (eds), *Beyond the Sociology of Development*, pp.208-28, London, Routledge and Kegan Paul.

Cleaver, H., 1977. 'Malaria, the politics of public health and the international crisis', *The Review of Radical Political Economics*, 9(1):61-80.

Cliffe, L., 1973. *Underdevelopment or Socialism?*, Brighton, University of Sussex, Institute of Development Studies.

Clifford, W., 1966. *A Primer of Social Casework in Africa*, Nairobi, Oxford University Press.

Cohen, R., 1972. 'Class in Africa: analytical problems and perspectives', in Miliband, R. and Saville, J., (eds), *The Socialist Register 1972*, pp. 231-56. London, Merlin.

Conroy, J.D., 1976. *Education, Employment and Migration In Papua New*

Guinea, Canberra, Development Studies Centre, Australian National University, Monograph, No. 3.

Coombs, P.H. (ed)., 1981. *Meeting the Basic Needs of the Rural Poor: the Integrated Community-based Approach,* New York and London, Pergammon.

Coombs, P.H. and Ahmed, M., 1974. *Attacking Rural Poverty,* Baltimore and London, Johns Hopkins University Press.

Court, D., and Ghai, D.P., 1974. *Education Society and Development: New Perspectives from Kenya,* Nairobi, Oxford University Press.

Davis, K., 1972. 'The urbanisation of the human population', in Breese, G., (ed)., *The City in the Newly Developing Countries,* pp. 5-20, London and Englewood-Cliffs, Prentice-Hall.

Djukanovic, V. and Mach, E.P., 1975. *Alternative Approaches to Meeting Basic Health Needs in Developing Countries,* Geneva, World Health Organisation.

Doherty, J., 1973. *The Location of Health Facilities in Tanzania,* BRALUP Service Paper, 732, Dar es Salaam, University of Dar es Salaam.

Dore, R., 1976. *The Diploma Disease,* London, George Allen & Unwin.

Dore, R. and Mars, Z., (eds), 1981. *Community Development: Comparative Case studies in India, the Republic of Korea, Mexico and Tanzania,* London, Croom Helm.

Doyal, L. and Pennell, I., 1979. *The Political Economy of Health,* London Pluto Press.

Drakakis-Smith, D., 1981. *Urbanisation, Housing and the Development Process,* London, Croom Helm.

Du Sautoy, P., 1958. *Community Development in Ghana,* London, Oxford University Press.

Du Sautoy, P., 1962. *The Organisation of a Community Development Programme,* London, Oxford University Press.

Dube, S.C., 1958. *India's Changing Villages: Human Factors in Community Development,* London, Routledge & Kegan Paul.

Dumont, R. and Cohen, N., 1980. *The Growth of Hunger: A New Politics of Agriculture,* London, Marion Boyars.

Dwyer, D.J., 1975. *People and Housing in Third World Cities: Perspectives on the Problems of Spontaneous Settlements,* London, Longman.

Eickelman, D.F., 1978. 'The Art of Memory: Islamic Education and its Social Reproduction', *Comparative Studies in Society and History,* 20: 485-516.

Etten, G. van, 1976. *Rural Health Development in Tanzania: A Case Study of Medical Sociology in a Developing Country,* Assen, Van Gorcum.

Evans, P., 1977. 'Multinationals, state-owned corporations and the transformation of imperialism', *Economic Development and Cultural Change,* 26(1):43-64.

Fanon, F., 1963. *The Wretched of the Earth,* New York, Grove Press. 1967 edition, Harmondsworth, Penguin.

Farrant, M. *et al.,* 1972. *Kampala's Children,* Kampala, UNICEF.

Farrant, M. (ed.), 1974. *An Investigation into Patterns of Destitution,* Department of Sociology, University of Dar es Salaam, mimeo.

Feacham, R., McGarry, M.G., and Mara, D.D., 1977. *Water, Wastes and Health in Hot Climates,* London, Wiley.

Fendall, N.R.E. 1963. 'Health centres: a basis for a rural health service', *Journal of Tropical Medicine and Hygiene,* 66:219-32.

Fendall, N.R.E., 1965. 'Medical planning and training of personnel in Kenya', *Journal of Tropical Medicine and Hygiene,* 68(1):12-20.

Fendall, N.R.E., 1968. 'The medical assistant in Africa', *Journal of Tropical medicine and Hygiene,* 71(4): 83-95.

Fendall, N.R., 1972. *Auxiliaries in Health Care: Programmes in Developing Countries,* Baltimore, Johns Hopkins Press.

Feuerstein, M.T., 1976. 'Rural health problems in developing countries – need for a comprehensive community approach', *Community Development Journal,* 11(1):38-52.

First, R., 1970. *The Barrel of a Gun,* Harmondsworth, Penguin.

Fitzpatrick, P., 1980. *Law and State in Papua New Guinea,* London and New York, Academic Press.

Food and Agriculture Organisation, 1970. *Lives in Peril,* Rome, Food and Agriculture Organisation.

Foster, P., 1965a. 'The vocational school fallacy in educational planning', in Anderson, C.A. and Bowman, M.J., *Education and Economic Development,* Chicago, Aldine Press.

Foster, P., 1965b. *Education and Social Change in Ghana.* London, Routledge & Kegan Paul.

Foster, P., 1966. 'A rebuttal', in Hanson, J.W. & Brembec, C.S. (eds). *Education and the Development of Nations,* New York, Holt Rhinehart and Winston.

Foster, P., 1968. 'Education for self-reliance: a critical evaluation', in Jolly, R. (ed.), *Education in Africa: Research and Action,* Nairobi, East African Publishing House.

Foster, P., 1975. 'Dilemmas of educational development: what we might learn from the past', *Comparative Education Review,* 19,iii.

Foster, P. and Sheffield, J.R., 1975. *World Year Book of Education 1974,* London, Evans Bros.

Foster-Carter, A., 1974. 'Neo-marxist approaches to development and underdevelopment', in de Kadt, E. and Williams, G. (eds.), *Sociology and Development,* pp. 67-108, London, Tavistock.

Frank, A.G., 1967. *Capitalism and Underdevelopment in Latin America: Historical Studies of Chile and Brazil,* New York, Monthly Review Press.

Frank, A.G., 1969. *Latin America: Underdevelopment or Revolution*, New York, Monthly Review Press.

Frankenberg, R., 1974. 'Functionalism and after? theory and developments in social science applied to the health field', *International Journal of Health Services*, 4(3):411-27.

Frankenberg, R. and Leeson, J., 1973. 'The sociology of helath dilemmas in the post-colonial world', in de Kadt, E. and Williams, G. (eds), *Sociology and Development*, pp.255-78, London, Tavistock.

Freire, P., 1972. *Pedagogy of the Oppressed*, London, Sheen & Ward.

Freyhold, M. von, 1979. *Ujamaa Villages in Tanzania*, London, Heinemann.

Friedlander, W.A., 1955. *Introduction to Social Welfare*, Englewood Cliffs, Prentice-Hall.

Furtado, C., 1973. 'Elements of a theory of underdevelopment – the underdeveloped structures', in Bernstein, H. (ed.), *Underdevelopment and Development*. pp. 33-43, Harmondsworth and Baltimore, Penguin.

Gaikwad, V.R., 1981. 'Community development in India', in Dore, R. and Mars, Z. (eds), *Community development: comparative case studies in India, the Republic of Korea, Mexico and Tanzania*, pp. 247-336, London, Croom Helm.

Gallet, P., 1972. *Freedom to Starve*, Harmondsworth and Baltimore, Penguin.

Gardiner, R.K. and Judd, H.O., 1954. *The Development of Social Administration*, London, Oxford University Press.

Garnaut, R., Wright, M. and Curtain, R., 1977. *'Employment, Incomes and Migration in Papua New Guinea Towns,'* Port Moresby, Institute of Applied Social and Economic Research.

George, S., 1976. *How the Other Half Dies*, Harmondsworth, Penguin.

Gershenberg, I., 1970. *The Distribution of Medical Services in Uganda*, Kampala, Makerere University.

Gil, D.S., 1976. 'Social policy strategies for social development', *Community Development Journal*, 11(2):86-93.

Gish, O., 1973. 'Resource allocation, equality of access and health', *International Journal of Health Services*, 3(3):399-412.

Gish, O., 1975. *Planning the Health Sector: the Tanzanian Experience*, London, Croom Helm.

Gish, O., 1977. *Guidelines for Health Planners*, London, Tri-Med.

Gish, O., 1979. 'The political economy of primary care and "health by the people": an historical exploration', *Social Science and Medicine*, 13C(4):203-11.

Godfrey. E.M. and Mutizo, G–C.M., 1974. 'The Political Economy of Self-Help: Kenya's Harambee Institutes of Technology', in Court, D. and Ghai, D.P. (eds), *Education, Society and Development*, Nairobi, Oxford University Press.

Golbourne, H., 1979. *Politics and the State in the Third World*, London, Macmillan.

Goldthorpe, J.E., 1975. *The Sociology of the Third World*, Cambridge and New York, Cambridge University Press.

Golladay, F., 1980. *Health Problems and Policies in the Developing Countries*, World Bank Staff Working Paper No. 412, Washington, World Bank.

Good, K., 1976. 'Class formations in colonial situations: some definitions and directions', *Australian and New Zealand Journal of Sociology*, 12(3):243-50.

Goody, J.R., 1968. *Literacy in Traditional Societies*, Cambridge, Cambridge University Press.

Great Britain, Colonial Office, 1945. *Social Welfare in the Colonies*, London, HMSO.

Great Britain, Colonial Office, 1948. *Summer Conference on African Administration*, African No. 1174, London, HMSO.

Great Britain, Colonial Office, 1958. *Community Development: A Handbook*, London, HMSO.

Great Britain, House of Commons Debates, 1940. *Second Reading of Colonial Welfare and Development Bill*, London, Hansard, House of Commons, Vol. 361.

Great Britain, Secretary of State for the Colonies, 1927. *Future Policy in Regard to Eastern Africa*, Cmd. 2904, London, HMSO.

Great Britain, Secretary of State for the Colonies, 1940. *Statement of Policy on Colonial Development and Welfare*, Cmd. 6175, London, HMSO.

Griffin, K., 1968. *Underdevelopment in Spanish America: An Interpretation*, London, Allen & Unwin.

Gunther, J.T., 1972. 'Medical Services, history', in Ryan, P. (ed.), *Encyclopaedia of Papua New Guinea*, pp. 748-56, Melbourne, Melbourne University Press.

Gunther, J.T., 1972. 'Medical services, history', in Ryan, P. (ed.), Guinea', *Papua New Guinea Medical Journal*, 17(1):4-7.

Gutkind, P.C.W. and Wallerstein, I., 1976. *The Political Economy of Contemporary Africa*, Beverly Hills and London, Sage.

Gutkind, P.C.W. and Waterman, P., 1977. *African Social Studies*, London, Heinemann.

Hall, T.L. and Mejia, A., 1978. *Health Manpower Planning: Principles, Methods, Issues*, Geneva, World Health Organisation.

Haq, M. ul., 1976. *The Poverty Curtain*, New York, Columbia University Press.

Hardoy, J.E. and Satterthwaite, D., 1981. *Shelter: Need and Response*, Chichester and New York, John Wiley and Sons.

Harrison, P., 1980. *The Third World Tomorrow*, Brighton, Harvester

Press, Harmondswoth and New York, Penguin.

Hayward, E.J.R., 1981. 'Basic services five years on', *UNICEF News*, 107(1):29-31.

Hecht, S., 1981. *Muruk and the Cross: Missions and Schools in the Southern Highlands*, Port Moresby, University of Papua New Guinea Education Research Report No. 35.

Heisler, H., 1970. 'Social welfare and African development', *Applied Social Studies*, Vol. 2 pp. 81-9.

Hellberg, J.H., 1973a. 'Health planning in developing countries', in May, R.J. (ed.), *Priorities in Malanesian Development*, pp. 138-41, Canberra, Australian National University.

Hellberg, J.H., 1973b. *Papua New Guinea: a Case Study of Integration of Government and Church Health Services*, Geneva, Christian Medical Commission, World Council of Churches.

Heller, T. and Elliott, C., 1977. *Health Care and Society: Readings in Health Care Delivery and Development*, Norwich, University of East Anglia, School of Development Studies.

Hinden, R., 1946. *Socialists and the Empire*, London, Fabian Publications.

Hollnsteiner, M.R. 1978., ' "Hope is whatever we find": the future of poor urban children in developing countries', *UNICEF News*, 97(3):20-6.

Hoogvelt, A.M.M., 1978. *The Sociology of Developing Societies*, (2nd edition), London, Macmillan.

Horvath, R.V., 1972. 'A definition of colonialism', *Current Anthropology*, 13(1):45-57.

Hughes, C.C. and Hunter, J.M., 1970. 'Disease and "development" in Africa', *Social Science and Medicine*, 3:443-93.

Hyden, G., 1980. *Beyond Ujamaa in Tanzania: Underdevelopment and an Uncaptured Peasantry*, London, Heinemann.

Hyden, G., Jackson, R., and Okumu, J., 1970. *Development Administration the Kenyan Experience*, Nairobi, Oxford University Press.

Independent Commission on International Development Issues, 1980. *North-South: a Programme for Survival*, London, Pan Books.

IDS Health Group, 1978. *Health Needs and Health Services in Rural Ghana*, 2 vols., Brighton, University of Sussex, Institute of Development Studies.

International Bank for Reconstruction and Development, 1965. *The Economic Development of the Territory of Papua and New Guinea*, Baltimore, Johns Hopkins Press.

International Council on Social Welfare, 1973. *Developing Social Policy in Conditions of Rapid Change. Role of Social Welfare*, New York, Columbia University Press.

ISSA, 1972. *Current Issues in Social Security Planning: Concepts and Techniques*, Geneva, International Social Security Association.

Jackson, R., 1978. 'Housing trends and policy implications in Papua New Guinea: flaunting the flag of abstracted empiricism', in Rimmer, P.J. *et al.* (eds), *Food, Shelter and Transport in South-East Asia and the Pacific,* pp. 171-88, Canberra, Australian National University.

Jain, S.C., 1967. *Community Development and the Panchayati Raj in India,* Calcutta, Allied Publishers.

Jazairi, N., 1976. *Approaches to the Development of Health Indicators,* Paris, OECD.

Jolly, R., 1964. 'Education', in Seers, D. (ed), *Cuba: The Economic and Social Revolution.* Chapel Hill, North Carolina.

Jolly, R., 1968. *Education in Africa: Action and Research.* Nairobi, East African Publishing House.

Jones, H., 1981. *Crime, Race and Culture,* Chichester and New York, John Wiley and Sons.

Juyal, B.N. and Vikashbai, 1979. 'The Ghandian approach to rural development: part 2 – in practice', *Ideas in Action,* 129:17-24.

Junquiera, H.I., 1971. 'Social changes and new welfare responses throughout the world. The welfare responses', in *Proceedings of the XVth International Conference on Social Welfare, Manila, Philippines, 1970,* New York and London, Columbia University Press.

Kalewold, A.I., 1970. *Traditional Ethiopian Church Education.* New York, Teachers' College Press.

Karunasatre, G., 1976. 'The failure of the community development programme in India', *Community Development Journal,* 11(2):95-119.

Kilama, W.L., Nhonoli, A.M. and Makene, W.J., 1974. 'Health care delivery in Tanzania', in Ruhumbika, G.,(ed.), *Towards Ujamaa: Twenty Years of Tanu Leadership,* pp. 191-217. Dar es Salaam, East African Literature Bureau.

Kimambo, I.N. and Temu, A.J. (eds), 1969. *A History of Tanzania,* Nairobi, East African Publishing House.

King, A.D., 1976. *Colonial Urban Development,* London, Routledge & Kegan Paul.

King, M., 1966. *Medical Care in Developing Countries,* Nairobi, Oxford University Press.

King, M., 1970. 'Medical manpower for occupational health in the tropics. II, the auxiliary – his role and training', *Journal of Tropical Medicine and Hygiene,* 73(12):336-46.

Kinyanjui, P.K., 1973. 'Education, training and employment of secondary school leavers in Kenya', *Manpower and Employment Research in Africa,* Centre for Developing Area Studies, McGill, 6, ii.

Kraut, H. and Cremer, D., 1971. *Health and Nutrition in East Africa,* Munich, Weltforum Verlag.

Kuitenbrower, J., 1976. *Premises and Implications of a Unified Approach to*

Development Analysis and Planning, Bangkok, United Nations, Economic and Social Commission for Asia and the Pacific.

Kuitenbrower, J., 1977. *Social Welfare and Dependence or Self-Reliance,* Bangkok, United Nations.

Lall, S. and Bibile, S., 1977. 'The political economy of controlling trans-nationals: the pharmaceutical industry in Sri Lanka, 1972-1976', *World Development,* 5(8):677-98.

Lambert, S.M., 1928. 'Medical conditions in the South Pacific', *Medical Journal of Australia,* 2:362-78.

Lambert, S.M., 1942. *A Doctor in Paradise,* Melbourne, Jabor.

Lea, J., 1979. 'Self-help and authority in housing: theoretical critics and empirical investigators', in *Housing in Third World Countries,* Murison, H.S., and Lea, J.P. (eds), pp. 49-53, London, Macmillan.

Leiner, M. and Ubell, R., 1974. *Children are the Revolution. Day Care in Cuba,* New York, Viking Press.

Lepani, C., 1976. *Planning in Small Dependent Economies – A Case Study of Papua New Guinea,* Port Moresby, National Planning Office, mimeo.

Levine, H.B. and Levine, M.W., 1979. *Urbanisation in Papua New Guinea,* London and New York, Cambridge University Press.

Lewis, A., 1955. *The Theory of Economic Growth,* London, Allen & Unwin.

Leys, C., 1969. *Politics and Change in Developing Countries,* Cambridge, Cambridge University Press.

Leys, C., 1975. *Underdevelopment in Kenya: The Political Economy of Neo-colonialism 1964-1971,* London, Heinemann.

Lipton, M., 1977. *Why Poor People Stay Poor: Urban Bias in World Development,* Cambridge, Mass., Harvard University Press.

Little, K., 1974. *Urbanisation as a Social Process,* London and Boston, Routledge & Kegan Paul.

Lloyd, P., 1979. *Slums of Hope?,* Harmondsworth and New York, Penguin.

Long, N., 1977. *An Introduction to the Sociology of Rural Development,* London, Tavistock.

Long, N. and Winder, D., 1981. 'The limitations of "directive change" for rural development in the Third World', *Community Development Journal,* 16(2):82-7.

Mabogunjie, A.L., Hardoy, J.E., and Misra, R.P., 1978. *Shelter Provision in Developing Countries,* Chichester and New York, John Wiley and Sons.

Maddocks, I., 1973. 'History of disease in Papua New Guinea', in Bell, C.O. (ed.), *Diseases and Health Services of Papua New Guinea: A Basis for National Health Planning,* pp. 70-4, Konedobu, Papua New Guinea, Department of Health.

Maddocks, I., and MacKay, J.S., 1974. 'Analysis of medical unit data

1972-73, *Papua New Guinea Medical Journal*, 17(2):203-09.

Madison, B., 1980. *The Meaning of Social Policy*, London, Croom Helm; Boulder, Westview Press.

Mair, L.P., 1944. *Welfare in the British Colonies*, London, the Royal Institute of International Affairs.

Mair, L.P., 1948. *Australia in New Guinea*, London: Christophers.

Mamdani, M., 1976. *Politics and Class Formation in Uganda*, London, Heinemann.

Mandl, P.E., 1979. 'IYC, a thrust to more effectively include children in development policies', *Assignment Children*, 47-8:7-13.

Manghezi, A., 1976. *Class, Elite and Community in African Development*, Uppsala, The Scandinavian Institute for African Studies.

Markovitz, I.L., 1977. *Power and Class in Africa: An Introduction to Change and Conflict in African Politics*, Englewood Cliffs, Prentice-Hall.

Marvin, R., 1975. ' "Economic Baba" – Is this a satisfactory explanation of why African parents value schooling?', *Journal of Modern African Studies*, 13,iii, 429-445.

Mayo, M., 1975. 'Community development: a radical alternative?' in Bailey, R., and Brake, M. (eds), *Radical Social Work*, pp. 129-43, London, Edward Arnold.

Mackie, R. (ed.), 1980. *Literacy and Revolution: the Pedagogy of the Oppressed*, London, Pluto Press.

McNamara, R.S., 1977. *Address to the Massachusetts Institute of Technology*, Washington, World Bank.

MacPherson, S., 1979. *Health and Underdevelopment in Papua New Guinea*, paper in 49th Congress of the Australian and New Zealand Association for the Advancement of Science, Auckland, January 1979.

MacPherson, S., 1980. *The Development of Basic Health Services in Papua New Guinea*, PhD. Thesis, University of Nottingham.

MacPherson, S., 1982. 'Mental Illness in the Third World', in Bean, P.T.(ed.), *Key Issues in Mental Illness*, Chichester, John Wiley and Sons.

McSweeney, B.G., 1980. 'Time to learn, time for a better life – the Women's Education Project in Upper Volta', *Assignment Children*, 49-50:109-27.

Mburu, F.M., 1979. 'Rhetoric – implementation gap in health policy and health services delivery for a rural population in a developing country', *Social Science and Medicine*, 13(a):577-83.

Mehmet, O., 1978. *Economic Planning and Social Justice in Developing Countries*, London, Croom Helm.

Michanek, E., 1975. 'The passing generation', in Nordberg, O. *et al.*, (eds), *Action for Children*, pp. 39-43, Uppsala, The Dag Hammarskjold

Foundation.

Midgley, J., 1981. *Professional Imperialism: Social Work in the Third World*, London, Heinemann.

Mitchell, S. (ed.), 1981. *The Logic of Poverty, The Case of the Brazilian North-east*, London, Routledge & Kegan Paul.

Moffett, J.P., 1955. *Tanganyika: A Review of its Resources and their Development*, Norwich, Jarrold.

Moore, W.E., 1963. *Social Change*, Englewood Cliffs, New Jersey, Prentice-Hall.

Mountjoy, A.B. (ed.), 1978. *The Third World: Problems and Perspectives*, London, Macmillan.

Munro, D.J., 1973. 'Man, state, and society' in Okensberg, M. (ed.), *China's Developmental Experience*, New York, Praeger.

Mushi, S.S., 1981. 'Community development in Tanzania', in Dore, R., and Mars, Z. (eds.) *Community development*, pp. 139-244, London, Croom Helm.

Mwambene, N.K.M., 1970. *Problems in the Implementation of a 'Socialist' Child Welfare Policy in a Rural Region of Tanzania*, University of Dar es Salaam, unpublished dissertation.

Mwansasu, B.U. and Pratt, C. (eds), 1979. *Towards Socialism in Tanzania*, Dar es Salaam, Tanzania Publishing House.

Myrdal, G., 1968. *Asian Drama: An Inquiry into the Poverty of Nations*, 3 vols, New York, Pantheon.

Navarro, V., 1972. 'Health services in Cuba: an initial appraisal', *New England Journal of Medicine*, 287(19):954-09.

Navarro, V., 1974. 'The underdevelopment of health or the health of underdevelopment', *International Journal of Health Services*, 4(1):5-27.

Nelson, H., 1972. *Papua New Guinea: Black Unity or Black Chaos?*, Harmondsworth, Penguin.

Nelson, J.M., 1979. *Access to Power: Politics and the Urban Poor in Developing Nations*, Princeton and Guildford, Princeton University Press.

Nenes, R.J., 1977. *Senegal. Syncrisis: the Dynamics of Health*, Vol. XiX, US Department of Health, Education and Welfare.

New, P.K.M., 1974. 'Barefoot doctors and health care in the People's Republic of China', *Ekistics*, 226:220-4.

Newell, K.W., 1975. *Health by the People*, Geneva, World Health Organisation.

Nigeria, Federal Ministry of Health, 1978. *Facilities and Manpower Survey*, Lagos, Ministry of Health.

Nilsson, S., 1973. *New Capitals of India, Pakistan and Bangladesh*, Uppsala, Scandinavian Institute of Asian Studies.

Norwood, H. (ed.), 1979. *Urbanisation and Housing in Papua New Guinea*,

Port Moresby, University of Papua New Guinea.

Nyerere, J.K., 1966. *Freedom and Unity,* Dar es Salaam, Oxford University Press.

Nyerere, J.K., 1968. *Freedom and Socialism,* Dar es Salaam, Oxford University Press.

Nyerere, J.K., 1973. *Freedom and Development,* Dar es Salaam, Oxford University Press.

Nyerere, J.K., 1977. *The Arusha Declaration Ten Years After,* Dar es Salaam, Government Printer.

Nyerinda, V.G., 1972. *Zambia's Response to Human Needs,* Lusaka, Zambia Council for Social Service.

Oliver, R., 1952. *The Missionary Factor in East Africa,* London, Longman.

Oram, N.D., 1976. *Colonial Town to Melanesian City: Port Moresby 1884-1974,* Canberra, Australian National University Press.

Oram, N., 1978. 'Housing, planning and urban administration', in Murison, H.S. and Lea, J.P. *Housing in Third World Countries.* pp. 43-48, London, Macmillan.

Oxall, I., Barnett, T., and Booth, D. (eds), 1975. *Beyond the Sociology of Development,* London and Boston, Routledge & Kegan Paul.

Palmer, I., 1980. 'Women in rural development', *International Development Review,* 22(2-3)pp.39-45.

Pan-American Health Organisation, 1978. *Health Conditions in the Americas 1973-1976,* Washington, PAHO.

Papua New Guinea, Department of Public Health, 1974. *Papua New Guinea National Health Plan, 1974-1978,* Konedobu, Department of Public Health.

Pathik, B. and Goon, E., 1978. 'Fiji School of Medicine', *Public Health Papers,* 70:79-96.

Payne, G., 1977. *Urban Housing in the Third World,* London, Leonard Hill: Boston, Routledge & Kegan Paul.

Perham, M., 1962. *Colonial Reckoning,* New York, Knopf.

Pettman, J. and Weeks, S.G. (eds), 1978. *The Foster Fallacy in Educational Planning, Occasional Paper No. 6,* Port Moresby, University of Papua New Guinea.

Prewitt, K., 1972. *The Functional Justification of Inequality and the Ndegwa Report: Shaping an Ideology,* paper presented to the 8th East African Social Science Conference.

Psacharopoulos, G. 1973. *Returns to Education,* San Francisco, Jossey-Bass.

Puffer, R.R. and Serrano, C.V., 1973. *Patterns of Mortality in Childhood,* Washington, Pan American Health Organisation.

Radford, A.J., 1972. 'The future of rural health services in Melanesia, with particular reference to Papua New Guinea', in Ward, M. (eds), *Change and Development in Rural Melanesia,* pp. 250-79, Canberra, Australian National University.

Ranger, T.O., 1969. *Colonialism in Africa, 1870-1960,* Cambridge, Cambridge University Press.

Rew, A.W., 1977. *Access and Implementation in Low-Income Housing in Metro Manila,* Bangkok, International Conference on Low Income Housing, mimeo.

Rhodes, R. (ed.), 1970. *Imperialism and Underdevelopment,* New York, Monthly Review Press.

Rifkin, S., 1981. 'Health, political will and participation', *UNICEF News,* 108/81/2, 3-5.

Rifkin, S.B. and Kaplinsky, R., 1973. 'Health strategy and development planning: lessons from the People's Republic of China, *Journal of Development Studies,* 9(2):213-32.

Riggs, F.W., 1964. *Administration in Developing Countries: The Theory of Prismatic Society,* Boston, Houghton Mifflin.

Ring, I., 1972. 'Budgeting and the national health plan', *Papua New Guinea Medical Journal,* 15(4):250.

Rodney, W., 1972. *How Europe Underdeveloped Africa,* Dar es Salaam, Tanzania Publishing House.

Rogers, B., 1980. *The Domestication of Women: Discrimination in Developing Societies,* London, Kogan Page.

Romanyshyn, J.M., 1971. *Social Welfare: Charity to Justice,* New York, Random House.

Roxborough, I., 1979. *Theories of Underdevelopment,* London, Macmillan.

Runawery, C. & Weeks, S., 1980. *Towards an Enga Education Strategy,* Port Moresby, University of Papua New Guinea, Education Research Unit Working Paper No. 3.

Ryan, P., 1968. *The Australian New Guinea Administrative Unit,* unpublished typescript. New Guinea Collection, University of Papua New Guinea.

Ryan, P., 1972. 'World War II', in *Encyclopaedia of Papua New Guinea,* pp. 1211-24, Melbourne, Melbourne University Press.

Ryan, W., 1971. *Blaming the Victim,* New York, Orbach & Chambers.

Santos, M., 1979. *The Shared Space: The Two Circuits of the Urban Economy in Underdeveloped Countries,* London and New York, Methuen.

Saul, J. and Arrighi, G., 1973. *Essays on the Political Economy of Africa,* New York and London, Monthly Review Press.

Schram, R., 1971. *A History of the Nigerian Health Services,* Ibadan, Ibadan University Press.

Seers, D., 1972. 'What are we trying to measure?', *Journal of Development*

Studies, 8(3): 21-36.

Segall, M., 1972. 'The politics of health in Tanzania', in Rwyemamu, J.F, *et al.* (eds.), *Towards Socialist Planning*, pp. 149-66, Dar es Salaam, Tanzania Publishing House.

Seidman, A., 1980. *An Economics Textbook for Africa*, (3rd edition), London and New York, Methuen.

Shah, G., 1978. 'The Ghandian approach to rural development', *Ideas in Action*, 125:3-6.

Sharpston, M.J., 1974. 'Health and development', *Journal of Development Studies*, 9(3):455-60.

Shivji, I.G., 1973. *The Silent Class Struggle*, Dar es Salaam, Tanzania Publishing House.

Shivji, I.G., 1975. 'Peasants and class alliance', *Review of African Political Economy*, 3 (May/October), 10-19.

Shivji, I.G., 1976. *Class Struggles in Tanzania*, London, Heinemann.

Sicault, G. (ed.), 1963. *The Needs of Children; A Survey of the Needs of Children in the Developing Countries*, New York, The Free Press of Glencoe.

Sidel, R., 1974. *Women and Child Care in China*, London, Sheldon Press.

Sidel, V. and Sidel, R., 1974. *Serve the People – Observations on Medicine in the People's Republic of China*, Boston, Beacon Press.

Sidel, V. and Sidel, R., 1977. 'Primary health care in relation to socio-political structure', *Social Science and Medicine*, 11 (6-7): 415-20.

Silvey, J., 1968. 'Unwillingly from school: the occupation attitudes of secondary school leavers in Uganda', in Jolly R. (ed.), *Education in Africa: Research and Action*, Nairobi, East African Publishing House.

Silvey, J., 1981. *'Recent Developments in Educational Selection Methods in Third World Countries*, paper given at Human Assessment and Cultural Factors Conference, August, Kingston, Ontario, Queens University.

Simmons, J., 1980. *The Education Dilemma: Policy Issues for the Developing Countries in the 1980s*, Oxford, Pergamon Press.

Simons, H.J., 1979. 'Zambia's urban situation', in Turok, B. (ed.), *Development in Zambia*, pp. 1-25, London, Zed Press.

Sorkin, A., 1976. *Health Economics in Developing Countries*, Lexington, D.C. Heath.

Stavenhagen, R., 1964. 'Changing functions of the community in developing countries', *Sociologica Ruralis*, 4:315-31.

Stein, H. (ed.), 1964. *Planning for the Needs of Children in Developing Countries*, New York, UNICEF.

Stohr, W. and Taylor, D.R.F. (eds), 1981. *Development from Above or Below? Radical Approaches to Spatial Planning in Developing Countries*, Chichester, Wiley.

Strang, P.J., 1973. *The Structural Relationships between Church and Government Health Services*, Konedobu, Health Planning Unit, Papua New Guinea, Department of Public Health.

Stretton, A.W., 1979a. 'A historical look at subsidisation of urban housing in Papua New Guinea', in Norwood, H. (ed.), *Urbanisation and Housing in Papua New Guinea*, pp. 17-24, Port Moresby, University of Papua New Guinea.

Stretton, A.W., 1979b. *Urban Housing Policy in Papua New Guinea*, Port Moresby, Institute of Applied Social And Economic Research.

Strong, W., 1926. 'Gonorrhoea in natives of New Guinea', *Medical Journal of Australia*, 1:340-1.

Symonds, R., 1966. *The British and Their Successors: A Study in the Development of Government Services in the New States*, London, Faber & Faber.

Tanganyika Development Commission, 1946. *Ten Year Development and Welfare Plan for Tanganyika Territory*, Dar es Salaam, Government Printer.

TANU, 1967. *The Arusha Declaration of TANU's policy on Socialism, and Self-reliance*, Dar es Salaam, TANU.

Tanzania, Ministry of Health and Social Welfare, 1970. *Ten Years of Development of Services in the Social Welfare and Probation Division*, Dar es Salaam, Ministry of Health and Social Welfare, Social Welfare and Probation Division, mimeo.

Tanzania, National Council of Social and Welfare Services, 1974. *Development and Participation – Operational Implications for Social Welfare*, Dar es Salaam, NCSWS.

Tanzania, National Council of Social and Welfare Services, 1974. *Development and Participation*, Dar es Salaam, NCSWS.

Taylor, J., 1979. *From Modernization to Modes of Production*, London, Macmillan.

Territory of Papua and New Guinea, Department of Public Health, 1966. *Annual Report 1965-66*, Port Moresby, Government Printer.

Territory of Papua and New Guinea, 1968. *Programmes and Policies for the Economic Development of Papua and New Guinea*, Port Moresby, Government Printer.

Thursz, D. and Vigilante, J.L., 1975. *Meeting Human Needs, An Overview of Nine Countries*, Beverley Hills, Sage.

Thursz, D. and Vigilante, J.L., 1976. *Meeting Human Needs, Additional Perspectives from Thirteen Countries*, Beverley Hills, Sage.

Titmuss, R.M., Abel-Smith, B. Macdonald, G. Williams, A.W. and Wood, C.H., 1964. *The Health Service of Tanganyika*, London, Pitman.

Todaro, M.P., 1971. 'Income expectations, rural-urban migration and employment in Africa, *International Labour Review*, 104(5):387-414.

Todaro, M.P., 1980. 'The influence of education on migration and fertility', in Simmons, J., (ed.), *The Education Dilemma*, pp. 179-186, Oxford, Pergamon Press.

Toure, M.P., 1979. 'The health revolution', *World Health*, November: 10-13.

Transnational Institute, 1974. *World Hunger — Causes and Remedies*, Washington, Institute for Policy Studies.

Turner, J.F.C., 1972. 'Housing issues and the standards problem', *Ekistics*, 33(196): 152-8.

Turner, J.F.C., 1969. 'Uncontrolled urban settlements: problems and policies', in Breese, G. (ed.), *The city in newly developing countries*, pp. 507-34, Englewood-Cliffs and London, Prentice-Hall.

Turner, J.F.C., 1980. 'What to do about housing — its part in another development', *Habitat International*, 5(1-2): 203-11.

Turshen, M., 1977a. *The Political Economy of Health in Tanzania*, unpublished D. Phil. thesis, University of Sussex.

Turshen, M., 1977b. 'The political ecology of disease', *The Review of Radical Political Economics*, 9(1):45-60.

Ueber, R. and Susan, M., 1978. *Health and Policymaking in the Arab Middle East*, Washington, Georgetown University, Center for Contemporary Arab Studies.

United Nations, 1964. *Patterns of Social Welfare Organisation and Administration in Africa*, New York, United Nations.

United Nations, 1968. *Proceedings of the International Conference of Ministers Responsible for Social Welfare*, New York, United Nations.

United Nations, 1970. *Social Welfare Planning in the Context of National Development Plans*, New York, UN.

United Nations, 1971a. *Report on the Symposium on Social Policy and Planning*, New York, UN.

United Nations, 1971b. *Popular Participation in Development: Emerging Trends in Community Development*, New York, UN.

United Nations, 1971c. *Improvement of Slums and Uncontrolled Settlements*, Geneva, UN.

United Nations, 1971d. *Report on Children*, New York, UN.

United Nations, 1976. *Global Review of Human Settlements*, Habitat, United Nations Conference on Human Settlements.

United Nations, 1979, *Social Development and the International Development Strategy*, Geneva, United Nations Research Institute for Social Development.

United Nations, 1980. *Report on the World Conference of the United Nations Decade for Women: Equality, Development and Peace*, New York, UN.

Valentine, C.A. and Valentine, B.L. (eds.), 1979. *Going Through*

Changes, Port Moresby, Institute of Papua New Guinea Studies.

Van Zijl, W.J., 1966. 'Studies in diaorrheal diseases in seven countries', *Bulletin of the World Health Organisation*, 35:pp.249-61.

Vaughan, J.P., 1971. 'Are doctors always necessary? A review of the need for the medical assistant in developing countries', *Journal of Tropical Medicine and Hygiene*, 74:265-71.

Vines, A.P., 1970. *An Epidemiological Sample Survey of the Highlands, Mainland and Islands Regions of the Territory of Papua and New Guinea*, Konedobu, Department of Public Health.

Vulliamy, G., 1981. 'The secondary schools community extension project in Papau New Guinea', *Journal of Curriculum Studies*, 13, 93-102.

Wagner, D.A. and Lotfi, G., 1980. 'Learning to read by "rote" in the quranic schools of Yemen and Senegal', paper given at the Annual Meeting of the American Anthropological Association Washington, D.C.

Waiko, J.D., 1977. 'The people of Papua New Guinea, their forests and their aspirations', in Winslow, J.H. (ed.), *The Melanesian Environment*, Canberra: Australian National University Press.

Wallerstein, I., 1974. 'Dependence in an interdependent world', *African Studies Review*, 17(1):1-26.

Ward, B., 1976. *The Home of Man*, Harmondsworth, Penguin.

Ward, P.M. (ed)., 1979. *Self-help Housing and Spontaneous Housing: A Critique*, Oxford, Alexandrine Press.

Weeks, J., 1972. *Employment and the Growth of Towns*, paper to the British African Studies Association Conference, mimeo.

Weeks, S.G., 1977. Inaugural Lecture, University of Papua New Guinea.

Weller, T.H., 1974. 'World health in a changing world', *Journal of Tropical Medicine*, 77(4): 54-61.

Wicker, E.R., 1958. 'Colonial development and welfare, 1929-1957', *Social and Economic Studies*, 7(4): 170-92.

Wigley, S.C. and Russell, D.A., 1972. 'Leprosy and tuberculosis', in *Encyclopaedia of Papua and New Guinea*. pp. 640-44.

Williamson, B., 1979. *Education, Social Structure and Development*, London, MacMillan.

Wolfers, E.P., 1976. 'Towards self-government, the perspectives of 1971', in Stone, D. (ed.), *Prelude to Self-Government*, pp. 1-24, Canberra, Australian National University.

Wolpe, H., 1975. 'The theory of internal colonialism: the South African case', in Oxall, I., et.al. (eds.) *Beyond the Sociology of Development*, pp. 229-52. London and Boston, Routledge and Kegan Paul.

World Bank, 1974a. *Education Sector Paper*, New York, World Bank.

World Bank, 1974b. *Sites and Services Projects*, Washington, World Bank.

World Bank, 1975a. *The Assault on World Poverty*, Baltimore, Johns

Hopkins Press.

World Bank, 1975b. *Health: Sector Policy Paper*, Washington, World Bank.

World Bank, 1975c. *Housing Sector Policy Paper*, Washington, World Bank.

World Bank, 1979a. *National Urbanisation Policies in Developing Countries*, Washington, World Bank.

World Bank, 1979b. *World Development Report, 1979*, Washington, World Bank.

World Bank, 1980a. *Health: Sector Policy Paper*, Washington, World Bank.

World Bank, 1980b. *World Development Report, 1980*. Washington, World Bank.

World Bank, 1980c. *Education Sector Policy Paper*, (3rd ed.), Washington D.C., World Bank.

World Health Orgnisation, 1973a. *Inter-relationships Between Health Programmes and Socio-Economic Development*, Public Health Papers, 49, Geneva, WHO.

World Health Organisation. 1973b. *Organisational Study on Methods of Promoting the Development of Basic Health Services*, Geneva, WHO.

World Health Organisation, 1974. *Training and Utilisation of Village Health Workers*, Geneva, WHO.

World Health Organisation. 1975a. *Fifth Report on the World Health Situation. 1969-72*, Geneva, WHO.

World Health Organisation. 1975b. *Promotion of National Health Services*, Geneva, WHO.

World Health Organisation, 1976. *Malaria: Processed Report for the Special Programme for Research and Training in Tropical Diseases*, Geneva, WHO.

World Health Organisation, 1977. *Training and Utilisation of Village Health Workers*, Geneva, WHO.

World Health Organisation, 1978a. 'The Alma-Ata conference on primary health care, *WHO Chronicle*, 32(11):409-30.

World Health Organisation. 1978b. 'The promotion and development of traditional medicine', *Technical Report Series*, Vol. 622, Geneva, WHO.

World Health Organisation, 1979. 'Training and utilisation of auxiliary personnel for rural health teams in developing countries, *WHO Technical Report Series*, Vol. 633, Geneva, WHO.

WHO/UNICEF., 1978. *Report of the International Conference on Primary Health Care*, Geneva, World Health Organisation.

Yeates, D.B., 1979. *Community Development in Papua New Guinea: A Study of the Port Moresby Community Development Group*, M.A.

thesis, University of Papua New Guinea.

Zeidenstein, S., 1980. 'A regional approach to women's needs: the Women and Development Unit in Honduras', *Assignment Children*, 49/50:141-54.

Subject Index

Name Index